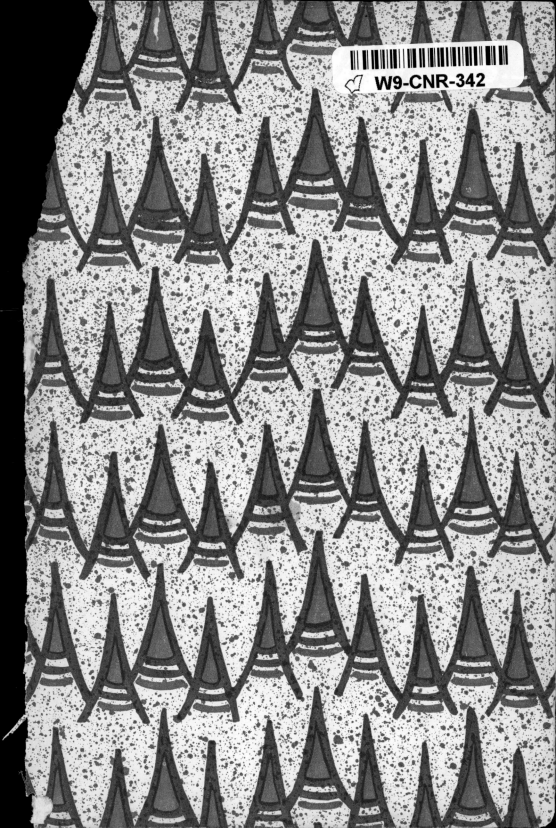

W9-CNR-342

5⁰⁰

Randolph Ray

The Real
SARAH BERNHARDT

(Photo, Henri Manuel)

Mme. Bernhardt in her Dressing-room during her Interpretation of *La Gloire,* by Maurice Rostand, in 1921.

The Real
SARAH BERNHARDT
WHOM HER AUDIENCES NEVER KNEW

BY

BASIL WOON

From material supplied by Mme. Pierre Berton

Illustrated

BONI AND LIVERIGHT
PUBLISHERS :: 1924 :: NEW YORK

Copyright, 1924, by
BONI AND LIVERIGHT, INC.

———

All Rights Reserved

PRINTED IN THE UNITED STATES OF AMERICA

First printing, February, 1924
Second printing, June, 1924
Third printing, October, 1924
Fourth printing, November, 1925

CONTENTS

5

Contents

Contents

Contents

ILLUSTRATIONS

INTRODUCTION

NEVER was more apt the German proverb, "Truth is its own justification," than in the telling of the story of that most remarkable of women, Sarah Bernhardt. During her life, in spite of the fact that she enjoyed more widespread publicity than any other person, man or woman, remarkably little was known by the public of her real life story. The very extent of this world-wide publicity served, in fact, as a sort of smoke-screen to conceal the intimate personality of the woman it vaunted.

To the playgoers of the world, and even to those who had never seen her act, Sarah Bernhardt was for ever acting a part. She shared her glory with the dozens of poets and playwrights whose inspired interpreter she was. The laurel wreath around her brow was of the same tinsel quality as the scenery which framed her personality.

It is hard to begin this work of telling the true, the intimate story of Sarah Bernhardt without laying oneself open to the charge of revealing secrets that were better left inviolate, of tearing down rather than building up the laborious character-structure of an international idol. But I refuse to allow these first pages to become a justification—the work itself will be that. What I am attempting now is simply an explanation.

If, in the course of this book, certain episodes are

recounted that may possibly wound the feelings of those who worshipped Sarah as an actress, I would point out that the enthralling story of her tremendous fight against the worst odds that ever faced a woman cannot be properly told if certain essential elements of her history are suppressed. Such elements, despite the character they seem to convey, are component parts of the amazing whole. We cannot reveal Bernhardt in her genuine greatness without revealing also certain things that in a less important biography had certainly better have been left unwritten.

For seventy-nine years Sarah succeeded in concealing the facts of her birth. Yet more than thirty years ago she said to Madame Pierre Berton, to whose remarkable and faithful memory the facts of this biography are due, "I hope that, when I am dead, you, who are younger than I am, will reveal to the world the real Sarah—the Sarah whom the audiences never knew!"

From time to time thereafter, throughout their long and intimate association, Sarah told Madame Berton the facts of her birth, of her childhood, of her absorbing up-hill battle towards celebrity and of her final conquest. These facts, together with matters of Madame Berton's own observation, are contained in this book.

Scrupulous to a fault, Madame Berton refrained from telling or publishing a word of what had been given her in confidence, until Sarah's death released her from her promise, and at the same time put her under the immediate obligation of fulfilling her old friend's wish and "revealing to the world the Sarah whom the audiences never knew."

A word about Madame Berton. She is the widow of Pierre Berton, the actor and playwright, who, before his marriage to her, was the adored intimate of Bernhardt. Their liaison, which is recounted hereafter, lasted two years, and even after they separated their friendship continued.

It was Berton who convinced Duquesnel, the director of the Odéon, of Sarah's genius as a tragedienne; it was Berton who encouraged her and taught her and who, more than any other man, was responsible for her early triumphs. It was Berton who stood beside her when all Paris sneered at and mocked her, and it was Berton who defended her when the co-directors of the Odéon wished to cancel her contract because of what they termed her "incorrigibility."

No living person, then, can be so fitted to tell Sarah's true history as the widow of the man who, himself, lived a part of it.

Madame Berton, after her marriage to Berton, accompanied her husband on many of Sarah's famous tours about Europe. Even after her marriage, Thérèse Berton remained Sarah's *confidante* and friend, though there were intervals of coldness that were natural enough in a temperament as self-centred, and as jealous as was Sarah's.

From now on the story will be as Madame Berton related it to me. I shall let her tell it here just as she told it me in Paris, without the addition of literary flourishes or anything that could detract from the dramatic power of the narrative itself.

BASIL WOON.

THE REAL SARAH BERNHARDT

The Real
SARAH BERNHARDT

CHAPTER I

For all my intimacy with Sarah Bernhardt (said Madame Berton), I find it difficult to believe that she loved me. I think that, on the contrary, she distrusted me, and I even believe that at times she hated me, because it was I, and not she, who had married Pierre Berton.

Yet she confided in me. She was at times hard-pressed for somebody to whom she could tell her secrets. She knew that I would keep my promise never to relate them during her lifetime, and I know she told them to me because she realised that one day even the most intimate details of her life would belong by right to posterity.

This great actress with Jewish, German, French and Flemish (and probably also Gypsy) blood in her veins, was born into that condition of life which even to-day spells ruin, hate, despair and poverty for the great majority. In those days illegitimacy was almost an insuperable obstacle to recognition and success.

To the fact that the union of her mother and father was never blessed by holy matrimony may with justice be ascribed the impunity with which she was assailed during the first forty or fifty years of her life by all manner of

23

critics, high and low. No less than three books or pamphlets were written attacking her before she had attained her fortieth year.

Articles in the Parisian press were sometimes so virulent as to be inconceivable, when it is remembered that the object of their venom was the world's greatest actress, the "Divine Sarah." Every blackmailing penny-a-liner in Paris essayed to make Sarah pay him tribute at some time or another. I do not think that she ever paid, but I do know that the fits of rage and despair into which she was thrown after reading these attacks often made her so ill that for days her understudy was obliged to play her part.

Her long fight to keep the truth of her birth from being published is known. In telling me one day of the sordid circumstances to which she owed her appearance in the world she pledged me to secrecy during her lifetime. I have kept that pledge, and it is only because she gave me express permission to write this book after her death, and because it is time that the world knew the true story of this extraordinary genius, that I tell it now.

The "Divine" Sarah was divine only in her inspiration; the "immortal" Sarah was immortal solely in her art. The real Sarah, the Sarah whom her intimates knew and adored, was not so much a divinity as an idol; a woman full of vanity and frailty, dominated since birth by ambitious egoism and a determination to become famous.

She was the supreme woman of the nineteenth and early twentieth centuries; but it was not her supremacy or her position at the pinnacle of theatrical success that made her lovable. She was loved, not because she was a saint but because she was not a saint; for to err is human and to be human is to be loved. Even on the stage her art was natural—she did not pose, she lived.

In the history of the Christian world only one other woman was born under a greater handicap than was Sarah Bernhardt, and few women ever rose to a similar fame. Yet Sarah, even at the height of her career, did things which were justly condemned by strict-living people and would not have been tolerated in the case of anyone else.

Consider this woman. She was born to an unwed Jewish mother whose birth-place was Berlin. Her father was a French provincial lawyer, a profligate, who afterwards became a world-traveller.

She was born a Jewess, baptized a Catholic. By birth she was French, and by marriage she was Greek.

Throughout her life she was, firstly, an actress; secondly, a mother; thirdly, a great, a tempestuous lover.

She was a sculptress of extraordinary merit; she was a painter whose pictures were exhibited in the Paris Salons before she became famous as an actress; she was a writer with many books to her credit.

A temperamental morbidity was, I think, supreme in her character, although many who knew her placed ambition first. After these came mother-love, vanity, affection and malice. She made more enemies than friends; more people feared her than loved her; yet her life was replete with great sentimental episodes with some of the most famous men of her time.

The happiest period of her life was during the infancy of her son Maurice; her greatest joy was in his abiding affection. The bitterest period of her life was her old age, when she was surrounded by jackals whose affection for her was chiefly purchased by the money she mistakenly lavished on them; and who reduced her to such a penniless condition that, practically on her death-bed, she was forced to pose for an American film company, so that her debts and funeral expenses might in part be covered.

Fifty years of constant association taught me the truth about Sarah Bernhardt. Others might have known her longer, but none knew her better. None certainly could speak with greater authority of her intimate life. I had the details of her birth, her life, and her loves that are here set forth from her own lips, and from the lips of others who figured in her career.

The first time I met Sarah Bernhardt will live in my memory for ever. A child of eight, I was taken to visit the actress—then beginning to taste the first fruits of success—in her *loge* at the Odéon Theatre.

I remember my fright as we crossed the vast, cavernous stage, on our way to the stairs which led to the dressing-rooms. Enormous pieces of scenery looked as though they might topple on one at any moment. Cardboard statues, which to my childish imagination seemed forbidding demons, leered at me from the shadows. Rough, uncouth scene-shifters, acolytes of this painted Hades, jostled me as we passed. The great height of the stage, ending in a gloomy mystery of ropes, pulleys and platforms which hinted at occult rites, awed me and made me feel smaller than I really was (and I was very small!).

From time to time voices, bawling from the gloom but whence exactly I neither knew nor could discover, echoed and re-echoed through the shadows. The curtain was up, and beyond the darkened proscenium I could faintly discern the four-storied auditorium, awesome in its resounding emptiness.

Whom could we be going to visit here, I wondered, and clung tighter to my mother's protecting skirts, while she inquired her way of a black-coated gentleman, who appeared with disconcerting suddenness as we reached the foot of the stairs. But I dared not voice the question, and now we mounted a bewildering number of steps, each bringing a more mysterious vista than the last.

Finally we reached the top of the stairs and my mother led me down a long passageway, lined with doors which had once been painted white but which were now a dirty cream colour. Some of these doors had simply numbers; others bore a name inscribed on a piece of pasteboard, inserted in a metal holder.

Almost at the end of the corridor my mother stopped before a door precisely similar to the others, except that instead of a number or a pasteboard it bore the name in golden letters:

SARAH BERNHARDT

Even then the young actress had evinced her preference for gold. She said that it matched her hair.

Receiving a summons to enter, my mother opened the

door and went in, dragging me resolutely after her. Inside this door was another, inscribed in like fashion, and when this in turn was opened, we found ourselves in a large room illuminated by two windows and shaded lights, for it was winter and the windows opened on a courtyard.

This room contained a settee, an armchair, two other chairs and a table, which had three movable mirrors above it. The table was littered with pots and vases of every description and a wild confusion of gold-backed brushes and toilet accessories. A great vase full of carnations stood on it, and another filled with the same flowers was on the floor near one of the windows. The room was carpeted, but the carpet was so littered with envelopes, pieces of paper and various articles of wearing apparel that its design could not be discerned.

Seated before the *table-de-toilette* was an angel.

Let the reader remember that he is dealing with a child's memory. My imagination had so been wrought upon by the fearful caverns below that I had fully expected to see, enthroned here, in the upper chambers, His Majesty Satan in all his glory. The sight then of this radiant creature, her head literally crowned with a tumbling glory of gold, came as a tremendous shock— until I recalled that, although that awful place down below must have been Hell, we had mounted upwards since then and must therefore by now have reached Heaven!

As my mother shook hands, I ran behind her and,

terror-stricken at I know not what, hid my face in her ample skirts. Then, as though from far away, I heard the divinity speak.

"So this is little Thérèse!" she said. "Come here, *ma petite,* and let Sarah Bernhardt kiss you!"

But I would not go, and only buried my face all the deeper in my mother's dress.

"*Mais, ma mignonne,*" remonstrated the angel, "I cannot see you if you hide like that! Come!"

My mother, excusably vexed, dragged me from my hiding-place.

"Come! come!" she said sharply; "speak to Mademoiselle! Go and kiss her!"

Thus commanded in a tone I knew too well, I advanced a step and stood there shyly, not daring to lift my head. Suddenly I was overwhelmed by two arms and a mass of golden hair, which literally covered my head and shoulders as Sarah Bernhardt caught me to her.

"*La pauvre petite . . . la pauvre mignonne!*" she kept repeating, punctuating the words with hearty hugs and an embrace on both cheeks. Then, holding me at arm's length:

"So, you want to be an actress?"

Now this, to my knowledge, was the first occasion on which I had ever heard that I was to be an actress. Certainly I had never mentioned the idea to anyone, least of all to my mother, who was not a person to whom one made confidences. I stood there dumb.

"*Ma foi,*" ejaculated the angel, in her glorious voice, "she is pretty enough!"

There followed a rapid exchange of remarks between my mother and Sarah Bernhardt—the connection between whom I have never been able to fathom—and during these I was ordered to sit on the chair (my legs did not touch the ground) and told not to open my mouth. As if I would have dared to! But I had become bold enough to feast my eyes on the divinity, and to study her at leisure.

How easily that first childish impression of Sarah comes to me now, fifty years later!

Those amazingly blue eyes, widely-spaced; that arched nose, a pulse beating in the sensitive nostril as she talked; that glorious mouth, full and red, the upper lip slightly projecting over the under one; that firm chin, with the dimple that Edmond Rostand afterwards raved about; those high cheek-bones, the line of them extending to where the hair covered the ears; above all, that extraordinary mass of unruly golden-red hair, tossed about in riotous confusion and every direction.

Many another face I might see and forget, this one, never!

When Sarah stood up to say good-bye, I saw that she was taller than my mother, and unbelievably slender.

As we went downstairs, I was in such an ecstatic state of bliss that I had not the slightest fear of the gnomes lurking in the shadows of the nether regions as we passed them again on our way out, nor do I remember my mother talking to me.

My heart was dedicated to a goddess. Sarah Bernhardt, from that day onwards, was my idol.

CHAPTER II

WHAT is the truth about Sarah Bernhardt's birth? Have I the right to tell it, even though I know the facts? Have I the right to divulge this secret of all secrets, for nearly four-score years locked in the breast of the greatest woman of five epochs? Who am I that I should venture into the cupboards of the dead Great for the purpose of rattling the skeletons I am certain to find there—yes, in the cupboards of *all* the dead great ones who later surrounded this celebrated woman, and not alone Bernhardt?

I have faced this problem squarely, fought it out with myself through long, sleepless nights, when publishers were bedevilling me for the truth, the whole truth and— scarcely anything but the truth. It is a problem that will raise a sharp conflict in the feelings of all my readers. It is a problem for Poe.

Have I the right—knowing what I do of the real circumstances surrounding not only the dead genius but her living relatives also—have I the right to tear the shroud from that dead face, and let the world gaze afresh on a long-familiar visage, only to find a new and wondrously changed entity beneath?

I will be frank. I had made up my mind not to do it: not for fear of giving offence to the dead, for 'twas from this very glorious clay that I had the truth with permission to publish it, but from respect to the living. Sarah Bernhardt not only left a son, Maurice Bernhardt; she left grandchildren and great-grandchildren, little ones whom I have watched joyously at play in the Parc Monceau, unknowing that at that very moment the great battle for life was being staged in the drab little house on the Boulevard Pereire. She had made up her mind that the sorrows which were hers should never blemish these innocent ones.

And yet—what a fallacy, what a heartrending fallacy it is to believe that such things can be concealed, or that, being concealed, they do not fester in their hiding-places!

Scarcely had the last, sad curtain been rung down on that greatest of real-life dramas than the scavengers of literature—those grisly people who lurk in the night of life, dealing in calumny and lies—began delving into the past of Sarah Bernhardt, just as the real *chiffoniers*, those horrible old women of the dawn, delve into the garbage cans of Paris, seeking for Heaven knows what filth.

The mystery of her birth was Sarah's great secret. Insatiable, the greedy public desired to rend this secret and to tear it into little bits. Literary ghouls fell upon the great woman's reputation and fought over it. They disinterred legends that Sarah, while living, had successfully and scornfully proved untrue. They sent out lies by the bushel, secure in the knowledge that the Golden Voice, which alone could brand them, was stilled for ever.

Perhaps it was to be expected that the first of these

legends came from Germany, a country that Sarah scorned and once refused to visit, although she had been offered a million marks to do so; a country, moreover, which had claimed Sarah as its own on more than one occasion.

In 1902 the Berlin *Lokal Anzeiger* published a "revelation" of the birth of Sarah Bernhardt. She was born, said the inspired writer, at Frankfort. Her father was a German, her mother a Fleming. She had been taken to France when a tiny child and there abandoned by her parents.

"We are aware," said the *Lokal Anzeiger,* "that Sarah herself claims to have been born in Paris. Our only retort to this is: let her produce her birth certificate!"

They knew, of course, that Sarah's birth was never registered. Later I will tell you why.

Sarah Bernhardt was interviewed about these statements at the time they were published. As always, she refused to comment on the extraordinary story, and contented herself with referring inquiring journalists to her Memoirs, entitled *"Ma Double Vie,"* which had been published some years before.

This was the only mention that she made of her birth. As far as the date goes, her version may have been correct, although her baptismal certificate, herewith reproduced, gives the event as having occurred on September 25, 1844!

Now comes George Bernhardt, a famous German, who ought to know better than to pander to the scandal-

L'an 1856 le 21 mai a été baptisée par nous soussigné Chapelain de la Communauté de Grandchamp ſaisant autorisé par Mgr l'Évèque de Versailles, dans la chapelle de ladite Communauté, Sara, Marie, Henriette née à Paris le 22e arrondiᵗ le 25 7ᵇʳᵉ 1844, fille de Mr Édouard Bernhardt, demeurant actuellᵗ au Havre, rue de ... Honoré Nº 2, et de Mᵈ Judith Van Hard, demeurant à Paris rue St Honoré 265. La marraine a été Mr Régis Lavolé rue de la chapelle St Antoine 65, représenté par Mr Nicolas Mercier, rue St Honoré 26 à Versailles, et la marraine Mᵉ Anna Van Hard ... fait ... l'enfant.   Sr M. J. Bernhardt.

De Bruck

J. Gourdan
Chapelain de la Communauté

L'an mil huit cent cinquante six le vingt deux mai a été baptisée

Baptismal Certificate of Sarah Bernhardt, May 21, 1856.

mongers, and who states positively that Sarah's father was his great-grandfather, George Bernhardt, and that her mother was a Gypsy woman for whom he experienced a temporary passion while living in Algeria.

But here he hedges. "At least," he says, "family records tell of the existence of the child, and of the allegation that George Bernhardt was the father; but they also say that the assertion was denied by him, which leads to the probability that Sarah Bernhardt had no claim whatever on the name she bore."

Frankfort, and now Algiers! A Flemish mother and a Gypsy mother! A fine haul for the scavengers!

Sarah had to fight rumours of this kind on several occasions during her lifetime. In a scurrilous book which was written many years ago it was asserted that she "never knew who her father was."

This, as might be expected, was untrue. Sarah not only knew who her father was, but knew him well. Though she never lived with him, he visited her frequently, especially when she was at school in the Convent at Grandchamps, and when he died he left her a portion of his fortune.

Sarah herself starts her Memoirs with this reference to him: "My father was travelling in China at the time—why, I do not know."

Here, then, was the answer to the problem that had been bothering me: it was clearly better to tell the truth once and for all, and to set at rest all doubts concerning this much-debated question of Sarah Bernhardt's birth, than to let every newspaper scavenger have his own way with it, prolong the agony, and incidentally contrive, by unscrupulous inference, to cast a shadow much blacker than the importance of the matter justified.

To aid me in coming to this decision I had the knowledge that Sarah herself, in telling the story to me many years ago, was aware that one day it would be made public, and wished things so. She knew that in time to come she would belong to history, and also how little of history is founded on actual fact. The last thing she wanted was for the facts of her life to be at the mercy of imaginative chroniclers, who would have nothing to base their story on except rumour.

Thus she told it to me, and thus I tell it to you. Let the world decide.

CHAPTER III

No. 5, rue de l'Ecole de Médecine was a weird, queerly-leaning tenement house in a black little side-street just off the Boulevard St. Germain, near the Boulevard St. Michel, in the heart of the students' quarter of Paris. It was a poor dwelling, at best, with a crumbling façade, ornamented with some scarcely-discernible heraldic device which told of past dignity. It had a low, wide doorway, with one of its great oak, iron-studded doors askew on its hinges, so that a perpetual draught whistled up the stone-flagged corridor that loomed darkly, like a cave, from the street to the crumbling stairs. A four-story building . . . each floor was just a trifle more weather-beaten, more decrepit, than the next. On the ground floor, next to the *loge du concierge,* was a wine-shop, smelling of last night's slops, where the brown-aproned proprietor leaned against his little wooden bar and filled new bottles with the dregs that had not been drunk the day before; next to the wineshop stood a cobbler's stall, with the tap-tap of the cobbler's wooden mallet resounding through the street to the courtyard at the rear; and next to the cobbler's, the stall of a *marchand des frites,* whose only merchandise was sliced potatoes fried in olive oil.

On the first floor was the *appartement* of the wine-dealer; on the second and third, *logements* for students —students who, returning nightly from the cafés of the Boul' Mich', enlivened the aged edifice with their cries.

And on the fourth floor of this building, a day in the early fall of 1844, in a modest flat of three rooms— bedroom, sitting-room and kitchen—was born the baby who afterwards became Sarah Bernhardt.

Her mother, then a beautiful young woman in her late teens, was named Julie Bernard, but sometimes she called herself Judith Van Hard. Among her intimates she was affectionately known as Youle.

It was eight o'clock at night. Youle was lying in bed, her mass of red-gold hair tumbling over her shoulders and down under the sheets. Her eyes of sapphire-blue were closed, and her breathing hard and spasmodic. Her features were drawn; her face pale.

Three other persons were in the room. One was a man—the doctor, busy packing up his instruments. The other was a young friend, Madame Guérard. The third was a tiny atom of humanity, barely a foot long and weighing certainly not more than half a dozen pounds. This infant's head was covered with a fuzz of reddish hair resembling the mother's; its tiny mouth was open and its little lungs were working at top-blast.

The temper for which Sarah Bernhardt was later to become notorious was making its first manifestation.

The delivery had been difficult, and Julie was not asleep but unconscious. Thus, though the baby cried all night, the mother did not awaken, and in the morning Madame Guérard sent off to the nearest synagogue for a Jewish priest.

But when the doctor came the crisis had passed; the girl on the bed had recovered consciousness and was already fondling her child. From then on her recovery was rapid, and before little Sarah had properly got her blue eyes open or begun to take an interest in things around her, the beautiful little Jewish girl was back at her work-table in the sitting-room, trimming hats for which she was paid a few sous each by the clients whose houses she visited in turn every week.

Julie Van Hard, or Bernard, was a Flemish Jewess born of a struggling lower-middle-class family in Berlin. Her father, originally from South Holland but a naturalised German, had worked in a circus, but had forsaken this occupation to go into the retail grain and seed business, first in Hanover and then in Berlin. Her mother was a German dressmaker and a great beauty. When Julie was thirteen, her father died and left her only a handful of marks with which to complete her education.

Instead of doing so she chose to leave school, and became an apprentice in a big Berlin millinery establishment. After working there a little more than a year, she fell in love with a non-commissioned officer in a cavalry regiment, who seduced and then callously left her. When the affair came to the ears of the girl's employer, she was discharged in disgrace.

After that she left Berlin and went to Frankfort, where she kept herself for a few months by making hats (at which she was very clever) and singing on occasion in *cafés-concert*. She was a lovely child, even in the poor dresses she could afford, and having a talent for music, had been taught the piano by her mother. She displayed, however, little of the great histrionic ability which was to develop in her daughter. In fact, Sarah Bernhardt never completely satisfied herself from which side of the family she derived her talent. Her father's relations, from what little she learned of them, were comfortable, mediocre middle-class people in the French provinces—with German or Dutch connections, to be sure, but with no "acting blood" as far as she could discover.

The Van Hard family, however, was an offshoot of the Kinsberger clan, who owned circuses and theatres in Northern Europe before Napoleon's day, and who later developed into wholesale dealers in grain. When Napoleon invaded Poland, in fact, a Kinsberger supplied him with grain for his horses. The exact relationship of this Kinsberger to Sarah she never properly knew, but he was probably a cousin of her grandfather.

Away back therefore in this maternal line, there probably existed someone with a talent for the theatre. Whether the ancestor in question ever used it is not on record. We know that her grandfather was a performer in a Dutch circus, but we do not know whether he was a clown or an animal-tamer.

In Frankfort, Julie Bernard, the modiste, met a young Frenchman, a courier in the diplomatic corps, and a wild love affair followed, which culminated in the girl following the young man to Paris.   There they continued their liaison for less than a month, however, since the courier's parents, people of noble birth, stepped in and forbade him ever to see the little German girl again.   He left her without warning, and without money.

For weeks afterwards little Julie, a stranger in a strange land and speaking little French, lived as best she might.   Paris is a hard city now, for the unprotected girl; it was harder then.   Often the German waif came perilously near starvation.   Once, according to a story that she later on in life related to Jeanne, her second daughter, who told it to Sarah, she tried to commit suicide by throwing herself under the wheels of a passing coach.   But she had misjudged the distance and the wheels passed within inches of her.

What she did to eke out a bare living in those terrible days we do not know.   It is unlikely that she ever confided the whole story to her daughters—even to Jeanne, her favourite.   What is known is that she continued to make hats whenever she could save sufficient sous to buy the material, and perhaps she sang or danced in the cabarets of the quarter; but this is unlikely, because of her ignorance of French.   Whatever she did, no one now can blame her.

Eventually, she struck up an acquaintance with a law student, who was registered on the books of the University of Paris as Edouard Bernhardt. The family name of this man, according to what Sarah learned later, was de Thérard, and his baptismal name was "Paul."

The exact reasons for the dual nomenclature I cannot give. Sarah herself knew of the matter only vaguely. I suggested that de Thérard was the student's right name, but that he carried on his liaison with Julie under the name of Bernhardt. Sarah admitted this was a plausible inference, but insisted that the attorney for her father's estate always referred to him as Bernhardt.

Bernhardt, or de Thérard, was one of the wildest youngsters in the Latin Quarter. He was constantly getting into scrapes, which his family at Le Havre had to pay for. Many of these scrapes were with women much older than himself, and *l'aventure amoureuse* was probably his strong—or weak—point. At any rate, he succeeded in studying as little law as possible, for he failed completely in all his examinations.

Where he and Julie met is unknown; probably it was a simple *rencontre de la rue,* which is common enough in Paris to-day. The nature of Julie's trade, when delivering her hats to her customers, took her frequently into the streets of the quarter in which young Bernhardt was studying and in which he prosecuted his love affairs. It is likely that, seeing a marvellously pretty girl (of a type then unusual in Paris), walking along the Boul' Mich', he followed her and, being of the handsome, devil-may-care type, pleased her so that she agreed to meet him again.

Be that as it may, the link between the little German girl and the reckless Havre student soon became public enough. Their appearance in any of the cafés or cabarets of the quarter was the signal for a chorus of congratulations and ironical greetings from Bernhardt's comrades.

The little flat at number 5, rue de l'Ecole de Médecine, was furnished and rented by Bernhardt for Julie, out of his slender student's purse.

Two weeks before the birth of his child, Bernhardt returned to Havre.

He wrote ardent letters to the forsaken mother and sent regular sums for the child's support. Sometimes he visited Paris, but rarely remained there longer than twenty-four hours. As his financial circumstances improved, for relatives bequeathed him fairly large sums, he began to travel, and before his first voyage, to Portugal, he suggested that the infant Sarah should be sent to his own old nurse, now become a professional dry-nurse, with a farm near Quimperlé, in Brittany.

About this time Julie's fortunes underwent a sudden change for the better. This came about through several circumstances which occurred within a few weeks of each other. First, a relative of the young girl died in Holland, and bequeathed to her and each of her three sisters an equal number of guelders. The sum was not large, but it sufficed to lift Julie above immediate want. She went to Holland to claim the money, and was gone six months.

A few days after the legacy reached her, she discovered to her astonishment that one of her sisters, Rosine, who was her elder by four years and who was supposedly in Marseilles, was in reality living in Paris. How she was living is rather a mystery. But she seemed to be well off, and she had been long enough in France to speak the language excellently.

When Julie returned from Holland, she came by way of Berlin and brought with her Henriette, her younger sister, then aged thirteen. There was still another sister, two years younger, and another aged twenty-eight, who was married and who lived in the French West Indies.

Julie and Henriette, when they arrived in Paris, went to live with Rosine, who had a flat in Montmartre. With baby Sarah safely in the country, in charge of a capable nurse, and with funds for the child's upkeep provided by the father, Julie felt free to look around.

She was a remarkable woman by this time. Eighteen years old, very fair, with a marvellous complexion and the wonderful head of hair that was to make her renowned later on, Julie Bernard possessed a gay and careless disposition that would have made her notorious anywhere. With her sisters, she began frequenting the cafés that were then fashionable, and it was not long before the trio began to meet interesting people.

Among these acquaintances was a man whom Sarah herself always referred to as "Baron Larrey," but who was probably another man of title with a similar name. Baron Larrey and Julie became first friends, then lovers, and the relationship lasted five years.

Far behind her now the dingy, decrepit old building at 5, rue de l'Ecole de Médecine! Far behind her the days when she had to trudge weary miles, in all weathers, to secure orders and deliver hats! Julie was now a *"fille à la mode."* She flaunted the latest fashions, the latest colours, the latest millinery on the Boulevards and in the exclusive restaurants. Her relationship with the Baron commanded for her a certain respect in the gay, care-free Bohemian world that was the Paris of 1845. Nobles at Court commenced to be interested in her. Famous personages of the stage consented to sit at her table.

She soon eclipsed in beauty and in accomplishments her less endowed sisters, although they, too, formed wealthy and prominent relationships.

All three sisters loved to travel. Julie took the younger one on many voyages throughout Europe, and Rosine made regular pilgrimages to Germany to the famous spas.

While Julie lived the gay, irresponsible life of a Parisian butterfly, her daughter Sarah, a weak, anæmic child, cursed with a terrific temper, remained on the farm in Brittany.

When she was nearly two years old she was still in her "first steps"; she did not begin to learn to walk until she was fourteen months old. Her nurse, who had married again, had other duties about the farm and could give scant attention to the little one during the day. In order to keep her quiet, the nurse got her husband to build a little chair, in which the baby was fastened with a strap. This was then pushed against a table, so that the child could amuse herself with pieces of coloured paper—the only toys Sarah Bernhardt knew until she was three years old.

One day the woman set her in the chair as usual but neglected to fasten the strap, and the baby, leaning forward to catch something, fell from the high chair and into the wide, Breton fireplace, in which a log fire was burning. Her screams brought the nurse and her husband running. The nurse picked her up and plunged her bodily, flaming clothes and all, into a huge tub of milk which was waiting to be churned.

Doctors were sent for from a neighbouring village and hasty messages sent to Paris. The only one of the sisters to be found was Rosine, who sent a message to Julie at Brussels, and herself hurried to Brittany. Four days later Julie arrived in Baron Larrey's coach, which had been driven at top speed all the way from Paris.

From this incident grew Sarah's nickname, which remained with her all her childhood, "Flower-of-the-Milk." She was three months recovering from the severe burns she had sustained, and until she died she bore scars to remind her of the accident.

For ever after, Sarah Bernhardt had a horror of fire. She could not bear even to look at one, and would shiver and turn pale when she heard the trumpets and bells of the fire brigade. Yet mother-love conquered this fear when, nearly twenty years later, her flat took fire and she dashed through a barrage of flames to rescue her own baby boy.

When little Sarah recovered, Julie proposed to the nurse, now a widow, that she should leave the Breton farm and live in Paris in a cottage Baron Larrey had taken on the borders of the Seine, at Neuilly. The nurse agreed, and a new existence began for the child on the fringe of the city, where her mother was earning a reputation as a gilded social butterfly.

CHAPTER IV

DURING the year which followed transfer of nurse and child to Neuilly-sur-Seine Sarah saw her mother but once, and then merely by chance.

Returning from a gay court party near St. Germain the coach, in which Julie was travelling with a resplendent personage, the Comte de Tours, broke down just after it had crossed the bridge over the Seine and reached the outskirts of Neuilly. The nearest coach-builder was a mile distant, and while the coachman walked this distance, Julie bethought herself of the neglected child living only a few streets away. So she and the Count daintily picked their way to the cottage, and found Sarah revelling in her bi-weekly bath.

This bath was an extraordinary affair, because it took place in the same tub as the family washing—and probably other washing that the nurse solicited in order to eke out her income. On the principle of killing two birds with one stone, the nurse would make a warm tub of soap-suds, put the linen to be washed into it, and then hoist in Baby Sarah!

The sight amused the Count and infuriated Julie, who gave the nurse a sound scolding. Sarah was hastily taken from the tub, dried, clothed and then handed to her fastidious mother, who fondled her in a gingerly way. But the baby failed to recognise the mother who had sacrificed so little for her sake, and burst into a storm of tears, pounding the finely-dressed lady with her puny little fists.

The Count thought it a fine joke, and laughed uproariously. "She is just like her mother, Youle!" he remarked, twirling his fine moustache.

Julie handed her tempestuous child back to the nurse. "If that is the way she behaves when her mother comes to see her," she said, "I shall not come again."

She kept her word to such good purpose that, eighteen months later, when the nurse married for a third time, and desired to take the child with her to her new home, letters to Julie's address were returned undelivered. The errant mother had not even thought it worth her while to keep her child's nurse informed of her movements.

The nurse's new husband was a *concierge,* one of those indispensable people who open the doors of Paris buildings, lose letters, clean stairs, quarrel with flat-owners, and generally make themselves as much of a nuisance as possible. This particular specimen was a big, upstanding man with sandy hair, about forty years of age, or ten years younger than his bride.

He was then *concierge* at number 65, rue de Provençe, in the heart of Paris, near where the Galeries Lafayette, the great stores, now stand. It was a dingy building, mostly devoted to commerce, and the *concierge* occupied one room on the first floor. This one room was bed-room, sitting-room and kitchen combined.

There was only one bed, a big four-poster, jammed against the window. There was also one kitchen table, on which he ate his meals; two chairs in varying stages of decrepitude; a small coal stove screened from the bed by a heavy velvet curtain—soiled legacy of some opulent tenant—and another small table, on which stood a wash-basin and pail. When water was wanted it was necessary to fetch it from a pump in the street.

It was into this sordid environment that little Sarah, "Flower-of-the-Milk," now almost five years old, was brought willy-nilly by her foster-mother. There was no room to put a cot for the child, so she shared a fraction of the bed. She was quickly put to work by her new lord, who soon initiated her into the mysteries of floor-washing and door-knob polishing, while it was generally *la petite Sarah,* when water was wanted, who was com-missioned to stagger down the stairs with the empty pail and return with the full one.

Living with two adults in this ill-ventilated, badly-lighted room—the sole window was one about twice the size of a ship's port-hole—and forced to do work which might well have proved too much for a child twice her age, it is small wonder that Sarah was frequently ill.

She lost appetite and colour, and grew weak, while the anæmia, which the bracing air of the country had almost cured, returned. Her eyes grew listless and had large puffs under them, so that neighbours, who pitied the child, prophesied that her days would soon be over.

Her only playmate, almost as unhappy as herself, was another little girl named Titine, the daughter of a working jeweller, who lived on the floor above; her playgrounds were the busy streets of Paris; her language the argot of the slums.   No one dreamed of sending her to school, which was not then compulsory.

There is very little doubt that the world would never have known Sarah Bernhardt if this state of affairs had lasted another year.   The child was fast going into tuberculosis, and could not even summon strength for the fits of temper that had distinguished her up till this time.

I have said that her only playmate was Titine, the daughter of the jeweller, but there was another for a month or so—the son of the butcher at the street corner.

One afternoon the janitor's wife returned from an errand and heard screams coming from the *loge*.   Hastening there she discovered the butcher's son, aged six, stripped to the waist, and the diminutive Sarah laying on to him with a strap.

"I am playing at being a Spaniard," she said in explanation, Spaniards having then a great reputation in France for cruelty.   The incident is interesting in the light of later incidents in her career, when charges of callousness and cruelty were brought against her.   For myself I have never doubted that a streak of the primitive existed in Sarah.   But, unlike others, I believe that she was the better for it, for out of it grew her single-mindedness and her will to conquer.

During all this time Sarah's mother gave no sign of life, despite repeated efforts on the part of the old nurse to find her.   In fact, the child's board had not been paid for nearly two years and, with her delicate health, she was becoming a charge which the couple could ill afford. Deliverance from this state of affairs came unexpectedly. One day Rosine, Sarah's aunt, paid a visit to a neighbouring house.   Sarah, who was playing in the courtyard of the building at the moment her aunt arrived, immediately recognised her, although the two had not met for more than a year.

"Tante Rosine!   Tante Rosine!"

The extravagantly dressed woman turned, hardly believing her ears.

"It is not?—why, it *is* Sarah, the daughter of my sister Youle!"

"Yes, yes!   It is I, Sarah!   Oh, take me away—take me away!   They suffocate me, these walls—always walls!   I cannot see the sky!   Take me away!   I want to see the sky again, and the flowers. . . !"

Sarah's cries had attracted a crowd, and much confused Rosine hurried the child into the *concierge's* room, and was there overwhelmed by the old nurse's explanations.

Something seemed to tell Sarah that she was not to be taken away at that moment.

"Oh, take me with you—take me with you!   I shall die here!"

It was the cry of a desperate child fighting for her life,

and it visibly wrenched at the heart of Tante Rosine. Yet—take her with her? How could she? What would her friend, the companion whom she lived with and who paid for her fine gowns and hats, say, if she brought home this little child of the gutter?

"Well," she conceded, as the woe-begone child clung convulsively to her skirt, "I will come back to-morrow, and take you away."

But with that curious intuition that characterises most children, Sarah sensed that she was about to be abandoned for a third time. She flung herself on the bed, sobbing, as her nurse accompanied her aunt down the stairs to the street below, where a fine equipage of box-wood and plush, prancing horses and liveried footmen was in waiting.

Rosine got into her carriage, dabbing a lace handkerchief at her eyes. She had a tender heart and was firmly resolved to write to Youle at once—Julie was in London —and make her take her child.

The footman regained his seat, the coachman clucked to his horses and the equipage moved away. But before it had gone two feet there was a heartrending wail and shriek, followed by a chorus of affrighted shouts, and a body came hurtling past the coach to the pavement. It was Sarah. The child had attempted to jump from the tiny first-floor window into the coach as it passed.

When Sarah awoke she found herself in a great, clean bed, surrounded by kind faces. She was at the home of her aunt in the rue St. Honoré. She had a double fracture of her right arm, and a sprained left ankle.

Julie, who was sent for immediately, arrived three days later, together with numerous other members of Sarah's family. For the first time in her brief existence, Sarah found herself a person of importance.

For the next two years little Sarah was an invalid, capable of walking only a step or two at a time. She passed this period sitting in a great arm-chair, unable to move without pain, dreaming childish dreams of splendour for the future.

"Never once," said Sarah in speaking of this period to me, "did I include in those dreams a suspicion that I would one day be an actress. I had never seen the inside of a theatre, and although many actors and actresses were among the friends constantly in and out of my mother's home at 22, rue de la Michodière—a rather meretriciously furnished flat with gilded salons and musty bedrooms—I was shy with them and they with me, and learned little from their conversation.

"In fact, the stage and all appertaining to it remained a deep mystery to me for nearly ten years after my accident. My actual going on the stage was an accident— or rather the solution of a problem which had worried my mother almost to death."

How this came about will be described in a later chapter.

At seven years of age, Sarah Bernhardt had so far recovered that she could walk and move without difficulty, and there was serious discussion about sending her to school. Her volatile mother, absent for the most part during Sarah's convalescence, nevertheless resented the presence of the child in her home as irksome, and chafed to place her where she would be in good hands and could do without maternal supervision and attention.

As a matter of fact, at the age of seven Sarah could neither read nor write, and had never heard of arithmetic!

When her mother explained that she was to go to live in a place where there were hundreds of other little girls, who were to become her playmates, Sarah was overjoyed. During the terrible two years when she could not run about like other children, Sarah had had no playmates whatever; and, during her airings in her mother's or her aunt's carriage, had often wistfully watched other and luckier little girls rolling hoops along the gravelled paths of the Champs Elysées, or in the fields which then fringed what is now the Boulevard de Clichy. She had been an intensely lonely child from her infancy and could scarcely contain her happiness at the thought that at last she was to be as other children, and have little friends with whom she could talk and play as an equal.

Probably the main reason for sending Sarah away at this juncture was the fact that Julie was again about to become a mother.

It may be as well to state here that Julie Bernhardt was the mother of four children including a boy who died. Sarah was the first, Jeanne the second, and Régine the third. More will be told hereafter concerning these two turbulent sisters of the actress. They both lived unfortunate lives and died still more unfortunate deaths.

A report of Sarah's parentage that has won considerable credence was published by a weekly Paris newspaper in 1886, and re-published again as recently as April 8, 1923, by *La Rampe,* a Paris theatrical paper. I quote from the latter:

"Edouard Bernhardt, grandfather of Sarah Bernhardt, was a Jew. He fulfilled the functions of chief oculist to the Court of Austria. He came to St. Aubin-du-Corbier, in Brittany, and there married the Marquise de la Thieulé du Petit-Bois de la Vieuville, by whom he had four daughters and one son: Julie, Rosine, Agathe, Vitty and Edouard. The Marquise died and Edouard Bernhardt married, secondly, Madame Van Berinth, who had been governess to his children. Rosine and Julie (mother of Sarah Bernhardt) ran away to Havre, where they obtained work as saleswomen in a confectionery establishment. Their father sent for them, and they fled to London. Shortly afterwards they returned to Havre, where Julie lived as the wife of a man named Morel, a ship-builder. They had fourteen children, of whom Sarah, born at Paris, 125, Faubourg St. Honoré, on October 23, 1840, was one."

This seems circumstantial but it is absolutely inac-

Sketch of Thérèse Meilhan (afterwards Mme. Pierre Berton)
by Georges Clairin, 1881.

curate. I give it here, together with the evidence to contravert it, because so many people believe the above to be the true story of Sarah's birth.

The rebutting evidence consists, first, in Sarah's own denial, which was published almost immediately after the story itself, and, secondly, in the fact that the certificate of her baptism, in which the truth was certainly given, states that she was then living (twelve years later) in the rue St. Honoré—not that she was born in that street; and the date is given in this certificate as September 25, 1844, not October 23, 1840, as is claimed by La Rampe; that her father was not "Monsieur Morel," but George Bernhardt; and that her mother was not "Julie Bernhardt" but Julie Van Hard.

And, as I have said, Julie had only four children, not fourteen!

The same paper (*La Rampe*) says that Sarah was baptised at the age of eight years. When she was eight, Sarah was still a Jewess and at the school of which we shall shortly give an account. Sarah was baptised, under the name of Rosine, five years later, at the Grandchamps Convent, Versailles.

When she was seven, then, and five months before Jeanne was born, Sarah was taken to Madame Fressard's school, at 18, rue Boileau, Auteuil. The building still exists, but it has been turned into a private sanatorium.

The journey to Auteuil, which one can now make from the rue St. Honoré in twenty minutes by underground railway or in half an hour by tramway or motor-bus, was

then quite a formidable affair.   Paris was left behind at
the Avenue Montaigne, and from there the way lay along
the banks of the smiling Seine, with only a roadside
estaminet bordering what is now one of the most aristocratic streets of all Paris.   It took over an hour for the
coach to reach the rue Boileau, in the little village of
Auteuil.   Sarah, needless to say, was enchanted with the
journey and with the happy prospects ahead of her.

It was quite a ceremony, the installation of Sarah in her
new home.   Besides Julie and Aunt Rosine, there was a
General and another man, who represented Sarah's father,
then absent in Lisbon.   They were very pompous and important, and inclined to exaggerate the wealth that was
so evident in the rich trappings of Aunt Rosine's coach.

After much talk and negotiation, during which the
party gathered around a bottle of wine opened by
Madame Fressard, Sarah was formally entered on the
books of the school as a pupil.

Amongst other things Julie insisted on presenting
Madame Fressard with eight large jars of cold cream,
with which she gave orders that Sarah was to be mas-
saged every morning.   Another order concerned Sarah's
mass of curly hair.   It was not to be cut or trimmed in
any way, but to be carefully combed night and morning.
And when Madame Fressard ventured a slight protest
at all these injunctions, Julie only waved her hand with
a large gesture, saying:

"You will be paid—her father is wealthy!"

The exact sum contributed by George Bernhardt

towards Sarah's maintenance was four thousand francs annually.

During all the conversation that attended her installation as a pupil at the Auteuil school, Sarah remained mute, too shy to say a word.

"What a stupid child!" said Aunt Rosine, who was years before she gained a very high opinion of Sarah.

"Naturally stupid, I'm afraid!" sighed her mother, languidly.

Only Madame Fressard, the stranger in the group, came to the forlorn little creature's aid:

"Well, she has your eyes—so intelligent, madame!" she said.

And with this the party left in their flamboyant coach, each scrupulously kissing the child farewell at the gate, and each, without any doubt at all, exceedingly glad to be rid of her.

Sarah was at last at school.

CHAPTER V

IN later years it was fairly well known amongst theatrical people that Sarah was subject to "stage fright." The only occasion, however, on which nerves actually stopped her performance, occurred at Auteuil school, when she was eight years and three months old. Sarah told this story to me on one memorable day at Ville d'Avray, when, during a fête given by the Grand Duke Peter of Russia, we had stolen away from the crowd into Bellevue woods. I have never seen the incident referred to in print.

"I had been at the school a little more than a year," Sarah told me, "when it was decided to give a performance of *Clotilde,* a play for children, which concerned a little girl's adventures in fairyland. Stella Colas, afterwards the wife of Pierre de Corvin, was cast for the name part. Another little fair girl (whose name I have forgotten) was to play the rôle of Augustine, the partner of Clotilde. And I was cast for the part of the Queen of the Fairies.

"At the rehearsals—we rehearsed all the winter— everything went well. My part was not an important one, but it involved some pretty realistic acting in the second act, when the Queen of the Fairies dies of mortification on hearing Clotilde affirm that the fairies do not really exist. This was the first 'death scene' in which I ever acted.

"I wore wings, of course, and many rehearsals were necessary before the stage-manager, who was our kindergarten teacher, could get me to fall without breaking them. Finally I learned the part, and managed to do it to the entire satisfaction of everyone.

"When the great night came, we were, of course, all very nervous, myself most of all, for my mother and two aunts had written that they would be present accompanied by no less a personage than the Duc de Morny, then considered to be the power behind Napoleon the Third's throne.

"Before the curtain went up, my knees were knocking together and I felt a wild desire to fly. I tried to run away and hide, in fact, but the teacher found me, petted me and made me promise to go on with the part.

"I had nothing to do until the end of the first act, when Clotilde and Augustine fall asleep at the foot of a great tree and dream of the fairies. My part was to descend from the tree, assisted by unseen wires, float to the middle of the stage, and then pronounce the words: 'On demande la reine des rêves? Me voici!' ('They want the Queen of Dreams? Here I am!')

"Clotilde and Augustine fell asleep, and trembling all over I floated down and advanced to the front of the stage. We had no regular footlights, and everyone in the little auditorium could be distinguished from the stage.

"Instead of pronouncing the sentence about the Queen of Dreams, I stood tongue-tied, unable to utter a syllable. Several times my mouth opened, and I tried to speak, but the words would not come.   All the time I was anxiously searching the audience for familiar faces.   It was only when I saw none, and realised that my mother was not present, that I managed to stutter:

"'*On d-d-dem-m-m-mande la reine d-des rêves? M-m-me voici!*'

"The last word I uttered in one breathless syllable; then rushed off the stage to the accompaniment of much amused applause.

"In the wings of the tiny stage I was met by the principal of the school, who, affecting not to notice my embarrassment, complimented me warmly on my 'success,' and then told me that my mother and her party had not arrived.   This, more than anything else, gave me the necessary courage to go through with my part.

"Even in later years when I was on the regular stage, the presence of my mother in an audience invariably made me so nervous that I could hardly play.   She was ever the harshest critic I had!

"The second act proceeded fairly well, since it was chiefly a dance by the fairies, with myself in the centre, wielding a mystic sceptre.   All I had to do was wave the sceptre, and the fairies would bow as it was raised and lowered.   Finally came the big moment when Clotilde awakens, and says: 'Pshaw, I was dreaming; there are no such things as fairies!'

"With these words I was supposed to stop and wave my sceptre indignantly, on which all the other fairies disappeared, leaving me alone with Clotilde and the sleeping Augustine. Clotilde advances to me and asks: 'Who are you?' To my reply 'I am the Queen of the Fairies,' she answers scornfully: 'You are a fraud, for there are no such things as fairies.'

"When she utters these words I stagger and then, moaning and clasping my hand to my heart, sink slowly to the ground. Clotilde, agonised, asks: 'What is the matter?' and I reply: 'You have killed me, for when a little girl says she doesn't believe in the fairies, she mortally wounds their Queen.'

"We had got as far as my reply 'I am the Queen,' when suddenly I perceived, in the front row of the audience, six beautifully-gowned ladies and two gentlemen, who had not been there before. In trepidation I searched their faces, standing stock-still and not listening to Clotilde's scornful reply. Yes! There was my mother, and there were my two aunts, as I had feared!

"All my stage-fright came back to me. And, instead of sinking to the ground as I was supposed to do, I burst out sobbing and ran off the stage, in the centre of which I left poor Clotilde standing, a forlorn little girl of ten. Instantly there was a storm of laughter and applause. Unable to stand it, Clotilde too ran off the stage, and the curtain was hastily rung down.

"Soon I was surrounded with teachers and elder girls, some abusing me, others begging me to finish the play.

But it was useless. I could act no more and the play, for lack of an understudy, was over. I was hustled, a weeping and very bedraggled-looking fairy, to the dormitory, where I was left alone with my thoughts.

"I would have given worlds to have been left alone for the remainder of the day! But it was not to be, for scarcely fifteen minutes passed before the door opened and my mother appeared, followed by my aunts and their whole party!

"I could have prayed for the floor to open and swallow me! I hid my head in the bedclothes, like an ostrich, and affected not to hear the words addressed to me. Finally I felt firm hands on my shoulders and I was dragged forth, weeping violently.

"If mother had only taken me in her arms and kissed and comforted me! I was only a tiny child, not yet nine years old and still constitutionally weak, with high-strung nerves. But she stood there holding me and looking coldly into my tear-filled eyes.

" 'And to think,' she said icily, 'that this is a child of mine!

" 'One would never think it,' said Aunt Rosine, sternly.

"All were hard, unsympathetic, seeming not to realise that they were bullying a child whose nerves were at the breaking-point and who was in reality almost dead from exhaustion. I broke into another storm of sobs and, kicking myself free from my mother, ran to the bed and threw myself upon it in despair. With some further unkindly remarks from my mother and aunts, the party finally left, but as he reached the door the Duc de Morny, the last to go out, turned and retraced the few steps to my bed.

" 'Never mind, my little one," he whispered. 'You will show them all how to act one of these days, won't you?'

"His comforting words, however, had come too late. I had sobbed myself into a fever and the next morning the doctor had to be called. For several days I was kept in bed and forbidden to see the other girls. Through these long four days I kept thinking constantly of my mother. Why had she been so cruel, so cold to her daughter? I knew that another child had been born the year before, and with childish intuition I hit upon the right answer. Mother loved the baby more than she loved me—if, indeed, she loved me at all. I was inconsolable at the thought. How lonely a vista the coming years opened to my immature imagination! Scores of times I sobbed out aloud: 'I would rather be dead! I would rather be dead!'

"Alas! this was not the last time that my mother's chilly behaviour towards me threw me into a paroxysm of misery resulting in illness. I never grew callous to her disapproval of me; her cutting criticisms had always the power to wound me to the heart. And yet I loved her! More, I adored her! Poor, lonely, friendless child that I was and had ever been, my starved heart cried out to the one human being whose love I had the right to claim, and who responded to my caresses sometimes almost as if I had been a stranger."

This was the only occasion on which Sarah Bernhardt ever bewailed to me or to anyone else, her mother's lack of affection for her.   She was scrupulously loyal to both her parents, and on the rare occasions when she mentioned them, it was always in terms of genuine love and respect.

During her two years in Auteuil, Sarah's mother went to see her only three times, and her father only once. Her father's visit took place at the end of the first year, in December, 1851.   It was the first time, to her recollection, that Sarah had ever seen him.   They met in the head-mistress's office, and the occasion must have been replete with drama.

"I was called from study one afternoon about three o'clock," said Sarah, "and taken to Mme. Fressard's *bureau*.   I found her waiting for me at the door with a peculiar expression on her face, and in the arm-chair near the fireplace I saw a very well-dressed man of about thirty, with a waxed moustache.

" '*Ma chérie,*' said Madame Fressard, 'here is your father come to see you.'

"*Mon père!*   So this was the mysterious personage whose wish and order governed my life; this the parent of whom my mother was apparently so much in fear, and yet whom she seldom saw; this the stranger who was responsible for my being!

"I advanced shyly and gave my face to be kissed, an

operation which my father performed twice, on both sides, his moustache giving me a prickly sensation on my cheeks.

" 'Why, she is growing into quite a little beauty!' he said to Madame Fressard, holding me so that he could look at me closely.   Then he asked me many questions: Was I happy?   Was I well?   Had I playmates?   What had I learned?   Could I read and write?—and spell? —and do sums?

"The interrogation lasted ten minutes and then my father took his tall grey hat and gloves, and prepared to leave.

" 'We will leave her with you for a little while longer, madame,' he said to Madame Fressard, while I listened with all my ears.

" 'I am going for a long journey and do not expect to return for eight or ten months.   When I come back we will consider what is best to be done.'

"Kissing me again, he took his departure and Madame Fressard drew me to her.

" 'I should think you would love your father very very much,' she said.   'He is such a handsome man!'

" 'How can I love him?' I replied wonderingly.   'I have never seen him before.' "

A year later Bernhardt had not returned from South America, but he sent Julie a letter, in which he urged that Sarah should be taken from Madame Fressard's preparatory school and sent to a convent; he suggested Grandchamps Convent, at Versailles.   He had written to the Superior, he said, explaining the circumstances, and the latter had replied that if little Sarah was sponsored by one other gentleman, preferably one in Paris, the matter could be arranged. Julie at once asked the Duc de Morny, who agreed to sponsor the child.

In the same letter Bernhardt said that he had made his will, in which he left 20,000 francs to Sarah, providing she had married before the age of twenty-one.

"I do not intend my daughter," he wrote coldly, "to follow the example of her mother."

Until she was twenty-one the income from the 20,000 francs was to pay for Sarah's schooling. Her mother was to pay for her clothes.

Although the letter said that Bernhardt did not expect to return to France for several months, he actually caught the next boat to that which carried his letter, and arrived in Paris just after Sarah had been withdrawn from the school at Auteuil.

This had not been effected without a storm of protest on Sarah's part. The two years had passed happily at Madame Fressard's, and she feared the future, surrounded by strange and cold relatives.

Julie had gone to London, and it was Aunt Rosine who went to the school to fetch the child.

Sarah delighted to tell of this departure from the school.

"I hated to leave," she told me, "and it was two hours before they could succeed in dressing me. Once this was accomplished, I flew at Tante Rosine like a young fury, and spoiled all her elaborate *coiffure*.

"She was furious and, bundling me into her coach, commanded me to keep silent. But I would not, and throughout the journey in the jolting carriage from Auteuil to 6, rue de la Chaussée d'Antin, where my aunt and my mother owned a joint flat, I tore at her hair and kicked at her legs, and otherwise performed like the disgraceful young ragamuffin I really was.

"I was no better on our arrival at the flat, and kept the whole household in an uproar until I heard the sudden announcement that my father had arrived! Then I collapsed and had to be carried to bed, where I lost consciousness for three hours. When I awoke, it was to find a doctor and nurse installed and an array of medicine bottles on the table. I felt utterly exhausted and I heard Doctor Monod, the great physician who had been called by the Duc de Morny, tell my father that I was in an extremely delicate condition and that my recovery depended upon my being kept absolutely quiet. 'Above all,' said he, 'she is not to be "crossed."' "

Sarah's father often visited her during her three days' convalescence from the fever brought on by a fit of temper, and on two occasions he brought with him Rossini, who lived in the same street and was an intimate friend.

Julie had been informed of Sarah's illness, but was herself ill at Haarlem, in Holland, where she had just arrived from London. It was a fortnight before she reached Paris, and in the meantime Sarah stayed at Neuilly, in the home of another and married aunt whose husband afterwards became a monk.

When Julie finally arrived, a dinner was arranged to

take place the night before Sarah was taken to the Convent. Edouard Bernhardt was present. This was the last time Sarah saw her father, for he died shortly afterwards in Italy.

Sarah's life at the Convent has been more or less faithfully described in her own Memoirs, and I shall not dilate on it here. She was expelled three times—the last time for good. She was baptised at the age of twelve under the name of Rosine, and from then on dated her determination to become a nun. For two years she was fanatical on the subject of religion, but this did not prevent her fits of temper from breaking out and disturbing the whole school.

"All my time at the Convent I was haunted by the desire to be a nun," she said to me once. "The beautiful life of the sisters who taught us at Grandchamps, their almost unearthly purity, their tranquil tempers, all made a tremendous impression on me. I dearly desired to take the vows and, had it been left to me, Sarah Bernhardt would have become Sister Rosine. But I doubt whether I would have remained a nun for life!

"I was never genuinely religious. It was the glamour and mystery and, above all, the tranquillity surrounding the life of a cloistered nun that attracted me. I should have run away from the Convent before many weeks."

Young Sarah was tremendously high-spirited and constantly in trouble. The nuns were always sending despairing reports to her mother.

Once, during a presentation of prizes, she pretended

to faint and acted the part so realistically that even the Superior was deceived and believed her pupil to be dead. It gave her such a shock that the poor lady was ill for days. Sarah was sent to her bedroom in disgrace.

"I spent the time reading forbidden books and eating *bonbons* that the *concierge* had smuggled in to me," she said, in telling me the story.

On another occasion she organised a flight from the Convent. In the dead of night she and six other girls of a similarly adventurous disposition climbed down torn and knotted sheets from their dormitory windows to the ground. Clambering over the high wall surrounding the Convent grounds, they took to their heels and were caught only at noon the next day, when in the act of throwing stones at horses of the Royal Dragoons.

For this exploit she was expelled, but was allowed to return on her promise never to give trouble again.

Scarcely two months afterwards, however, she was discovered by the mother-superior on top of the Convent wall, imitating the Bishop of Versailles, whom the day before she had seen conducting the Burial Service at a graveside. Expelled again!

On still another occasion she was caught flirting with a young soldier, who had tossed his cap over the wall. When the nuns tried to catch her, she climbed the wall and stayed there for hours until long after dark. On this occasion she caught a chill which nearly resulted in her death, and when she had recovered she left the Convent for good.

CHAPTER VI

At the age of fifteen Sarah was a thin, weedy, shock-headed girl, about five feet tall, but undeveloped. Her complexion was pale and dark rings under her eyes told the story of unconquered anæmia. She had a chronic cough that would shake her thin body to paroxysms. She was extremely subject to colds and chills, and the slightest indisposition would send her to bed with fever. Doctors shook their heads over her and predicted that she would die of consumption before reaching the age of twenty.

Her anæmia gave to her face a species of sombre beauty which was enlivened by the extraordinary play of expression in her eyes as she talked. Her features reflected every change of mood, and her moods were many. Judged by her face alone, she was not so much beautiful as striking. Character fairly leapt at one when she spoke.

Her character was a curious composite of morbidity, affection, talent and wilfulness. Her mother and her governess, Mlle. de Brabender, a probationer nun, were often reduced to despair by her temper, which seemed to grow worse as she became older. At other times, but more rarely, she was tractable to the point of docility.

Sarah's first visit to the theatre was to the Opéra-Comique. This great event occurred when she was

slowly recovering from the illness which followed her
expulsion from the Convent at Grandchamps. One day
she was at her music lesson with Mlle. Clarisse, when
her mother's maid came to say that her presence was
desired in the salon. There she found her mother, the
Duc de Morny, and her younger sister Jeanne, who was
never far from her mother's side when the latter was in
Paris.

Putting his hand on her curly head the Duke said:

"We have a great surprise for you."

"A wonderful surprise," added her mother.

Sarah clapped her hands excitedly. "I know—I
know! You are going to let me enter the Convent—I
am to be a nun!"

She was overwhelmed with joy; never doubted but
that her fondest dream was to be made true.

"What is this?" demanded the Duke in amazement.
"Our beautiful little Sarah wants to be a nun? And why
do you wish to condemn yourself to that living death,
may I ask?"

Living death! To the child, whose memories of the
Convent were so recent, the life of a nun was a living
joy—a joy of service, sacrifice and peace. To her rest-
less, turbulent, almost exotic temperament the thought
of the calm, well-ordered existence of the tranquil *religie-
uses* was a beautiful one, a sacred memory. She could
not bear the harsh laughter with which her mother
greeted the suggestion.

"Expelled from a convent and wants to be a nun!"

said Julie, scornfully.   She could never bring herself to
believe that this amazingly complex creature was her own
child.

"Hush!" commanded the Duke, frowning.   "Now,
my little one, my question is not answered.   Why do you
wish to be a nun?"

Sarah looked fearlessly at her mother's protector.

"The doctors say I am soon to die—I have heard them
talk," she said.   "I would like to die with my soul dedicated to God."

To Julie, who was still a Jewess, this was cause for
further laughter; but the Duke, a man of much sentiment
and some honour, was much affected.

"Nonsense!" he said.   "You are not going to die for
many years!   The doctors are fools!   We shall dis-
charge them for idle talking. . . . No, my little one,
the great surprise is not what you thought.   We are
going to take you to the Opéra-Comique to see a play."

Instead of the stammered thanks he expected, Sarah
began to cry.

"I do not want to go to the Opéra-Comique!" she
cried, stamping her foot.   "I won't go!   Mother Saint-
Sophie (the superior at the Convent) said that the
theatre was wicked.   I do not want to be wicked: I want
to be a nun!"

Threats and persuasion were both necessary before
Sarah consented to don the new gown her mother had
purchased for her and accompany her parent and the
Duke to the latter's box at the Opéra-Comique.

This theatre was then in the Place du Chatelet, and little did the child dream, as she entered it, that twenty-five years later she herself would lease it from the city and call it the "Théâtre Sarah Bernhardt"—which is its name to-day. Thus, the last theatre in which she acted was also that in which she saw her first play.

Sarah fell an immediate victim to the theatre. The piece she saw that night—Sarah herself did not remember its name—held her enthralled. It was necessary for her companions to drag her away after the curtain had fallen on the last act.

She had been transported to a new world, an unreal sphere of delight. For days, for weeks thereafter she spoke of little else. She besieged her mother with demands to be taken to the theatre again. The latter, however, was too wrapped up in her own pleasure-loving life to take much heed in the desires of her wilful daughter.

One day Sarah went off to the art school, where she was learning to paint—her ambition to become a nun was almost forgotten now, and she would spend feverish hours in preparation for the career she was convinced was ahead of her as a great portrait-painter—and did not return until the next morning.

All that night searchers hunted throughout the city for the truant; the police were informed and it was even suggested that the Seine should be dragged, for it was remembered that to come home from the art school, which it was ascertained she had left at the usual hour, it was necessary for her to cross the Pont Neuf.

At nine o'clock the next morning a tired, sleepy and very dirty Sarah returned to her mother's flat and, in reply to a storm of questions and reproaches from her almost frantic mother, explained that she had spent the night in the Opéra-Comique.

She had gone there direct from her art school and had succeeded in entering the theatre unobserved. Hiding under a seat in one of the galleries, she had waited until the play began and had then appropriated a chair. After the play, seized with panic, she was afraid to go out with the rest of the audience and had hidden herself again, only leaving when the doors were opened to the cleaners in the morning.

After that the Duke gave her regular tickets for the theatre, and she saw many plays. Frequently she would visit the same theatre a dozen times, learn several of the parts by heart and surprise her friends by reciting them.

It was at this period of her life that Sarah began to have friends of the opposite sex, but she assured me that she loved none of them.

"I had no foolishness of that kind in my head!" she told me on one occasion. "My mother's house was always full of men, and the more I saw of them the less I liked them.

"I was not a very companionable child. I had few girl friends and fewer male acquaintances, but these latter were assiduous in their attempts to make me like them.

"The first man who asked me to marry him was a wealthy tanner's son, a young fellow of twenty who was earning forty francs a week in his father's establishment, but who expected to be rich one day.

"His father used to frequent my mother's house and one day he brought his son with him. I was sent for to complete the party and, though I was haughty and kept the young fellow at a distance, I could see that I had made a conquest.

"He came again and again, and would waylay me on my journey to and from the art school, insisting on carrying my books. I did not dislike him, for he was a handsome, earnest young man, but neither did I like him particularly; and when he capped his attentions by asking me to marry him I laughed in his face. He went away vowing revenge.

"That night my mother came into my bedroom and asked me whether the tanner had not proposed that day.

" 'Yes, mother,' I said.

" 'And you accepted him?'

"I gave her a look of horror. 'Accept him?' I cried. 'But no, of course I did not accept him! I do not love him—that is one reason——'

" 'It is a poor reason,' said my mother angrily. 'Do you suppose I wish you on my hands for ever? Are you never going to marry? Your sisters are growing up and soon they will marry and you will be left, an ugly *vieille fille!* Love always comes after marriage!'

" 'I do not care,' I persisted. 'I will not marry your

tanner! He has large ears and his teeth are bad and he cannot talk. I will not marry him, and if he comes here again I shall slap his face!'

"My mother was angrier than I had ever seen her. 'Very well, then, you shall do as you like! I wash my hands of you!' she exclaimed, and left me.

"I burst into a storm of tears and cried half the night. What a lonely child I was! My only friends were Madame Guérard, who was under the domination of my mother, and Mlle. de Brabender, a timid soul, who would fondle and talk to me affectionately when we were alone, but who was afraid to open her mouth in the presence of my lovely mother."

The tanners—father and son—ceased to frequent the Van Hard house, and for a long while Julie did not speak to her daughter except formally. To make up for it, she was tremendously and ostentatiously affectionate with her two other daughters, Jeanne and Régine, who had been born four years previously.

Régine had a childhood somewhat similar to that of Sarah; that is to say, she was bundled from here to there, never nursed by her mother, alternately the recipient of cuffs and kisses, and from the age of three left pretty much to her own sweet devices. It is not to be wondered at that she grew into a perfect terror of a child.

At the time of which we are writing now, Régine was forbidden the reception rooms of the house, and spent most of her time in Sarah's room. Sarah became her nurse and teacher, and this relationship continued until, fourteen years later, Régine died.

Julie Van Hard had become a fashionable personage in Paris, owing to her relationship with the Duc de Morny, who was then one of the most powerful men in France. The Duke kept her plentifully supplied with money, and her gowns were the rage of Paris.

Beautiful, of commanding stature, her glossy reddish-gold hair without a streak of grey in it, Julie was an idol to be worshipped by the youthful *dilettantes* of the gay city. No reception, no first night at a theatre, was complete without the presence of Julie Van Hard.

Dressmakers besieged her to wear their gowns for nothing, in return for the advertisement she gave them. It was Julie Van Hard, mother of Sarah Bernhardt, who launched the famous Second Empire style of tightly-wound sleeves, with lace cuffs, square *décolleté* and draped gowns with long trains. She was a great coquette, and almost certainly the Duc de Morny was not the only recipient of her favors.

Julie Van Hard's home was spacious, and was invariably filled with visitors. There was a dinner or an entertainment of some kind every night. Gathered in the two gorgeously-decorated salons one would see such people as Sarah's two aunts, Rosine Berendt and Henriette Faure; Paul Régis, who stood as her godfather at Sarah's baptism; General Polhés, an old friend of Julie's and godfather of Régine; Madame de Guérard, Count de Larry, Duc de Morny, Count de Castelnau, Albert

Prudhomme, Viscomte de Noué, Comte de Larsan, Comte de Charaix, General de la Thurmelière, Augustus Lévy the playwright, Vicomte de Gueyneveau, and many others.

Sarah seldom appeared at the parties in which these people figured. Their activities did not interest her. She had refused to continue with her piano studies, to the great disappointment of her mother, who was an accomplished pianiste.

"I have always hated the piano!" Sarah told me once in 1890. "I think it is because Mlle. Clarisse, my teacher, used to rap me on the fingers with a little cane she carried to mark the tempo. Whenever I hit a false note, down would come the cane, and then I would fly into a fury, charge the poor lady like a small tigress and try to pull her hair out. She did not remain to teach me very long and she was never replaced!"

The next candidate to Sarah's hand was a worthy glove-maker, named Trudeau. He was wealthy, as wealth was counted then, and while not precisely the son-in-law Julie would have wished, he would doubtless have been welcome enough in the family had he succeeded in breaking down the barriers Sarah had erected before her heart.

Sarah's chief objection to Trudeau was that he was too fat. Then, again, he was smooth-shaven, and it was accounted very ugly in those days not to have a moustache. Clean-shaven men, on entering a theatre, would often receive a jeering reception from the audience. The hirsute fashion of that period was long side-whiskers, a short, double-pointed beard, and a pointed, waxed moustache.

Julie did not urge her daughter to marry Trudeau. She probably knew that any such effort would have been doomed to failure from the start. Trudeau, however, laid determined siege to the young girl for several months, during which he sent her, among other expensive gifts, a brooch of the sort that was afterwards known as a "la Vallière." This brooch was among those recently sold by auction in Paris.

To all his many proposals of marriage, however, Sarah turned a deaf ear. She would taunt him about his figure, which was short and broad, and above all she would jeer at his lack of a moustache.

"Never will I marry a man who cannot grow hair on his face!" she once declared.

He persisted, until one day Sarah called him a "fat old pig" and threw the contents of a glass of champagne in his face. Then he accepted his *congé*, and went out of Sarah's life for ever.

Following Trudeau came a chemist, who had a shop at the corner of the Boulevard and the rue de la Michodière. He had been captivated by the red-haired long-legged youngster who used to come to him to have prescriptions filled. I do not recall the name of this man, but I know that when Sarah refused him he consoled himself less than a month later by marrying a widow. Years later Sarah broke a parasol over his head, when he refused to promise not to supply her sister Jeanne with morphine.

After that a succession of young men unsuccessfully petitioned for her hand. In a space of two years she had nearly a dozen proposals, all of which she refused with equal disdain. She was becoming a noteworthy character in Paris herself, but she, the child, was of course eclipsed by the brilliant beauty of her mother.

These suitors came from all classes and conditions of society. At least one—the Vicomte de Larsan, a young fop whose father was a frequenter of Julie's house— was of noble birth and heir to a considerable fortune. He was twenty-two years of age, and when he asked her to marry him, Sarah slapped his face.

I had many long talks with Sarah about these early romantic episodes. She loved to repeat reminiscences of her girlhood and she had an astounding memory.

As far back as 1892, she told me that in her life she had received more than a thousand proposals of marriage, and that she could remember the name and the date of every one of them!

I was curious about these thousand proposals of marriage, and often tried to get her to give me the names. But she said that to do so might cause harm to some of the men concerned, many of whom were then happily married, and had children. She told me of many episodes, however, in which such secrecy was not necessary, and these episodes will be found in detail later in this book.

Sarah Bernhardt.

One of the best of the earliest pictures.

"In my teens I cared nothing for men—they disgusted me!" she said. "I was called a great little beauty, and men used to kneel at my feet and swear that they would jump in the Seine if I refused them. I invariably told them to go and do so!

"I was indifferent to all men. My mother's flat at 22, rue de la Michodière, which had been beautifully furnished by the Duc de Morny, was full of men visitors from early afternoon until late at night. I would keep out of their way as much as possible, and once I ran away for three days, because one of my mother's admirers persisted in making revolting proposals to me.

"Finally I returned one day from the painting school and found my mother and the servant out and P—— installed in the salon. Before I could escape, he had seized me and covered me with kisses. They were the first love-kisses I had ever received, and I was not to give one for years afterwards

"I struggled violently, bit him on the chin and scratched his face frightfully, but I was a weak child and he would have overpowered me eventually had not the door opened and my mother, followed by the Duc de Morny, come in. Neighbours had heard my screams and were congregated outside the door. My mother was white with passion.

"The Duke challenged P—— to a duel in secret, his rank preventing him from making the affair a public one. The duel was never fought, however, for P—— left that night for his home near Arcachon, and a few months later I heard he had been killed in a coaching accident near Tours.

"The Vicomte de Larsan was the most persistent suitor, after P——, and he was only a boy. I could not bear the sight of him, with his rouged cheeks, his scented hands, his powdered hair and his shirts covered with expensive lace. He used to wait outside the house for hours until I came out, and would make fervent declarations of love in the street. I grew to hate him, and I told him so!

"But at that time I hated nearly all men, except the Duc de Morny. That nobleman was my mother's most faithful protector, and he gave her large sums, which helped to pay for my education and my art lessons. He used to predict a great future for me. Not only did he stand sponsor for me for the Versailles convent but also procured my entrance into the Conservatoire.

"Many people in those days thought that I was the Duke's natural daughter, and the legend has persisted. It was not true, though, for when I was born my mother was in exceedingly humble circumstances, and she did not meet the Duke—a meeting which changed her fortunes—until several years later."

CHAPTER VII

THE first press notice that Sarah Bernhardt ever received
was published in the *Mercure de Paris* in October, 1860,
when she was sixteen years old. Curiously enough it did
not concern her histrionic talent—then just beginning to
develop—but related to a painting entitled "Winter in
the Champs Elysées," with which Sarah had won the
first prize at the Colombier Art School in the rue de
Vaugirard.

Sarah gave me the clipping to copy—it was among her
most prized possessions—and, translated, it read as
follows:

"Among the remarkable candidates for admission to
the Beaux Arts should be mentioned a young Parisienne
of sixteen years, named Mademoiselle Sarah Bernhardt,
who is a pupil at Mlle. Gaucher's class in the Colombier
School. Mlle. Bernhardt exhibits an extraordinary
talent for one so young and her picture 'Winter in the
Champ Elysées,' with which she has won the first prize
for her class, is distinguished for its technical perfection.
Rarely have we had the pleasure of welcoming into the
Beaux Arts a young artist of similar promise, and there
can be no doubt that very soon Mlle. Bernhardt will be

classed as one of our greatest painters and thus win glory for herself and her country."

The painting in question was bought by an American friend of Sarah's some forty years later. I do not know how much was paid, but other early paintings of hers, which have sold privately during the past twenty years, have brought very large prices indeed.

My mention of this first press criticism of Sarah's work brings to mind the day she brought me, a little girl, into the library at her house 11, Boulevard Malsherbes, and showed me four fat volumes each filled with newspaper clippings, and another one only just begun. On a chair was stacked a collection of envelopes each dated, containing other clippings, and these Sarah showed me how to paste in the book. It was a great honour for me.

Later in the afternoon Maurice Bernhardt, then a small boy, came in and helped me, but I remember that he was more of a nuisance than a help, and he ended by tipping over the paste-pot and making a mess which I had to clean up.

When she died Sarah possessed many of these fat volumes of press-clippings, from every country in the world. It was said that if all the newspaper notices she received during her career could have been placed end to end, they would have reached around the world, and that if all the photographs printed of her could have been stacked in a pile, they would have reached higher than the Eiffel Tower.

Somebody even calculated once that the name Sarah Bernhardt alone had been printed so often in newspapers and magazines, and on bills, programmes and the like, that the letters used would bridge the Atlantic, while the ink would be sufficient to supply the needs of *The Times* for two months!

I cannot vouch for this, but there can be no doubt whatever that, if the number of times one's name is printed is a criterion, Sarah Bernhardt was by far the most famous person who has ever lived. For nearly sixty years never a day went by without the words "Sarah Bernhardt" being printed somewhere or other. When she returned from her American tour in 1898, the press-clippings she brought back with her filled a large trunk.

The interesting point in all this is that only a very few writers concerned themselves with her painting and sculpture. Out of all the millions of articles written about her, a bare sixty or seventy concern her capabilities outside the theatre.

If little was known of Sarah the artist, still less was known of Sarah the woman. That is why this book is written.

Thousands of people who loved her as an actress never knew that she had been married! Those who knew that she was a Jewess born were few indeed. Nothing was known of her intimate home life, of her *affaires du cœur,* of her attempts at authorship, of the many plays she either wrote or revised.

In all the multitudinous clippings in that wonderful

collection of hers, how many reveal the fact that Sarah
Bernhardt was a certificated nurse? How many persons
know that she once studied medicine and was highly
proficient in anatomy? How many know that she was
a vegetarian, and often said that her long life was due
to her horror of meat? How many know that, for
many long years, until infirmity intervened, Sarah Bernhardt, the Jewess born, was a practising Catholic, seldom
missing her Sunday attendance at Mass?

Is it not extraordinary that so little should *really* have
been known of the most famous woman in the world?
Is it not amazing that Sarah was able to conceal her
home life under the glorious camouflage of her stage
career?

Yet, looking back into history, how little is known of
the great men and women who decorate its pages!

We know where Jean d'Arc was born; we know she
saved the French armies from defeat; but never has it
been written where she went to school, and little or
nothing is known of her family, of the mother who produced her, of the father who brought her up a heroine.
Oliver Cromwell had a wife, yet what do we know of
her? George Washington was one of the greatest
warriors of his day, yet we know little of the private
life of the Father of America.

I have always felt this lack of personal knowledge of
our own great ones. Only recently have biographers
realised the true scope of their task. Until the intimate
story of Victor Hugo was published, some few years

ago, how little we knew of the man who wrote three times as many words as there are in the Holy Bible!

This is somewhat of a digression, but one justified perhaps by the considerations involved. If the great and successful deeds of men of genius make entrancing reading, how much more absorbing can be the tale of their spiritual struggles and "mental fights"?

And with her graduation from the art school—she was entitled to enter the Beaux Arts but never did—the real struggles of the lonely, temperamental child who was Sarah Bernhardt began. Though she did not know it, a war of impulses was going on within her soul.

There was her great, her undoubted talent for painting and sculpture, which her teachers were convinced would soon make her a great personage. There was her budding dramatic talent which she was only beginning to suspect. There was her fundamental morbidity, that would plunge her into moods during which she dreamed of and longed for death. There was the craving of her turbulent nature for the peace and tranquillity investing the life of a cloistered nun. There was her inherited unmorality—I know of no other word with which to describe it—which was for ever tugging at her and endeavouring to drag her down into the free-and-easy existence led by her mother. There was her maiden heart, starving for affection. There was her delicate health, which made prolonged effort impossible. And lastly there was her iron will, inherited probably from her father.

A phrase in one of the pathetic writings of Marie
Bashkirtseff comes to my mind: "At the age of fourteen
I was the only person remaining in the world; for it was
a world of my own that could be penetrated only by
understanding, and no one, not even my mother, understood."

How could the frivolous nature of Julie Van Hard
have comprehended the deep waters that ran within the
soul of her unwanted child?

Julie would be enormously vexed at Sarah's seeming
dullness. When she had said something particularly
witty—and Julie was witty according to the humorous
standards of the period—and Sarah did not smile, Julie
would cry: "Oh, you stupid child! To think that you
are mine. . . !"

Not even Sarah's achievements in the school of painting could convince Julie that she had not given birth to
a child of inferior mentality. For what success Sarah
had with her pictures, Julie took credit to herself.

She was exasperated by Sarah's attitude towards the
life she herself loved so well. Julie would remain for
hours at table, surrounded by wits and half-wits, dandies
and hangers-on at court, proud in the assumption that
she was an uncrowned queen. At such parties Sarah
would sit speechless, unable or unwilling to join in the
coarse sallies of her mother's guests. Her mother used
constantly to refer to her in the presence of others as
"That stupid child," or "That queer little creature."

When she had an exceptionally important personage

to entertain, Julie would forbid Sarah to show herself, fearful that her daughter's "stupidity" would injure her own chances.

As constantly as she blamed Sarah, she praised and lavished affection on Jeanne, her "little Jeannot." Jeanne seemed to take naturally after her mother in all things, and when she grew older she even surpassed her mother by the frivolous way in which she lived.

The sad story of Jeanne will be told later, but it may be said that she had none of Sarah's vast intelligence, none of her good taste, none of her tremendous capacity for affection. Jeanne was without talent—a pretty but vapid shell. Her father was not, of course, Edouard Bernhardt.

Régine, on the other hand, took after Sarah, who practically brought her up. But Régine had Sarah's temper and wild, erratic temperament without Sarah's talent and Sarah's stubborn will. Where Sarah was firm and unyielding, Régine was merely obstinate. Where Sarah was clever, Régine was only "smart." She was a "pocket edition of Sarah," as her mother once remarked, without Sarah's depth of character.

Two months after Sarah attained her sixteenth birthday, her mother moved to No. 265, rue St. Honoré, not far from the Théâtre Française—better known as the Comédie Française—and Sarah delighted in loitering about the stage entrance and making friends with the actors and actresses who passed in and out.

Sometimes she passed whole afternoons and evenings

thus employed.   Occasionally she would run errands for her idols, to be recompensed by a free ticket to the balcony.   On one never-to-be-forgotten occasion Jules Bondy, one of the actors, took the eager little red-head into the theatre itself and installed her on a case in the wings, from which she could see the play without herself being seen.   It was Molière's *Le Médecin Malgré Lui,* and from that time dated Sarah's love for the works of the actor-playwright to whom the Comédie Française is dedicated.

In later years Sarah played Molière several times, but she made no notable success in this author's works.

Sarah always longed to be a comédienne; she might have been a great one, in fact, but for her greater gifts for tragedy, which prevented managers from risking her appearance in lighter drama.   Great comédiennes of merit are less rare than great tragediennes.   In fact, I doubt whether there is living to-day an actress who will ever be called Sarah Bernhardt's equal in tragedy.

Shortly after the household moved, Sarah fell down the stairs and broke her leg.   An infection developed and it was two months before she was able to walk. When she finally recovered she was thinner than ever— a veritable skeleton.   Her face maintained its eerie beauty, the large blue eyes retained their occasional fire, but the flush of fever relieved her habitual pallor and beneath her neck her body was little more than a bag of bones.

She ceased wearing short dresses and took to long

ones, for very shame of her thin limbs. She wore thick clothes and corsets to pad herself out. She grew introspective, spending long hours alone or playing silently with her infant sister Régine, or reading books. Once Mlle. de Brabender discovered her on her knees and, on inquiry, obtained the confession that she had been praying steadily for nearly three hours.

The religious habit again grew on her. The subjects for her brush were mostly saints, surrounded with the conventional halo. She hung her room with religious pictures, some done by herself and some bought cheaply at a shop near the Church of St. Germain l'Auxerrois. Over her bed was a crucifix, modelled by herself from wax.

She was confirmed at the age of sixteen years and five months, and wore the virginal white for days afterwards —until it grew so dirty, indeed, that her exasperated mother made her throw it away.

A priest had given her a rosary that had been dipped in the holy waters of Lourdes, and this she wore continually. In the quarter she became known as *"la petite religieuse."* Doctors shook their heads, and predicted that she was falling into a decline, from which she would never recover. Her suitors fell off, one by one, until only a retired miller, Jacques Boujon, a man of fifty, remained.

To English readers it may seem incredible that a girl of sixteen should have had actual suitors, and among them men of position and wealth. This was nevertheless common in France in the middle of the last century, and it is by no means rare in the France of to-day. Added to this was Julie Van Hard's intense desire to rid herself, once and for all, of this strange child she had brought into being, whose sombre presence in her house of gaiety seemed to be a perpetual mockery.

One day Sarah was visited in her bedroom, where she was studying, by her mother and Mlle. de Brabender.

"I want you to put on this new dress I have bought you, and then come down to the salon. There is something particularly important we have to say to you," said Julie.

Sarah shivered. There seemed something extraordinarily portentous in her mother's manner. Who were "*we*"? The child felt, as she told me years later, that that moment represented a cross-roads in her life.

Overwhelmed with a dread she could not define, Sarah put her new dress on with trembling fingers and descended to the salon. There she found quite a company awaiting her. Foremost in the party was the Duc de Morny. Next to him was her mother. Across the table was Jean Meyedieu, her father's notary-public. Next to him was Aunt Rosine. Madame Guérard, wearing an anxious look, occupied a seat near the fireplace. Mlle. de Brabender, accompanied by Jeanne, followed Sarah in.

The door was closed. Then Julie turned to her daughter. "Some months ago," she said, "you refused

to consider a proposal of marriage from an honourable
gentleman."

Sarah remained mute.

"To-day another honourable gentleman asks you to
marry him."

Storm signals flashed from the girl's eyes. "I will
marry no one except God!" she declared. "I wish to
return to the Convent!"

"To enter a convent," put in Meyedieu, "one must
have money, or else be a servant. You have not a sou!"

"I have the money my father left me!"

"No, you have not! You have only the interest until
you are twenty-one. If, at that age, you have not
married, the terms of your father's will stipulate that you
shall lose the principal."

The Duc de Morny intervened.

"Do you think that you are right, dear, in thus going
against the wishes of your mother?"

Sarah began to sob. "My mother is not married, yet
she wants me to be a wife! My mother is a Jewess, and
she does not want her daughter to become a nun!"

"Leave the room!" ordered Julie, angrily.

Thus ended the second family council over the future
of Sarah, and the problem was not yet solved.

After this Sarah's existence in her mother's house
became a torment. She seldom saw her parent; and
when she did, the latter hardly looked at her. She took
her meals with Régine and Mlle. de Brabender in the
nursery. She abandoned art, and spent her days looking

after her baby sister in the Champs Elysées and on the *quais* of the Seine.

She still attended the theatre as often as she could, and became a faithful devotee of the Comédie. Often she would venture as far afield as the Châtelet, or the Boulevard Bonne Nouvelle, to witness plays at the Gymnase.

One evening she returned, after a solitary evening at the theatre and, finding the salon empty, began to recite one of the parts she had seen. She had seen the play so often that the rôle of the heroine was practically graven on her memory. Believing herself entirely alone, she went right through with the piece, finishing with a dramatic flourish at the place where the heroine—I forget the play—was supposed to stab herself to death.

There was a hearty "Bravo, bravo!" and the Duc de Morny rose from a chair in which he had been sitting behind a screen.

The Duke went out and called to Julie and Rosine, and, when the two sisters entered, he asked the child to play the part again. At first bashful, Sarah eventually plucked up courage and finally did as she was asked. The Duke was much affected.

"That memory and that voice must not be lost!" he cried. "Sarah shall enter the Conservatoire!"

"She has no sense, but she is not bad at reciting," agreed Julie, scenting a happy compromise.

The Conservatoire? Sarah began to worry. What

was this new horror to which they were so easily condemning her?

"What is it, the Conservatoire?" she asked, hesitating.

"It is a school, my dear," said the Duke; "a school for great actresses."

"To the Conservatoire, by all means!" cried Aunt Rosine. "She is too stupid to be a good actress, but it will keep her out of mischief!"

The Duke was quite excited.

"We have solved the problem!" he cried. "Our Sarah is to become an actress!"

"But I don't want to be an actress!" cried poor Sarah.

Her objections were overridden, and that very night the Duke wrote to his friends at the Conservatoire, demanding that Sarah should be inscribed on the lists for admission.

Sarah was now within a month of seventeen.

CHAPTER VIII

WHEN application had been made to Auber, then director of the Conservatoire—who, on the Duc de Morny's recommendation, had agreed to inscribe Sarah on his lists —it was found that only nine weeks remained before the examinations!

Even to-day, a conservative estimate of the time required for preparation for the Conservatoire is eighteen months. Many children start studying for it when they are ten or eleven. Rarely has any pupil succeeded in entering without at least nine months' preliminary study. And Sarah had only nine weeks!

Aunt Rosine was sceptical of Sarah's ability to pass the examinations. The Duc de Morny was consoling.

"You will not pass this time," he said, "but there are other examinations next year."

As to Julie Van Hard, she was inexorable with her daughter.

"You are my daughter. You shall not disgrace me by failing!" she said to Sarah.

Julie took the child out, and bought her books by the dozen. They consulted Hugo Waldo, an actor acquaintance, and on his advice chose the plays of Corneille, Molière and Racine. Julie wanted the child to select a part in *Phèdre* for her examination, but Mlle. de Brabender, the probationer nun, said that this could not be permitted, as *Phèdre* was too shocking a rôle to place on the lips of a *jeune fille*.

In the end, Sarah learned the part of Agnes in Molière's *Ecole des Femmes,* but never used it in the examination. She passed most of her time learning to pronounce her "o's" and "r's" and "p's," and in practising the art of pronouncing each syllable separately and in putting the accent in the tone, rather than on the syllabic divisions. Nowhere is French spoken entirely purely, except on the stage of the better Paris theatres.

The day of the examinations came, and Sarah was by now word-perfect. To enable her to say her part, however, it was necessary for someone to give the cues. This had not been thought of.

Julie, whose taste in dress was exquisite but a trifle exotic, had out-done herself in her purchases of things for Sarah to wear on the great day. The gown was black, deeply *décolleté* about the shoulders; a corset accentuated the extreme slenderness of her waist; the skirt was short, but lacy drawers, beautifully embroidered, descended to the beaded slippers.

Around her neck, Sarah wore a white silk scarf. Her hair, after an hour's tussle with the hairdresser, had been combed and tugged into some sort of order and was bound tightly back from the forehead with a wide black ribbon. The effect was bizarre. One of George Clairin's best-known sketches of Sarah showed her in the hands of the hairdresser on this occasion, her mother standing near.

After what seemed an interminable wait in the hot, stifling auditorium of the Conservatoire, Sarah's name was called. Trembling, she ascended to the stage. On the way she tried to loosen the painful ribbon about her head, with the result that it came unpinned and her glorious red-gold hair tumbled forthwith about her face. Indeed when she mounted to the stage where the jury sat in uncompromising attitudes, her face could hardly be seen.

"And what will you recite?" asked the chairman, a man named Léataud.

"I have learned the part of Agnes, but I have no one to give me my cues," said Sarah.

"Then what will you do?"

Sarah was at a loss, but she regained courage suddenly on seeing two of the jury smiling at her encouragingly.

"I will recite to you a fable: 'The Two Pigeons,'" she said.

When she had finished, Professor Provost, one of the jury, asked that she should be accepted. "I will put her in my class," he said. "The child has a voice of gold!"

This was the first occasion on which Sarah's "golden voice" was thus referred to.

Sarah, who was eighth on the list at the Conservatoire, took no prize, but she was admitted. She was mad with joy. Her mother condescended to praise her a little. Mlle. de Brabender and Madame Guérard overwhelmed her with caresses. Little Sarah was a member of the Conservatoire! Her career had begun!

She had no conspicuous success at the Conservatoire. She obtained indeed one second prize for comedy, but her great talent for the drama had not yet developed. With the exception of Camille Doucet—the jury voted unanimously that she could not be included among those to be given certificates of merit. Sarah, despite her second prize, returned home in tragic mood.

"It was the second great disappointment of my life,' she said, when she related it to me years later. "I crept up to my bedroom and locked the door. Had there been any poison at hand I would have taken it. I was seized with a great desire to end my life. I thought of the Convent, of Mère Saint-Sophie. Oh, if they had only let me become a nun, instead of entering this vast, unkind world of the theatre! I cried my eyes out and finally went to sleep.

"When I awoke, it was late at night. There was not a sound in the house. My fury had spent itself, and only a great despair remained. The thought that I would have to face my mother the next day seared my soul. How could I stand her sarcasm, that cutting phrase I knew so well: 'Thou art so stupid, child!'

"I determined I would end it all for ever. I would die. I would creep out of the house while no one watched, run down to the *quai* and throw myself in the Seine. . . .

"I approached the door, unlocked it, opened it

cautiously. As I did so a piece of paper, that had been thrust into the jamb, fluttered to the ground. I took it nervously. It was a letter from Madame Guérard, my faithful old nurse. I retraced my steps into the room and held the letter to the candle as I incredulously read the message it contained:

" 'While you were asleep the Duc de Morny sent a note to your mother saying that Camille Doucet has confirmed that your engagement at the Comédie Française is arranged for. . . .'

"My mood changed miraculously. I shouted with joy. I rant to the door, flung it open, ready to cry out my news to anyone who heard me. But the household slept. I went back to bed and cried myself to sleep for very happiness."

The next day Sarah received a formal letter summoning her to the Comédie. The day following she was engaged, and signed her contract. Almost immediately she began rehearsing in the play *Iphigénie*.

About two months before her eighteenth birthday Sarah made her *début* at the *Comédie,* in a minor part. As a *débutante* from the Conservatoire, she was naturally fair prey for the critics. The greatest of these was Francisque Sarcey, who was credited with the power to make or break an actress. Managers hung on his verdicts.

This is what that powerful critic had to say about Sarah on the occasion of her *début*.

"Mlle. Bernhardt is tall and pretty and enunciates well, which is all that can be said for the moment."

Another critic, James Berbier, wrote:

"A young woman named Sarah Bernhardt made her *début* at the Comédie on September 1. She has a pretty voice and a not-unpleasing face, but her body is ugly and she has no stage presence."

Still another, Pierre Mirabeau, declared:

"Sarah Bernhardt has no personality; she possesses only a voice."

After Sarah's second *début*, in *Valérie*, this same Mirabeau wrote:

"We had the pleasure of seeing in the cast at the Comédie the young woman Sarah Bernhardt, who made her *début* recently in *Iphigénie*. She has improved, but she still has much to learn before she can properly be considered worthy of the House of Molière."

When Sarah appeared in *Les Femmes Savantes*, Francisque Sarcey, who had ignored her in *Valérie,* devoted several lines to her:

"Mlle. Bernhardt took the rôle of Henriette. She was just as pretty and insignificant as in *Iphigénie* and in *Valérie.* No reflections on her performance can be extremely gay. However, it is doubtless natural that among all the *débutantes* we are asked to see there should be some who do not succeed."

Sarah was furious at these critiques, but not as furious as her mother, who bitterly exclaimed:

"See! All the world calls you stupid, and all the world knows that you are my child!"

Her mother did not perhaps realise that her words cut the young actress straight to the heart. Above all things Sarah had wanted to please Julie; above all things Sarah had feared her mother's harsh criticisms.

That night she was found moaning in her dressing-room. A doctor, hurriedly called, declared she had taken poison, and she was rushed off to the hospital.

For five days Sarah hovered between life and death, finally rallying after four of the best doctors in Paris had been called into aid in the fight.

In response to questioning by her old friend, Madame Guérard, Sarah confessed that she had swallowed the contents of a bottle of liquid rouge. Asked the reason for this strange and terrible act she answered:

"Life was useless; I wanted to see what death was like!"

I have always believed that it was her mother's want of sympathy for her which caused Sarah's desperate act, and if there was another reason the world never knew it. Newspapers of the day attributed it to a love affair, but this Sarah denied when she related the episode to me— an episode, by the way, which is not included in her Memoirs.

"I was wrapped up in my art, and had no serious love affairs at that time," she said. "I was simply despondent because I did not succeed fast enough. Why! not a single critic praised me!"

It was the famous authoress Georges Sand who took Sarah in hand afterwards, preached love of life to her and persuaded her that a great future lay ahead. To Georges Sand Sarah one day confided:

"Madame Sand, I would rather die than not be the greatest actress in the world!"

"You are the greatest, my child!" said Madame Sand with conviction, and added: "One day soon the world will lie at your feet!"

Sarah's morbidity continued to be one of her chief characteristics however. She delighted in going to funerals; and visiting the Morgue, that grim stone building with its fearful rows of corpses exposed on marble slabs, was one of her favorite diversions.

Death had a weird fascination for her. Shortly after she entered the Comédie she had a love affair with an undertaker's assistant, but she broke off her engagement to him when he refused to allow her to be present at an embalming.

She used to describe the robe she wished to be buried in: "Pure white, with a crimson edging, and with yellow lilies embroidered about the girdle."

The crimson edging and the embroidery were absent when she was finally laid to rest.

Later on we shall hear again of this morbid streak in the divine actress—how she designed and even slept in the very coffin in which she was buried; how once she shammed dead in her dressing-room at the Odéon to such purpose that a hearse was sent for and the curtain rung down, while a tearful director announced her demise!

Her notorious temper had not left her. If anything, it was more violent than ever. The stage door-keeper at the Comédie on one occasion called her "Young Bernhardt," omitting the honorary prefix of "Mademoiselle." Without a word she broke her parasol across the man's head. Seeing him bleeding, she hurried for water, tore her silk petticoat into pieces, and bathed and bound his wound.

Twenty years later, when her name was beginning to echo round the world, this same door-keeper came to her house and told her that he had lost his position through infirmity and was now at the end of his resources.

With one of those gestures of munificence which mark the *tragédienne's* career like flashes of light, Bernhardt turned to her secretary and instructed him to buy the old man a cottage in his native Normandy, and to place a sufficient sum in trust to keep him for the remainder of his life.

Bernhardt made many enemies during her first years on the stage, and some of them remained her adversaries until their deaths.   She outlived almost all of them.

The afternoon of her *début* at the Comédie was a *matinée* exclusively for professional folk and critics.   One of the latter, an old and embittered man named Prioleau, was credited with being almost as powerful as Sarcey. He was the doyen of the critics, and as such occupied a privileged position in the wings.

The better to see the performance, he shifted his chair until it partly blocked one of the exits.   Sarah Bernhardt, going off the stage backwards, tripped over the legs of the critic's chair and nearly fell.   On recovering herself, she seized the chair by its legs and pitched the critic to the floor.   Then she turned on her heel with a fiery admonition to "keep your legs to yourself."

Horrified actresses told the angry girl that the man she had insulted was Prioleau, the great critic.   Returning to where the choleric old gentleman was picking himself up, Sarah set herself squarely in front of him, her eyes glinting fire.

"If you dare to say or write a word about me," she warned him, "I will scratch your eyes out!"

The next day she sent him a written apology and a bunch of flowers, following this with a personal visit, in which she pleaded with the old man to forgive an act of which she would certainly not have been capable had she been in her right senses.   Prioleau never forgave her, but he never used his heavy weapon of sarcasm against her.   Perhaps he always secretly believed in her threat. He died not long afterwards.

Sarah was an extraordinary mixture of pugnacity and sentiment.   One day she found a dog investigating her overturned bottle of smelling-salts.   Infuriated she dropped the poor little creature out of the dressing-room window on to a small ledge from which, if it had moved, it would have fallen four or five stories to the ground.

Five minutes later shouts attracted a crowd to the dressing-room, where they found a maid desperately hanging on to Sarah's feet, while the young actress hung head downwards outside the window, in order to rescue the dog.   Having got the animal up safely, she took it home and smothered it with kindness, never permitting it to leave her until it died of old age fourteen years later.

Sarah's love for animals—particularly ferocious ones —was one of the abiding passions of her life.   At different times she owned a pink monkey given her by an African explorer, a wildcat which was presented to her during one of her American tours, and two lion cubs, baptised "Justinian" and "Scarpia."   All four were tame and often accompanied her to the theatre, remaining in her dressing-room while she played.

She also once brought back with her from Mexico a tiger cub, which terrorised her household and, when she took it to the theatre one day, nearly broke up the performance by eating and tearing the curtains. The cub was finally poisoned by somebody in Sarah's entourage. On one occasion I saw Sarah feeding live quails to this tiger cub in her dressing-room. The same day it bit Madame Joliet, the prompter.

Another savage creature Sarah once owned was a dog. She had only to say to him "Allez!" (Go!) and he would spring at any one's throat. One day when we were at the Hotel Avenida, Lisbon, Sarah asked me to go to my room to fetch something for her. As I went out I heard her say "Allez!" and the dog sprang at me. Fortunately my husband arrived just in time, and tore the dog away. White with fury, Pierre said to Sarah: "If that happens again, I'll kill the brute!"

But I never believed Sarah did the thing deliberately. She was very apologetic.

But this is digressing from our story. We left Sarah as a *débutante* at the Comédie Française. Her *début,* as we have seen, was not very brilliant. But if her entrance into France's most famous theatre was not particularly exciting, her exit was the reverse.

CHAPTER IX

In the Comédie Française stands a statue: the bust of
Molière, the great actor-playwright to whom the theatre
is dedicated. Each year, on the anniversary of his
death, every actor and actress belonging to the company
attached to the playhouse must file past the statue and
salute.

It was due to an incident occurring during this annual
ceremony that Sarah Bernhardt left the Comédie for the
first time.

The actresses were assembled in a corridor giving
access to the statue—the *sociétaires* (actresses who had
completed their period of apprenticeship) naturally taking precedence over the *débutantes*. All were in costume,
and over the costumes they wore the long mantle, showing their badge of membership of the Comédie. These
mantles had long trains and, in endeavoring to avoid
treading on one of them, little Régine Bernhardt, who
held Sarah's hand, inadvertently stepped on that worn
by Madame Nathalie, one of the oldest actresses of the
theatre, whom Sarah described as "old and wicked."

Madame Nathalie turned and, roughly seizing the child
pushed her so violently that she was flung against a
stone pillar, bruising her side and cutting her face.

Sarah Bernhardt forgot the solemnity of the occasion,

forgot the distinction of the company, forgot everything except that her little sister had been wantonly struck.

"Beast!" she cried, and, running to the old actress, slapped first one side of her face and then the other, as hard as she could strike. The blows resounded throughout the corridor.

Madame Nathalie remained rooted to the spot. Sarah stood before her, with panting bosom and eyes flashing fire. For an instant it looked as though the ceremony would be spoiled, but other members of the company rushed between the two and they were hurried in different directions.

The next day she was summoned to the office of M. Thierry, director of the Comédie.

"Your conduct has been disgraceful, mademoiselle!" he said, "and your engagement should be cancelled immediately, but I have decided to give you one chance to make amends. Waiting in the next room are Madame Nathalie, and two other *sociétaires*. You will apologise to Madame Nathalie, in their presence, and in mine."

"Apologise to that woman who injured my baby sister?" cried Sarah. "Never!"

"Think, mademoiselle," urged Thierry. "Unless you do so you leave the Comédie!"

Leave the Comédie! After all the torturing months of preparation, after all the help she had received from the Duc de Morny, from Camille Doucet and her other friends, after the hard struggle at the Conservatoire.

Sarah saw her mother's bitter eyes, heard her scornful tongue.

She knew that her admission to the Comédie Française had been an honour and a favour which her performance at the Conservatoire did not justify. She knew that if her engagement was cancelled it was possible that she might look in vain for other employment; that every manager in Paris might be turned against her. More, she knew that her family would regard her leaving the Comédie as a personal insult to them, and it would, she realised, be no longer feasible for her to live at home. Sarah thought of her Aunt Rosine's triumphant "I told you so," and shuddered.

But on the other hand, she knew that she was in the right. A sense of tremendous injustice weighed upon her. This woman had struck her little sister, and she had administered a deserved correction. What though she was one of the oldest *sociétaires* at the Française, *She* should be the one to apologise!

It took Sarah some five minutes to arrive at this, her final conclusion, and then, turning to M. Thierry, she said:

"If Madame Nathalie will apologise to Régine, I will apologise to her!"

M. Thierry looked at her incredulously.

"You mean that you will allow a question of pure pride to interfere with your career and perhaps spoil your future?" he demanded.

"I mean that if the whole incident occurred again, I

would slap Madame Nathalie twice as hard!" said Sarah angrily.

M. Thierry turned back to his papers.

"Very well, mademoiselle," he said; "you have until to-morrow afternoon to change your mind!"

Sarah did not apologise, and she was not immediately sent away. Her powerful friends who had supported her in her effort to enter the theatre made representations to M. Thierry, and, much against his will, he agreed to give the young actress another chance.

But Madame Nathalie nursed her spite, and when, a few weeks later, Sarah was given the rôle of Dolorès, in the play of that name by Brouihet, she contrived to influence the director to take the part away from the girl, almost on the eve of production, and give it to Madame Favart.

No sooner did Sarah learn this than she bounded into M. Thierry's office.

"Give me my contract!" she cried. "I resign! I will have nothing more to do with your theatre!"

The same evening she was again a free agent. She had left the Comédie. When she returned home to inform her mother of her action, the latter took it coolly.

"Very well," said Julie, "you need look for no further help from me, or from my friends. Hereafter you can do with your life as you wish! You are emancipated!"

Sarah was then eighteen years old. From that day on she was free of maternal control, and a few weeks later she secured a minor part at the Gymnase. After playing this, she was promised a leading part in a play called *Launching a Wife,* but this promise was not kept. In her anger, Sarah left the theatre, packed her trunk, and, with less than a thousand francs, left suddenly for Spain.

In Madrid she developed a passion for bull-fighting. At one moment, according to Caroline, her maid, she became engaged to Juan Lopez, a famous matador, but at a dinner given to celebrate the engagement, which was attended by famous personalities of the *corrida,* Lopez drank too copiously of the strong vintages of Spain, and Sarah, disgusted, left him and the dinner party and returned to her hotel. This incident decided her return to Paris, and, borrowing the necessary money from the manager of the hotel, who had known her father, she left the next day.

This was the first of two mysterious visits Sarah paid to Spain. Of the second, which occurred some eleven years later, practically nothing is known.

Now began the most painful period of Sarah Bernhardt's life. No longer able to face the daily tirades of her mother and her aunts, who called her lazy, idle and wilful, she left the former's flat and took one of her own in the rue Duphot, close by the Madeleine.

She drifted away from her family and the friends of her childhood and made questionable acquaintances in the fast-living set where her beauty, originality and wit made her much sought after. She became a well-known figure in certain salons and in the restaurants *à la mode.*

Now and again she played small parts in various thea-

tres, but long intervals occurred between the occasions
on which she worked.   Her figure remained excessively
slender, boyish and agile.   It never became really full,
but its slenderness was less noticeable after she had given
birth to her son, Maurice.   It then to some extent
rounded out, only to become thin again when she was
forty, at which epoch she invented the shoulder-length
glove to conceal the skeleton-like outline of her arms.

The birth of her son was the event which changed
Sarah's whole life.   It gave her something to live for.
Until then she had been a wilful, spoiled, eccentric girl,
given to tremendous fits of temper which were invariably
followed by prolonged periods of despondency.

She had few intimates, and the friends who gathered
round her were not of the sort likely to set her feet in
the right direction.   She had spells of strenuous energy,
which would be succeeded by fits of laziness lasting sometimes for months, during which time she would live par-
simoniously on small sums borrowed from stage acquaintances or from her mother's friend, the Duc de Morny,
who still remained faithful to the child for whom he had
done so much.

Nothing, unless it was her eccentricity, distinguished
her from the hundreds of other lovely girls at that time
adorning the Paris stage.   She had given up her attempts
at painting, after moderate successes gained at several
salons; the passion for modelling had not yet seized her,
and, although she had undoubtedly immense talent for

acting, she neglected to develop it, with the result that her theatrical engagements were few and far between.

She and her young sister Jeanne, then aged only fourteen, would often be seen at public balls of the better class, dancing with a cohort of young men, amongst whom were included some of the wildest members of society. She was frequently a guest at smart but somewhat questionable entertainments in the homes of titled acquaintances, whose riches were expressed in the luxury and the beautiful women with whom they surrounded themselves, and in the amount of rare wines they and their friends consumed.

Of average height, exceptionally slim, with blue eyes alternately flashing wit and fire, and invariably costumed in the latest fashion, Sarah, as she neared her majority, was in danger, despite her great talent, of falling into that bottomless pit which still exists in Paris for beautiful girls, and out of which it is so difficult to climb.

She was a member of one of the fastest sets of a fast city, and only a miracle could have been expected to save her. Her health was bad, she had frequent spells of coughing, and the tell-tale flush of fever was constantly on her cheeks. To all admonitions, however, she would reply that, if her life was to be a short one, she had better enjoy it to the full while there was yet time.

But the needful miracle happened. As the result of an ardent love affair, almost certainly with a man of princely family, she gave birth to a boy, whom she named Maurice.

As in her own case, the *accouchement* was a difficult one,

(Photo, Nadar)

Sarah Bernhardt.

(1859)

and complications ensued which rendered her recovery doubtful. The child was under-sized but robust, and from his birth he resembled his mother.

Motherhood to Sarah was at once a boon and a scourge that whipped her flagging consciousness of right and wrong.

It brought her face to face with the hard realities of the pathways of error, but it gave her the strength of character she had lacked and which was to lead her up from and out of these dangerous pathways. It provided her with the one thing that had been so far lacking in her character.

Motherhood gave Sarah Bernhardt ambition.

If from then on she became greedy of praise and publicity, she at the same time became a strenuous worker; if she was hard with those whom she used as stepping-stones, she was harder with herself; if she allowed her tongue to become caustic and her manner overbearing, it was because life had been revealed to her in its veritable aspect, and because she realised the supreme necessity of building a wall between herself and her past.

Intolerant of criticism, exquisite in her art, mighty in labour, Sarah Bernhardt lavished on her tiny son a love she had never believed she could feel for any human being.

Every aim of her existence was to provide for him while he was young the shield of respectability she herself had never known.

Proud though she might be to the exterior world, she was humility itself before the cradle of her child.

And her struggle was no easy one. She told me of it one day on board ship while we were travelling to the Near East, and so deep an impression did her words make on me that I can remember them almost textually.

"When my son was born," she said, "I had, for all my fortune, the sum of two hundred francs. If it had not been for Madame Guérard, who officiated at the birth of my child as she had officiated at my own, I do not know what I should have done.

"I owed ten times two hundred francs in small tradesmen's bills, scattered about the city. My mother was ill, and could not be appealed to. I was ashamed to go to my other friends, such as the Duc de Morny, who would have been only too glad to have helped me, and I forbade Madame Guérard to say a word to anyone about my predicament.

"When my sister Régine came to see me, she was told that I had a contagious disease and could not be seen. Later on it was given out that I had left Paris for a holiday in the country.

"When the first week was up I had scarcely a sou. It was then that I determined to appeal to the one man whom duty should have compelled to aid me, and I sent a letter to the Prince, imploring him to take pity upon me and upon our child.

"The Prince's reply was brutality itself: 'I know a woman named Bernhardt,' he wrote, 'but I do not know her child.' The note enclosed—fifty francs!

"I persuaded myself that there was a mistake. I could

not believe that the man I had loved could be so cruel.

"I dragged myself out of bed and went, faint and ill, to a mansion in the rue de Lille, where the Prince was that night giving a joyous *fête*.

"I was shown into an ante-room and waited nearly an hour before the Prince finally condescended to see me.

"Standing there in the doorway like a magistrate come to judge—to judge me, the mother of his child whom I carried in my arms—he asked me what I wanted. I could not believe his attitude.

" 'I have come to show you your child, and to demand your recognition of him!' I answered.

"The Prince's reply was to become purple with anger, to thump his fist on the table, and not only to deny the child, but to make the most monstrous allegation conceivable.

"Nearly fainting, I went from the house in tears, my baby's cries mingling in my ears with the music of the dance and the shouts of the reckless party within."

Such was the first great trial of the woman who was to become the most famous tragic actress on the world's stage.

The fortitude that Sarah Bernhardt gave proof of then became the basis of the strong character which slowly formed from that day onwards. Scorned by the man who of all men had best the right to help her, Sarah bitterly determined to make the males of the species pay for the agony of her calvary.

This was the turning point of Sarah Bernhardt's life.

In one respect the world owes the evil Prince —— a
debt, for had he recognised the child, had he lavished
money and tenderness upon the mother, there is a probability that she would never have found the will and determination which were the earnest of her future success.   Never was the adage that courage is born of necessity truer than in the case of the young Sarah Bernhardt.

Forced to work to support her child, whom she sent to
a professional nurse in Normandy, Sarah laboured with
a fierceness and a tenacity unequalled in the history of
the stage.

She found work at the Gymnase, at the Porte St. Martin, at the Vaudeville, at the Lyric and at other theatres.
Never allowing herself a moment's rest, studying her
parts far into the night, arriving always the first for rehearsals, she gamely set foot on rung after rung of the
ladder which she had herself set up.

Her reputation, which had been so sadly tarnished
by her previous mistakes, became once more satisfactory.
She enjoyed the friendship of influential managers and
playwrights.   It was not long before she became marked
for success.   Critics began to comment favourably on
her work, especially in *La Biche au Bois,* a play at the
Porte St. Martin, which gave her her first opportunity
as a star, and which resulted in her being offered a contract by M. Fournier for three years.

Before she accepted this contract, however, Lambert
Thiboust, a well-known playwright, asked her to take the
name part in *La Bergère d'Ivry,* and she accepted—sub-

ject, of course, to the approval of the directors of the Ambigu theatre, where the piece was to be played.

These directors were two men named Faille and Chilly. Chilly had a mistress, Laurence Gérard, whom he desired to have the part. To please Thiboust, however, they consented to give Sarah a hearing in the rehearsal room of the Ambigu, and thither she went and recited a part she had learned at the Comédie Française in *On ne badine pas avec l'amour*. There was complete silence until she had finished, and then Faille rose and shook his head sadly.

"My poor little girl," he said, with assumed sympathy, "you cannot take this part! You are too thin—and, besides, you are in no way equipped for the theatre! You are not even a good actress!"

Sarah could hardly believe her ears.

"*Tenez*," pursued Faille, "here is Chilly, who has heard you from behind that curtain. Ask him what he thinks."

Sarah turned to Chilly, the little director who was later to be intimately associated with her career.

"Lambert Thiboust is crazy!" said Chilly shortly. "You would be no good in the part, mademoiselle! We cannot give it to you!"

As Sarah went out, more or less in a daze, she passed Laurence Gérard on her way in. Then she realised why she had lost the part.

Later on, Chilly became famous as co-director of the Odéon. Faille never succeeded, and years later, taking pity on him, Sarah Bernhardt acted in a benefit performance to establish a fund for his old age.

Sarah was ever generous in such matters. She never forgave an enemy who remained powerful, but she could always forgive and forget when poverty or misery overtook those who had done her harm.

CHAPTER X

FOLLOWING the fiasco of her lost engagement at the Ambigu, Sarah Bernhardt visited her old and faithful friend, Camille Doucet. She was kept waiting some minutes in an ante-room, and, on being bidden eventually to go into his office, almost ran into a tall, handsome young man, who had been in conference with Doucet. The man stopped and apologised, and Sarah was conscious of two deep-set blue eyes regarding her with a real interest.

"Is this not Mademoiselle Sarah Bernhardt?" the tall man asked. On Sarah's hesitating admission that he was right, the man continued:

"I have just been talking to Doucet about you. Come in, and we will see him together."

Sarah followed him, not knowing who her new acquaintance was, nor understanding the nature of his business with her. Once in Camille Doucet's office, however, she was quickly informed.

"This is Pierre Berton, junior," said Doucet, introducing her. "He would like to see you a member of his company at the Odéon."

Sarah was overwhelmed. Pierre Berton was then one of the most popular actors on the French stage; he was also, after Mounet-Sully, the handsomest. To have been singled out by him for a part at the Odéon was an honour she had never dared dream of. There was no actor in France with whom she would sooner have worked.

Sarah was too much taken aback at the sudden proposition to say much. Extending her hand to Berton, she thanked him with a smile.

"There is, however, an obstacle," went on Doucet. "I have just learned this morning that the Odéon staff has been reorganised and that Chilly has been named co-director with Duquesnel."

Sarah's spirits fell like lead. How could she hope for an engagement at the Odéon, when one of the men who would have to sign her contract was the same who had, only a few days previously, said publicly that she could not act? Seeing her downcast Berton tried to reassure her.

"You need not be afraid of Chilly!" he said. "I have spoken to Duquesnel, and he is on our side. Chilly will have to agree!"

An appointment was made for Sarah to see Duquesnel on the following day and, after some further conversation, Berton offered to accompany Sarah home. In the cab Sarah asked him what was the reason for his interest in her.

"Since the day I saw you in *Les Femmes Savantes* at the Comédie Française," Berton answered, "I have believed that you would one day become a very great actress, but I believe also that you need someone to aid you with the directors, who do not understand your temperament.

I have watched you for two years, and I am prepared to help you at the Odéon, as far as possible, if you will allow me to do so."

Sarah's reply, Berton told me in later years after I had become his wife, was to seize and kiss his hand impulsively.

From that moment began the wonderful romance which developed between these two—Pierre Berton, the accomplished and successful actor, and Sarah Bernhardt, the *débutante* of twenty-two. Their relationship lasted a little over two years. When it finished—we shall see why presently—Sarah was as great an actress as he an actor. In two short years she had leaped to fame.

They met, as arranged, in Duquesnel's office at the Odéon, on the day following Sarah's meeting with Berton and Doucet. Sarah was immediately taken with Duquesnel, a mild, blue-eyed man, endowed with prodigious activity and with the name of being possibly the greatest *metteur-en-scène* in Paris. He was exceedingly courteous to her and set her at ease immediately by declaring that he thought her engagement could easily be arranged.

She asked about Chilly. "You shall see him to-morrow," promised Duquesnel. Sarah looked at Berton.

"I have spoken to him," said the actor, "and he has promised to leave the engagement of the company in my own hands, providing the salaries and the lengths of the contracts are supervised and agreed to by him and Monsieur Duquesnel."

Later on Sarah discovered that what had actually happened was that Chilly, spoken to the evening before, had flatly declined to consider Sarah as a member of the company.

"She is not an actress, and shows no promise of ever being one!" he repeated.

And then Pierre Berton had threatened to resign, so that in face of this threatened calamity Chilly had given way. He had insisted, however, that the responsibility for Sarah's engagement should rest with Berton and Duquesnel.

The next day Sarah went to Duquesnel's office again, and was introduced to Chilly, who presented her with her contract.

"Believe me, mademoiselle," he said, "had I been alone in this matter, you would not have been engaged!"

"If you had been alone here I would not have consented to sign!" said Sarah haughtily.

For months after that, she told me, she hated Chilly. In reality, however, he was a decent little fellow, and a man of great ability, whose only fault was his obstinacy. Later on he and Sarah became fast friends, and when Sarah left the Odéon, to return to the Comédie Française as the triumphant idol of the French stage, it was Chilly who went on his knees to her and implored her to reconsider her decision.

Sarah entered the Odéon in 1866. In 1868 she was famous. In 1872 she re-entered the Comédie Française, where she remained eight years.   In 1882 she was married, and in 1889 became a widow.

I give these dates now because the period comprised by them was that in which Sarah Bernhardt reached the supreme pinnacle of her glory, and it was during this period, also, that the most romantic episodes of her life occurred.

Le Jeu de l'Amour et du Hasard (The Game of Love and Luck), by Marivaux, was the piece in which Sarah made her *début* at the Odéon.   Berton and Duquesnel were mortified, Chilly was triumphant: Sarah had failed!

There was no mistaking the failure.   Scarcely any applause was vouchsafed the young actress and so conspicuous was her lack of success that the piece was withdrawn within a few weeks, after playing to half-empty houses.

Chilly wanted to break her contract, but Berton and Duquesnel restrained him.   Berton gave it as his opinion that Sarah was made for tragedy, whereas the play by Marivaux was a comedy, and Sarah's part obviously unsuited to her.

Among the famous people who were in the audience the night Sarah Bernhardt made her *début* at the Odéon was Alexandre Dumas the elder.   After the play was over Sarah overheard Duquesnel ask him:

"What do you think of the young Sarah?"

"She has the head of a virgin and the body of a broomstick!" retorted Dumas, dryly.

Sarah was then earning the munificent sum of 100

francs (four pounds) a month. From the estate of her father she still received a small amount—not more than 200 francs monthly, and on this income was obliged to live.

For several months she worked as an understudy, Chilly obstinately refusing to consent to her taking any important rôles.

During this period the love of Pierre Berton for his erratic little *protégée* grew enormously. On more than one occasion he asked her to marry him, but Sarah refused, on the ground that it would be unfair to the woman who for years had lived with Berton as his wife, and who had presented him with four children.

The fact that Berton was willing and even anxious to abandon this woman (his wife in all but name) and his family indicates the depth of his passion for Sarah Bernhardt. He confessed to me in later life after our marriage that "the days that Sarah Bernhardt consented to devote to me were like pages from immortality. One felt that one could not die!"

That Sarah returned his love is a fact too well known to need confirmation here, but I have always doubted whether she gave to Pierre the full and sincere depth of the passion he brought to her. Sarah's was a nature too complex to harbour any deep feeling for long.

There is also the indisputable fact that at this moment she was living solely for the stage, the animating force within her being a determination that her baby son should

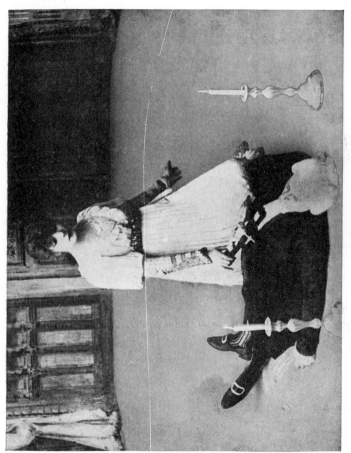

Sarah Bernhardt in a Scene from *La Tosca* with Pierre Berton, when their Romance was at its Height.

never lack for money or advantages. Neither has he, throughout his long life.

Life at the Odéon was toil fierce and unremitting, but Sarah loved it. She would wake at nine o'clock and read over her parts, both in bed and while she was dressing. At eleven o'clock, and often again in the afternoon, there were rehearsals of plays quite different from the one that was to be given at night.

Her evident desire to work, combined with the glorious quality of her voice, which was already becoming renowned among playgoers, brought even the manager, Chilly, round to her side. Reliability and hard work were his two fetishes. He could not forgive Sarah her thin legs, but he was madly enthusiastic over her voice.

"Oh! if you could only act!" he said to her on more than one occasion.

Fine acting is not precisely a gift of the gods; it is the ultimate result of a willingness to acquire technique by constant attention to petty details. No actor ever became great over-night who had not spent weary months in the acquisition of technique.

Now, three principal acquirements go to make up stage technique. First, there is what is known as stage presence, or the ability to lose one's own individuality in the part one is playing. Secondly, there is the speaking voice, which should be so perfected that a whisper may carry drama, pathos or humour to the topmost gallery and be understood. Thirdly, there is memory.

Sarah had the voice and she certainly had a marvellous

memory. She could take the book of a new part at
night and return on the following afternoon with the rôle
committed to memory.   Once she had learned it, Sarah
never forgot a part, even though she might be playing
two different pieces, afternoon and night.

When Berton wrote *Zaza,* the play for which he is
best known in England, she went over it with him, taking a whole night to do it.   The next day Berton was to
read it to an audience of managers and producers. While
he was reading the third act, Sarah objected to his way
of interpreting one of the parts.

"It should go like this," she said—and forthwith she
recited for fifteen minutes words which she had only
read once.   On comparison with the book it was found
that she had not made a single mistake.

In the '80's I attended a picnic at St. Germain, and
heard Sarah recite a part in *Iphigénie,* the first play in
which she appeared at the Comédie Française, and in
which she played only on two occasions during her long
career.   There was never a moment after she became
internationally famous when Sarah could not recite out
of her prodigious memory the whole of the words of
any one of fifty or sixty different plays.

I have said that her voice was becoming known in
Paris.   One day Georges Sand came to her dressing-
room.   Looking very mysterious, she said:

"There is a gentleman outside who has fallen in love
with your voice!"

"Send him away!" retorted Sarah petulantly.   She

was in a bad humour, in consequence of a quarrel with Berton.

"You cannot send this man away, my dear!" said Madame Sand. "He is the Prince!"

"Never mind; I do not want to see him, Prince or no Prince," declared the young actress.

After much coaxing, however, she consented to meet the "gentleman in love with her voice," and descended to the stage, where she found Prince Napoleon talking with Louis Bouilhet. Sarah shook his hand, instead of kissing it, as was the custom, and said never a word. The Prince was furious.

"She is spiteful, your little kitten," he said to Georges Sand.

"She is a Madonna, sire!" said the authoress.

"A Madonna who acts like a devil!" retorted the Prince, shortly, and, turning on his heel, he walked away.

He came back many times, however, and was often one of a party in Sarah's dressing-room. The news that she was the recipient of royal favour soon got abroad, and sarcasms were printed in some of the liberal weeklies. When she read them, Sarah sent a note to the editors:

"Criticise my performances on the stage if it pleases you, but my private life should be free of insult. Furthermore, I have loyal friends who will protect my name with their swords."

This, too, was published, and all Paris laughed at the actress who thought it an insult that her name should be linked with that of a prince. Other people in the profession thought it a pose, but Sarah was quite sincere. She was fascinated by the smooth, cynical flow of the Prince's conversation, and she could not openly bid him remove himself from her presence. At the bottom of her heart, however, she disliked him profoundly and was at small pains to conceal it.

Once an artist of revolutionary tendencies, one Paul Deshayes, entered Sarah's dressing-room, to find there Prince Napoleon, Madame Sand and several others. Deshayes was seeking his gloves, which he had left in the room a few minutes before. Turning to the Prince he said curtly:

"You are sitting on my gloves, monsieur!"

The Prince, turning red with anger at this unceremonious mode of address, took the gloves and flung them on the floor.

"I thought the chair was clean!" he said contemptuously.

Sarah Bernhardt jumped to her feet, picked up the gloves, and handed them to Deshayes.

Then, turning to the Prince, she said hotly:

"Politeness used to be considered a privilege of kings, sir, but I perceive that they do not teach it to princes!"

This incident also found its way into print and Sarah's reputation gained another notch. All this time she had yet to score a genuine success on the stage.

This came towards the end of her first year at the Odéon, in circumstances which were much commented on at the time. All Paris was in arms against Alexandre Dumas, the most maligned author who has ever lived. On the night of the *première* of *Kean,* Dumas appeared in a box at the Odéon accompanied by his mistress, Ada Montrin.

Cries came from all over the house calling on him to "send the woman away." Dumas tried to speak, but his voice was drowned in cat-calls. Hundreds of students stood on their seats, chanting an obscene song that had been written about Dumas.

Finally the woman and Dumas both left—the latter to take refuge behind the wings, and the former to depart from his life for ever.

Duquesnel, Chilly, Berton and the whole company were in terror when the curtain was about to be raised. They expected a warm reception and—they got it. Berton, who was playing the part of Kean, could not make his voice heard beyond the footlights. For a moment there was a question of cancelling the performance.

Then Sarah Bernhardt, in the first big rôle of her career—that of Anna Danby—came upon the stage, and, from the first words, a hush settled over the house. Her glorious voice filled the theatre.

Calm and unflurried, though in reality intensely nervous, Sarah continued speaking her part. The words of the poet were given their exact intonation, every syllable distinct from its neighbour, and fell upon the breathless house like the limpid notes of a flute.

When she had finished, there was at first silence, and then a roar of approval. Sixty students, their hands locked together, rushed round the house and threatened to invade the stage. Sarah, appalled, believed it was a demonstration against her. Her cue came to leave the stage. She rushed off and up to her dressing-room, whence she could dimly hear the unceasing roar from the theatre.

Duquesnel, rushing in, found her white as a sheet with terror. Duquesnel himself was pale, and perspiring in great drops.

"Come!" he said to Sarah, extending his hand, "they want you!"

Sarah shuddered and shrank backwards.

"Come!" said Duquesnel again, impatiently. "I tell you they *want* you!—Hark, cannot you hear them calling?"

Through the open door the din from the house came with greater volume. Sarah could not distinguish a word.

"They are mad about you, child!" cried Duquesnel, as he saw she did not believe him. "They will not let the play go on until you go on and speak to them!"

Then Sarah understood that this was not failure. It was triumph, success, glory! She took Duquesnel's arm and went hesitatingly on to the stage, not even noticing that she was still attired in the kimono which she used as a wrap between the acts.

When she appeared before the curtain pandemonium broke loose. "Sarah!" "Sarah!" "Our Sarah!" the audience yelled.

And "Our Sarah" she was to the populace of Paris from that day onwards.

She was famous. She hurried back into the wings and brought on Berton Senior, and they gave him an ovation too. But always there was the chant: "Sarah!" "Our Sarah!"

The students were mad. Sarah resolved to win them over to Dumas, and sent word for him to come on the stage. But Dumas had gone, suffocated by tears at what he believed bitterly to be the assassination of his brain-child. The next morning, when he learned the truth, he sent Sarah a note thanking her.

Sarcey was the only critic who did not join in the chorus of praise which followed in the press. Writing in the *Courrier de la Semaine* he stated:

"I have nothing to add to my previous opinion of Mademoiselle Sarah Bernhardt, who, it appears, had some success with the noisy students the other night. Her voice is exquisite, certainly, but she is just as certainly not an actress."

The original means Sarah took to humble Sarcey and to bring him to her side will be described in the next chapter. Meanwhile, he remained her most bitter and most persevering critic.

CHAPTER XI

OUT of a multitude of aspiring actresses Sarah Bernhardt, at the age of twenty-four, had jumped into celebrity practically in a single night. The success of *Kean* continued; the theatre was packed night after night. Berton, hitherto the greatest figure on the stage of the Odéon, himself had to bow before the woman whose genius he had been the first to perceive.

Their intimacy continued, though necessarily in secret, on account of Berton's other attachments. Success turned Sarah's shock head a little, but for many months she remained faithful to the loyal man who had befriended her and had made her victory possible. Their idyll was the talk of the theatre. No one then dreamed how bitterly she would turn against him in later years.

She had no lack of other admirers. They flocked round her. There was Jules Garnier, and most notable of all perhaps François Coppée, whose genius Sarah discovered in an odd way.

She was dining in the house of a friend and was introduced to a small, pale-faced young man, whose wealth of dark hair was smoothed back from his brow. "He had," Sarah told me later, "the eyes of a dreamer and the head of a saint."

Coppée shyly shook her hand, and seemed to want to say something, but to be too bashful.

"Come, François," urged Madame Agar, the great *tragédienne,* who was the hostess, "you have been wanting to meet Mlle. Bernhardt for weeks, and now that you have the chance you are dumb!"

"He has written a play," she explained to Sarah, "and he thinks that you should be the one to play in it."

"It was written for you," said the young poet, simply.

François Coppée was then unknown, and Sarah had never heard his name before. But the subtle compliment of writing a play round her touched her heart, and she determined to grant him his wish.

"We will hear it at once!" she decided.

Two hours later she had enthusiastically promised to make Duquesnel and Chilly produce the piece, which was called *Le Passant,* and within four months it was produced at a benefit matinée. Then, after it had proved an enormous success, it was included in the regular Odéon repertoire, which it has never since left.

If *Kean* had been a triumph for Sarah, *Le Passant* was a vindication. There had been many to hint that her success in *Kean* was only an accident due to fortuitous circumstances and to the fact that she was popular with the students who thronged the theatre on the first night. But when she carried all before her in *Le Passant,* she proved herself to be the great actress that she really was.

Every critic except the dour Francisque Sarcey, who still persisted in ignoring her talent, joined in an enthusiastic chorus of praise, and they said much more about her than they did about Agar, who was in reality the star of the piece.

Duquesnel was triumphant; Chilly was delighted. They had found another star worthy of the greatness of their theatre. They were summoned to play *Le Passant* at Court, in the magnificent setting of the Tuileries. The Emperor Louis Napoleon, after the performance, descended from his throne and kissed Sarah on both cheeks, afterwards presenting her with a diamond brooch set with the Imperial initials.

This brooch was not among the property of the *tragédienne* which was recently sold by auction in Paris, and I believe there was a story that, pressed for funds during a trip to London after the revolution, she pawned it and never subsequently regained possession of it. She was like that all her life. Always the desperate need for money, always the large extravagance, the royal expenditures that she could not afford!

This was the age of literary giants. Neither politics, nor even religion, had half the power to stir the passions of the educated masses that a literary war between two editors or two dramatists possessed. The two great rivals for public popularity were Victor Hugo and Alexandre Dumas the elder, and there was a deal of fanaticism in the fervour of their respective partisans. Public meetings were held denouncing one or the other. Victor Hugo's political martyrdom was of recent memory, and this gentle character, this splendid genius, was the prey of attacks which were at once unscrupulous and false. Newspapers were started by chiefs of the different literary factions, and dozens of duels, some of them mortal, resulted from the wanton attacks on the reputations of two of the greatest men of the time.

Sarah's first meeting with Victor Hugo occurred about a week after the *première* of *Le Passant,* in which she took the adolescent male rôle of Zanetto. It suited her to perfection, for she had retained her boyish slimness and her general allure of *gaminerie.*

After the performance she was presented to Hugo, who had been watching the play from the depths of a *loge.* Public opinion was running high in Paris at the moment, and it was considered inadvisable that either Victor Hugo or Alexandre Dumas should show themselves in public.

Sarah had ignorantly allowed herself to be carried away by the fulminations of the Dumas clique at the Odéon, and actually shuddered when she held her hand out to Hugo to be kissed.

"Ah, mademoiselle," remarked the great author, with a sad smile, "I see that my greatest trial is to come in your prejudice against me!"

Sarah was touched, and could not bring herself to believe that this meek man, with the deep marks of suffering about his eyes, was really the monster his enemies would have the world believe. It was currently rumoured that Hugo was an anarchist, that he had deserted his wife, that he had five mistresses at one and the same time, and that his life consisted of one immorality after another.   He was accused of many political crimes also —and with as much reason.

"I am my own judge of men, monsieur," said Sarah.

Victor Hugo bowed low, muttered a word of adieu and later wrote Sarah as follows:

"MADEMOISELLE,

"Yesterday I was presented to you, trembling lest you might not accede to my request and play in my *Ruy Blas*.   But I was tongue-tied in the presence of your beauty and your charity; I, who am a man of words, was dumb.   I pray you, see Chilly; he knows my wishes.   Believe, mademoiselle, in my sincere admiration,

"VICTOR HUGO."

Sarah saw Chilly, only to be informed by him that it had been decided to put off the revival of *Ruy Blas* until the following season.   Instead, when *Le Passant* was finished, Sarah played as star in three plays which definitely established her position as one of the greatest actresses of the period.   These plays were *L'Autre,* a delicious comedy by Georges Sand, *Le Bâtard* and Theuriet's *Jean Marie.*

Before she could play *Ruy Blas,* the war of 1870 broke out.

Before we go into the war experiences of Sarah Bernhardt, experiences which, moreover, forged her character into a species of flexible steel, two episodes must

Sarah Bernhardt in *Le Passant*.

be mentioned which have been published before, but which, in my opinion, have been scurrilously misinterpreted. One refers to the fire in her flat in the rue Auber, near the Opera, and the other to the serious illness that followed one of Sarah's everlasting practical jokes—which this time took the form of trying to make the world believe that she was dead!

Sarah had, as before stated, taken a seven-room flat in the rue Auber which, with the aid of certain of her family, who were now only too willing to resume their relationship with her, she had somewhat luxuriously furnished. That in this connection she went heavily into debt to various furniture dealers, decorators and the like I do not doubt, for such became her invariable practice in later life. From the day she jumped into fame, she was invariably surrounded by dealers anxious to sell her all sorts of things, from jewelry to houses, and from pianos to horses and carriages. These men knew that her salary at the Odéon was still only 160 francs per month, on which she could certainly barely afford an attic. They knew also that the income she received from her father's estate had been greatly diminished, and was now less than 200 francs monthly.

With less than 500 francs—twenty pounds—a month, and with the inevitable extra expenses incidental to her career, what could Sarah Bernhardt be expected to afford? Her mother could spare her nothing. Her aunt Rosine, in an effort to placate the girl for the many slights of childhood, had given her two ponies and a smart little carriage, but this, at the same time, cost a good deal to keep up. None of her other relatives gave her anything. When she appealed to them they would say: "Why do you ask us? You are a famous actress, and famous actresses can always have money!"

How true that was, Sarah had early found out. I do not think it was any particular regard for morality which kept her from treading the path so many of her sister actresses were obliged to tread, and from procuring herself one or more rich protectors; it was rather that Sarah's whole life now was bound up with the stage, and that in her love-affairs she consequently never strayed beyond its charmed circle.

I do not say that Sarah Bernhardt was any less or any more "immoral"—and we must try and remember, we readers of a different race, that the moral code of 1870 was not that of to-day—than were the half-dozen other leading actresses of the time; but I do assert that she never formed a liaison merely for the sake of the protection and wealth it could give her.

When Sarah loved, when this brilliant woman gave herself, it was always for her art, and to someone who could assist her in the material realisation of her lofty and ambitious dreams. Such a thing as forming an alliance merely to rid herself of the burden of poverty probably never even entered her mind, which was always lifted above the sordid things of life. But when, as in the case of Pierre Berton, she was offered the love of a great and a noble character, or when, as in the case of

Damala, she was swept off her feet by a romantic passion, she succumbed willingly enough.

A list of the men whom Sarah Bernhardt loved and by whom she was loved reads like a biographical index of the great Frenchmen of the nineteenth century. It includes actors, painters, sculptors, architects, cartoonists, poets, authors, and playwrights, but not one idle rich man or rich man's son!

It is to be doubted whether Berton, Chilly or Duquesnel helped her to furnish the flat in the rue Auber, and it is therefore somewhat of a mystery how she managed to assemble the strange setting which framed her at this period of her life. Her taste was all Louis XV, and quaint bowlegged chairs and tables were scattered round her in great disorder.

Sarah's was ever a careless nature and, being extremely imperious as well as chronically penniless, she could not keep a maid. She had her aged grandmother living with her for a period, and she had taken her baby from its hired nurse and installed him in a nursery at her own home. The child took up the grandmother's time, and the household work seldom got done, except when Régine, Sarah's wild and hoydenish little sister, could be persuaded upon to do her share.

"I shall never forget my first visit to Sarah's flat," said my husband to me once. "It was on a Saturday afternoon; we were going over a part together, and I had promised to finish the recital at Sarah's home. I arrived about three o'clock, and was met at the door by a tumble-haired whirlwind in an old chemise and skirt, whom I with difficulty recognised as Régine, Sarah's little sister. Régine looked as if she had not had a wash for a week, and perhaps she hadn't. She had great smudges of grime on her face, and her hands were black.

"She dragged me into the salon, and here I got another shock, for the room was in the most frightful mess you can imagine. Empty wine bottles rolled about on the carpet; the remains of a meal stood partly on the mantelshelf and partly on the table, all mixed up with sheets of manuscript, which I saw were books of the plays which Sarah had appeared in. Photographs in gilt frames were here and there, most of them tumbled on their faces, and over all was a thick layer of dust. I had to dirty two of my handkerchiefs before one of the chairs could be trusted not to soil my trousers.

"From another room a baby kept up a wail, and I could hear Sarah talking to it, trying to calm it. Sarah's child was then nearly five years old, but had the development of a normal child of three.

"When Sarah finally appeared, it was in a long smock covered with paint and grease. Her hair was done anyhow, and her wide-set eyes sparkled with fun as she viewed my distaste for her surroundings."

During all the time Sarah and he remained intimate friends, Pierre told me, he could never bring himself to set foot again in her home.

"It spoiled all my conceptions of her," he said. "In

the theatre she was such a fairylike, delightful creature. One could not help loving her. But at home——!"

One night, after a gay supper following the theatre, Sarah returned home to find her flat, in a building situated at the corner of the rue Auber and the Boulevard Haussmann, in flames. The fire had started in her own apartment, from a candle incautiously left burning by a maid-of-all-work who occasionally came to clean up. The blaze had been discovered shortly before midnight, and at one o'clock in the morning, when Sarah arrived, it was still confined to three rooms of the flat, but showed symptoms of spreading, in spite of the efforts of the firemen.

To her horror, Sarah discovered that nobody knew whether her baby had been saved or not!

There had been nobody but Maurice in the flat when she had left it for the theatre that night, with the exception of the charwoman, who had long since gone. The grandmother and Régine were both absent in the country. Unless one of the firemen had seen and rescued the child, therefore, there was every chance that it was inside the burning building.

The flat was of peculiar construction, because of the angle of the two streets. One end of it was disconnected from the other by a passage-way which had doors at both ends. The fire had started on the rue Auber side, and though it had spread upwards and downwards, it had not jumped across the court in the rear, or worked around the corner to the Boulevard Haussmann side, in which was the nursery.

Sarah took all this in at a glance.   Her intense horror and dread of fire was not even thought of.   Brushing aside those who tried to hold her back, she dashed into the Boulevard Haussmann entrance, ran up the stairs and into her flat.   Groping her way through the smoke to the nursery, she found her son safe and sound in a deep sleep.   She wrapped him in a blanket and came down with him into the street.   There she collapsed, and was ill for two days.

When she was well enough to hear the news, they told her that the whole building had been burned down and that, but for her courageous intervention, her child would undoubtedly have been burned to death.

The best proof that Sarah even then possessed a number of jealous enemies was the statement openly made in the theatrical world that, weighed down with debt, she had caused the fire herself in order to collect the insurance.

This story, which has since been still more widely spread, is refuted by the following two facts: firstly, if Sarah had caused the fire, she would hardly have left her baby to run the risk of being burned to death; secondly, she had not yet paid the premium on the insurance, and it was consequently null and void.   Instead of her collecting from the insurance company, it was this company, La Foncière, as the proprietor of a flat set on fire through carelessness, which collected from Sarah.

She was forced to pay the fabulous sum of forty thousand francs in damages, which she was enabled to do by the proceeds of a benefit performance at the Odéon, at which Adelina Patti, then at the height of her fame, sang.

The receipts of this benefit were more than the necessary forty thousand francs, and with the remainder Sarah was able to take a flat at No. 4, rue de l'Arcade. It was furnished, however; and Sarah was still without the means to furnish a flat for herself until her late father's man of affairs came and proposed to arrange a cash payment to her out of her father's estate providing she would insure her life in his favour for 250,000 francs. This was done, and Sarah rented a large flat at the corner of the rue de Rome, almost opposite the one which had been burned. This she was careful to insure immediately.

The other episode for which Sarah was much criticised was her famous practical joke at the Odéon, after a quarrel with Duquesnel.

A call-boy rushed through the theatre screaming: "Bernhardt is dead! Bernhardt is dead!"

With one accord the entire cast rushed off the stage to Sarah's dressing-room, where they were met by an extraordinary sight.

Sarah was reclining, dressed completely in white, on a flat couch placed in the middle of the floor. Her hands were crossed over her bosom, which appeared to be motionless, and a red stain was visible on her chin and neck.

At the four corners of the couch were placed gigantic candles, like the *cierges* used in churches.

Who had placed her like that? Nobody knew. Her dressing-maid was in hysterics, and could not be questioned. Duquesnel came in and, taking in the tableau in a glance, burst into tears.

The performance was stopped and the curtain rung down. A doctor and an undertaker were hurriedly sent for, and the audience was informed by the grief-stricken Duquesnel that "Mademoiselle Sarah Bernhardt had suddenly passed away."

Then, and then only, did Sarah sit up, kick over the candles with a sweep of her legs, and amaze and scandalise the mourners by going into screams of helpless laughter. Duquesnel was white with anger. Running to his office, he wrote and signed a note cancelling her contract, and stating that after that night her services would not be required.

Sarah threw the note in his face and flung herself out of the theatre. For hours she drove about in the Champs Elysées, careless of the falling snow. Next day Duquesnel sent her a note that, on reconsideration, she would be permitted to return, but that an apology would be expected.

A few hours later an emissary from Sarah arrived at the theatre. "She will not come back until you ask her to do so on your knees!" he told Duquesnel. The latter, realising that he stood in danger of losing his most popular star, went to Sarah's home and apologised. Sarah reconsidered her remarks about making him get on his knees, and admitted that she had only meant to play a little joke, and had had no idea that it would go as far as it had.   There, except for satirical comments on the "crazy Bernhardt" in the weekly papers, the matter ended.

CHAPTER XII

SARAH was twenty-six years old when war was declared between France and Germany. At three o'clock in the afternoon of July 19, 1870, I, a child still in short frocks, was present with my mother at her apartment in the rue de Rome.

A rehearsal was in progress for some play, the name of which I have forgotten, and Sarah was reading the script in her beautiful, expressive voice, running her hand through my hair as she did so, when a servant came in and announced that she was wanted at the door.

"What is it?" Sarah demanded, angry at the interruption.

"A messenger from the Foreign Ministry," said the servant. "He is in a great hurry and has instructions to deliver his message to none but yourself, madame, personally."

Sarah laid down the manuscript and went out of the room. Two minutes later she was back, and I can remember to this day how white her face was, how brilliant her marvellous eyes. She held up her hand, in which was a long envelope, and bade everyone be silent. The twenty or twenty-five people present were quiet at once and looked at her expectantly.

"We have declared war!" she cried, and the echo of

that golden voice, vibrating with emotion, is with me yet.

At once the room was in a buzz of excitement.   Everybody was speaking at once.   Théophile Gautier, the bookworm, who was present, made his voice heard through the din.

"They are mad—mad!" he exclaimed.   Then he went to Bernhardt.

"From whom comes your information, mademoiselle?" he asked.

"From Captain Lescouvé, deputy of the *chef du cabinet* of Monsieur Ollivier."

Ollivier was the Premier who had declared war under the pressure of the "imbecile emperor."

Jane Essler, a famous artiste of her time, who had been sitting in a chair lazily watching the scene with an expression of calm indifference, suddenly jumped to her feet.

"Come, let us go to the Boulevards!" she cried.

"Aux boulevards!"   We were swept away by excitement.

"No; let us go to the Odéon!" shouted Sarah, and this new suggestion met with a frenzy of approval.

"A l'Odéon!   A l'Odéon!   Vive la guerre!"

When we came down from the flat the Boulevard Haussmann, or the street now known by that name, was alive with people.   Any passage of vehicles was impossible, so we went on foot through the rue Auber as far as the Opéra.

Here there was an enormous crowd.   The great Place

was literally surging with people. On the walls of the
Opéra itself huge posters had been pasted but a few
minutes before. I remember that some of our party
tore them down and stuffed them into their pockets as
souvenirs. The posters explained the abrupt action of
the Government, and enjoined the people to remain calm.

"Victory is assured," was one phrase that stands out
in my mind.

Carried along by the crowd, we were swept down the
Avenue de l'Opéra. Opposite the Théâtre Française was
another huge crowd. Marie Lloyd—an actress, who, by
the way, had been Sarah's competitor at the Conservatoire, and who had gained the first prize which Sarah
had coveted—was standing by the statue of Molière, singing the Marseillaise. Every time she came to
"Marchons! Marchons!" the thousands of people present took up the refrain, and again and again the words of
the magnificent old song were repeated.

Our party got separated here, and only five of us managed to reach the Pont Neuf, which, crossing the Seine,
led almost directly to the Odéon. I was being partly
carried, partly dragged by my mother, and was so wildly
excited that I felt no fatigue, in spite of the considerable
distance we had come.

An empty fiacre passed. The poet, Robert de Montesquiou, then a boy of nineteen, but even at that time
one of Sarah's firm friends, hailed it. The *cocher*
looked at him insolently.

"*A l'Odéon!*" said Robert.

"It is five francs!" replied the *cocher*.

The distance was not more than seven hundred yards, and the fare ordinarily should have been only one franc. De Montesquiou was indignant and started a violent protest, but suddenly the *cocher* caught sight of Sarah Bernhardt.

"It is 'our Sarah'?" he exclaimed. "Then I'm a dog! Come, I will take you all, and for nothing!"

I remember that Sarah climbed up on the box next to the old coachman and gave him two resounding kisses, one on each bronzed cheek. It appeared that the *cocher* was a regular subscriber at the Odéon!

When we arrived at the theatre we hurried round to the stage-door and trooped up into the wings. There we found Chilly, Duquesnel and others talking on the stage in loud voices. When they saw us, they set up a shout.

"Voilà Bernhardt!"

Chilly hurriedly explained that the Government had requested that the theatre should be reserved that night for a patriotic demonstration, at which some of its members would be present.

"The Emperor will be here also," he went on, "and has specially requested that you will open the proceedings by singing the Marseillaise."

The doors opened at six o'clock. By 6.30 the theatre was packed. The speeches were to begin an hour later. Sarah was supposed to open the meeting, but when the time came she could not be found anywhere.

Distracted officials searched the theatre high and low.

shouting for the missing actress.   At last the meeting began without her.

At eight o'clock Pierre Berton walked in through the stage-entrance, followed by Sarah.   Berton looked as black as a thunder-cloud.   Sarah's eyes were flashing, and red spots of temper were on her cheeks.   Her friends recognised the signals and the word was passed around: "Something has gone wrong between Pierre and Sarah . . . they have had a row."

Sarah went straight to Duquesnel, who began scolding her for being late.   But she cut him short.

"I have acted for the last time with that man!" she declared, pointing to Berton.

Pierre looked on bitterly.   (All this I had years later, of course, from friends who saw the scene.   I had been sent to bed after my fatiguing afternoon.)

"What is the matter?" asked Duquesnel, puzzled but not despairing, for he knew Sarah and her fits of temper, although he feared her obstinacy.

"He is disloyal!   He is a pro-German!"

Pierre Berton darted forward with a loud protest.

"It is a lie!" he shouted angrily.   "She asked me to come on the stage and sing the Marseillaise with her, and I said I would not, because I disapprove of the war and of the crazy Emperor who has declared it, as does every sensible man in all France.   But I am not disloyal!   I am not pro-German!"

Sarah refused to listen.   "You hear him?" she cried.

"He admits it himself! I will not appear with him again! I will not act with traitors!"

At this remark flung at him with a hiss of a whip-lash by the woman he loved and whose career he had made, Berton turned away hiding his face in his arm. Then he walked out of the theatre and was seen no more that night.

A famous journalist of the time, de Girardin, was making a fiery speech, the gist of which was that within a fortnight our troops must be in Berlin.

"*A Berlin!*" howled the crowd, mad with frenzy. And then, glorious in its full-toned strength, came the voice of Sarah, singing the Marseillaise.

She was standing at the back of the dress circle, and had not been noticed until she began to sing. She was dressed in a white robe with a green girdle—a costume taken from one of her plays—and standing there, as those inspiring notes issued from her splendid throat, she personified the very spirit of France.

"*Allons, enfants, de la patrie . . .*"

The whole audience was on its feet singing, but ever above that volume of sound rose the golden tones of Sarah Bernhardt. Hers was not a singing voice, but now it rang out pure and clear as a bell.

Just as a crystal glass, tapped with the finger-nail, will be heard above the din of a great railway station, so was Sarah Bernhardt's voice heard above the din and uproar of the Odéon that night.

When she left the theatre, bands of students seized

her and carried her shoulder high along the Boulevard St. Michel, and across the Pont de la Cité to the Place de Notre Dame, where still another demonstration was in progress.   Again she sang the Marseillaise, and then *"Mourir pour la Patrie,"* and other patriotic songs.

She was exhausted when she reached home, and had caught a bad cold, which kept her indoors for several days.   During this period, however, messengers arrived almost every hour bringing her the news.

Paris, they said, was full of marching troops.   The city was still in the throes of excitement.   The Opéra was giving patriotic performances every night, at which Marie Sass was singing the Marseillaise from the balcony, so that all Paris could join in.

The Emperor had gone to the front.   The first clash had occurred sixty miles south of Mayence.

The theatres were still open, but there was talk of closing them.   The actors were organising a volunteer corps, and some had gone already to the front, but there was a lack of uniforms.

MacMahon had sent word from Reichshoffen that all was well; the *morale* was fine; they would be in Berlin in a few weeks!

The papers were talking about a rumoured big victory.   The Germans in Paris were not to be interned, but were to be kept to do the work of the city.

Sarah Bernhardt shared the popular belief that victory was in sight, that the war was all but over.   All the newspapers, every lounger on the boulevards said it—so why should she not believe it to be true?

She went on playing as usual at the Odéon, singing the Marseillaise whenever requested to do so, but she adhered to her resolution not to play with Pierre Berton; and Duquesnel, deciding that discretion was the better part of valour, had carefully arranged the bill so that they would not be called upon to act in the same pieces.

The two seldom met and never spoke. Berton came rarely to the theatre; he was engaged in secret work, which some declared was of a revolutionary nature, but it turned out later that he had organised a corps of volunteers amongst the theatrical people out of work, and was drilling them on the fortifications! Sarah did not know of this at the time.

Victor Hugo, of course, had disappeared from Paris, where his last visit had been made only under pain of instant arrest, if seen; for he had been banished from the capital for his revolutionary writings. But among the papers of Hugo, which were found at his death, was a letter from Pierre Berton, written in August 1870, a month after the declaration of war, and smuggled out of Paris, in which Berton appealed to Hugo to "return and save France!"

And France was in need of saving! No longer were the boulevards filled with maddened patriots, excited by wine and shouting of victory; instead, these same patriots walked about with a grave air, or joined squads of men under training; and when they spoke there was no bravado, but only great determination.

Wissembourg, with the defeat and death of General Douay, had been the first event to startle the Parisian out of his self-satisfaction and ignorance. Then, two days later, came the defeat which definitely turned the tide against France—the route of Marshal MacMahon, which army was literally cut to pieces at Freischwiller and Reichshoffen. A human torrent of four hundred thousand men poured over the fields of France. The country was invaded; Paris was in danger.

Paris in danger! The Parisians were not so much inclined to laugh as they had been at first. It was ridiculous, of course—it would take a million and a half men to besiege Paris successfully—but still, but still, there was Wissembourg, and the undeniable evidence of Freischwiller and Reichshoffen!

Count de Palikao, the new head of the Government, was a friend of Sarah's; that is, he had seen and spoken to her once or twice, and would stop and bow when he met her. One day he sent for her from his office, at the Chamber of Deputies.

"Mademoiselle," he said, taking her hand, "you can do a great work for your country, if you will!"

Sarah asked him to explain. The Count then said that the Government had noticed how enthusiasm for the war was dying; and that something like panic was imminent in Paris, unless optimism and hope could at once be restored to the hearts of the people.

"That is your task!" he finished.

The Count's plan was for Sarah to organise a committee of artistes, authors and newspaper writers of her acquaintance, the object of which was to instil into the people of Paris renewed belief in the success of the campaign. More patriotic performances were to be given; patriotic posters were to be drawn up and posted; and every member individually, whether by word of mouth or by articles in the Press, was to affirm his or her belief that victory was near.

Sarah undertook the task with enthusiasm. There is no doubt now that her part in the defence of Paris was a glorious one. There is no doubt, either, that wily old Count de Palikao, being a general and a fine strategist himself, was perfectly well aware even then that Paris was doomed.

Towards the latter part of August the efforts of the volunteer committee fell more and more flat. The people seemed to have sunk into an apathy out of which they could be aroused, only at infrequent intervals, by rumours of victories—which generally turned out to be false. When Sarah sang the Marseillaise now she met with but a feeble response.

And then came Sedan, the overthrow of the Emperor, and the Declaration of the Republic.

Magically, as it seemed, the whole city, which had been shouting its plaudits of Napoleon III but a few months ago, had turned republican. Nobody would admit to having ever been a royalist! *"Vive la République"* sounded on all hands.

When Sarah Bernhardt arrived at the Odéon that afternoon of September 4—there was no performance and no rehearsal, but she could not stay away—it was to find a group of actors surrounding Pierre Berton, who, with a hammer and chisel, was carefully chipping away the plaster "N" from the front of the royal box.

Sarah stood and watched them for some time and then Berton, descending from the ladder, saw her.

"Mademoiselle," he said, "I was hoping that I should see you!"

Sarah stood speechless.   Taking her by the arm, Pierre led her unresistingly aside.

"I leave with my regiment for the front to-night!" he said.

"Where is your uniform?" demanded Sarah.

"You shall see it!"

Running up to his dressing-room, Berton came down a few minutes later garbed in one of the pitifully non-descript uniforms of the National Guard—a grey *képi* with a leather peak, a white-and-blue coat and red trousers.   On his arm were three *galons,* showing his rank to be that of captain.

Sarah threw her arms about his neck and kissed him before the entire company.   Before nightfall all the-atrical Paris knew that Sarah Bernhardt and Pierre Berton were again lovers.

By now thousands of wounded were arriving in Paris, and the temporary hospitals were totally inadequate. Great canvas hospitals were erected on the fortifications, but these had to be withdrawn into the city as the German advance continued. There was an appalling lack of trained nurses, and almost as great a lack of doctors and surgeons.

The theatres were closed, and Sarah disappeared for two weeks. When she re-appeared, it was in the uniform of a nurse. She had earned her *brevet* from working in one of the temporary hospitals, and even in that short time had learned not a little of the art of caring for wounded.

Her next act was to ask permission from the Comte de Kératry to re-open the Odéon as a hospital. This permission was readily accorded, but no beds or supplies were forthcoming, and it took all her energy and influence to procure these.

She was alone in Paris. Her son had been sent to Normandy, and her mother and aunts had left at the same time, presumably for Normandy but in reality for England and Holland, whither they took the baby boy. While Sarah imagined her son safely in a small village near Havre, he was really in London, and later at Rotterdam.

During the siege of Paris her family left Rotterdam and went into Germany, and at the very moment when Sarah was caring for the wounded with untiring and devoted energy, her baby boy, in charge of her mother and aunts, was living in the country of the enemy at Wiesbaden. This she did not discover until after the siege was raised. It certainly is the best possible confirmation of the nationality of her mother's family.

CHAPTER XIII

SARAH grew to know at least two members of the revolutionary government extremely well. One was Jules Favre, who was given the portfolio of Foreign Affairs, and the other Rochefort, the notorious editor of *La Lanterne,* who was taken out of prison by the mob on the night the Empire was overthrown.

Two more opposite characters it would be hard to imagine. Favre was a man in middle life—calm, rigidly upright, a thinker and a statesman. Rochefort was little better than a literary apache, and was the idol of the worst quarters of Paris. His speeches were calculated to appeal to the baser instincts of the mob; those of Favre were the measured words of the lawyer. Rochefort, if he had ever seized the reins of power, might have been another Marat; while Jules Favre, if he could not save France from mutilation and humiliation at the hands of Germany, at least aided her in retaining her honour and self-respect.

When Jules Favre, with Paris ringed by enemy steel and guns capable of shelling the Opéra point blank, and its population all but starved, said to Bismarck: "Not one foot of soil! Not one stone from our fortresses!" he was establishing for all-time-to-come the immortal spirit of Republican France.

Think! Paris could have been laid in ashes on the morrow, the whole of France ravished within a month, the last soldier put to the sword, all without any possibility of resistance—and there was found a Frenchman who could say defiantly to Bismarck: "Not one inch of soil! Not one stone from our fortresses!"

Who shall dim the glory of a nation like that?

If I seem to lay unwonted stress on the Franco-Prussian war—now a matter, even for the French, of cold, unsentimental history—it is because it occurred at perhaps the most impressionable moment of Sarah Bernhardt's life, and has thus a direct bearing on our story.

We have just gone through a war so big that, although the Armistice was signed five years ago, it seems only yesterday. We have had living evidence ourselves of the influences of war upon the generation which fought it. We know how war can alter the characters of men, for we have seen it react on our own brothers and fathers and sisters. In France, in 1870, the women did not go to the war as they did in those terrible years from 1914 to 1918, but they bore their share—possibly the heaviest share—of suffering behind the scenes. In 1870 the army in the field was at least on the move, engaged in active operations; or, if it had been compelled to capitulate, it was, at least, not hungry. But at that time the women of Paris were very nearly starving. It is hard to keep up courage, let alone enthusiasm, on an empty stomach; but this the women of Paris did!

As the Germans drew closer and closer to Paris and

the outer defences began to fall, the flood of wounded that poured into the hastily-contrived hospitals increased, until it became a matter of serious doubt whether there were sufficient beds to hold them.   Almost everything was lacking—bedding, medicines, bandages, doctors, nurses and food.

Starting with five wounded soldiers, Sarah's hospital in the Odéon was soon taking care of more than a hundred.   I remember visiting it with my mother during the siege, and the frightfully fetid odour that assailed one on entering the door still lingers in my nostrils.

The wounded lay both in the theatre proper and on the stage.   The beds were placed in great semi-circles, leaving wide aisles between, along which the doctors and nurses walked.

The nurses were nearly all actresses and friends of Sarah Bernhardt whom she herself had trained.   Their efficiency, naturally, left much to be desired, but to the wounded they seemed like ministering angels.

Among the patients were many German prisoners, and during the siege these always had the best and choicest food obtainable, so that when cured they could be released and sent back to their army, to refute the impression of a starving Paris!

Sarah told a story of one man, a corporal, who taunted her on his arrival with the words: "Oh ho!   I see the stories were true!   You have nothing to eat for so long that you are a skeleton!"

This uncomplimentary allusion to Sarah's slimness

angered her excessively, but she went on bandaging the man's leg, which was broken. The next day the corporal was astonished at being served with chicken soup for his dinner. On the following one he was given boiled eggs and some young lamb.

"Chicken, eggs and lamb in a starving city!" he exclaimed. "Why, you have everything you want! All these stories of a starving Paris, then, are untrue?"

He did not know that Sarah's own dinner for days had been black bread and beans, and that she had not eaten meat for more than a month! Whatever delicacies were brought to the hospital were for her wounded.

Her face grew thinner, but took on an added beauty. She did not spare her frail body, but worked from early morning until late at night. More than once, when an exceptionally late convoy of wounded arrived, she worked all night as well.

Her character became stronger and nobler; forged in the fires of suffering, the metal rang true. "La Bernhardt" became a password of homage among the soldiers. From a careless *gamine,* flattered by the adulation of the multitude, she became a serious woman, striving only for one thing: the alleviation of suffering among the soldiers who were giving their all for their country.

It might be said that the war came at an opportune moment in Sarah Bernhardt's career. It demonstrated to her that, despite the plaudits of Paris and the flattery of the multitude, she was only an ineffectual morsel of the universe. It served to tame her conceit, to teach her how insignificant individual success and glory are compared to the welfare or suffering of a nation.

Her character became more subdued, her fits of temper less violent and more rare.   Her beauty had not suffered, however; rather had it been enhanced.   Her eyes, always enigmatic, had themselves gained something of the sentiment which animated her being.   Dressed in the white of a military nurse, with the red-and-green cross on either arm and on her hooded cap, she was ethereally lovely.

She used to go round begging overcoats from her rich acquaintances.   The Odéon was large, coal scarce and heating difficult.   It became a proverb among the men she knew: "Don't go down to the Odéon with your overcoat on, or you will lose it: 'la Bernhardt' will take it for her wounded!"

Nevertheless, they were generous to her.   The Ministry of War, established in the Palace of the Tuileries, allowed her the same rations at those allowed to the regular hospitals—and, in fact, Sarah's personal appeals probably obtained for her something extra.

At any rate, even in the darkest days of the siege, Sarah Bernhardt's wounded never lacked for anything essential.   She set every woman and child of her acquaintance to work making bandages and folding lint. I myself worked eight hours a day so doing.   How I loved Sarah Bernhardt in those days!   She seemed to me to be glory personified.

When the siege began there were, according to official statistics, 220,000 sheep, 40,000 oxen and 12,000 pigs within the city limits. This, said the authorities, was ample to provide for the wants of Paris for five or six months. And so it would have been—if they had not forgotten that a live lamb or ox or pig needs to be fed as well as the human beings who are subsequently to eat them! They had brought this vast army of animals to Paris, but they had forgotten to bring in sufficient quantities of forage to feed them.

All the public buildings were used for storing either food or munitions. The Opéra, which had not then been officially opened, was organised as a gigantic warehouse by Charles Garnier, its architect, and it was discovered that a river of fresh water flowed underneath its cellars.

Sarah Bernhardt had had her hospital in full working order for six weeks before she discovered that all the cellars underneath the Odéon were filled with boxes of cartridges and cases of shells! Since the Germans could have shelled the Odéon point blank from the heights of Bellevue or Montretout, there was some excuse for the urgent protest she made in person to Rochefort, that these munitions should be removed and her wounded relieved from the necessity of lying on a powder mine. Rochefort saw that the necessary orders were given.

As winter dragged on, the siege became a wearisome thing, but the courage of the Parisians could not be daunted. Cut off from all communication with the outside world, and even from their fugitive armies in the South; starving and nearly at an end of their resources, there was nevertheless no real thought of surrender. The Germans said Paris could not hold out a month. It had already held out two.

The hardest thing was to keep up the spirits of the people, and in this Sarah Bernhardt again took a leading part. The police had closed the theatres, and many of these, like the Odéon and the Opéra, were being used for purposes of national defence. But it was felt that some amusements should be provided, so Pasdeloup, the famous conductor, was asked to organise a committee of singers, musicians and stage-folk to see if some way could not be found of getting over the difficulty. Eventually, on October 23, Pasdeloup gave his first concert, and shortly afterwards Lescouvé re-opened the Comédie Française.

Sarah Bernhardt organised a scratch theatrical company from among those of the actors and actresses of the Odéon who were available, rehearsed several stock plays and gave them in the open air, for the benefit of the troops of the National Guard, who were encamped on the fortifications and in the parks.

In November Pierre Berton re-appeared—an older, bearded, strange-looking Berton. He had been in that part of the army which was cut off from Paris, and had only reached the capital by slipping past the German sentries at the peril of his life.

"But why did you not stay in the country, where you were safe, and where your family is?" he was asked. It was true—his mistress and his children had long ago escaped to Tours.

"What?—stay out of Paris, and *she* here?" he demanded, pointing to Sarah Bernhardt.

Their intimacy continued, but without the great passion of other days. Sarah was tender to him, but made him see that her days and nights belonged now to the wounded. Nevertheless, Berton complained that others had taken his place in her heart.

There were four men, in particular, who excited his jealousy. These were the Count of Kératry, under-secretary for food supplies; Paul de Remusat, one of the prevailing moderate elements in the new Government and a great friend of Thiers; Rochefort, who certainly had for Sarah a strange and somewhat uncanny attraction, in view of his violence and his dissolute character (Sarah says of him: "It was Rochefort who caused the downfall of the Empire"); and finally Captain O'Connor, a cavalryman, who was a much more serious competitor for Sarah's affections than the other three. O'Connor will figure in these memoirs later on.

There is considerable doubt as to whether Count de Kératry was ever a lover of Sarah Bernhardt's. He had known her since she was a child at Grandchamps, when he used to visit the Convent to spend an hour with a niece, who was a pupil there. Later, he had been introduced to her family, and by the time he received his commission as a lieutenant of cavalry and was sent to command a unit in the campaign of Mexico, had come to be a rather frequent visitor in the house in the rue Michodière. From then on Sarah Bernhardt did not see

Sarah Bernhardt in her Studio Dress.

him until he returned, just before the Franco-Prussian war, and was given an appointment on the Staff. After the revolution he was made a *préfect,* with special charge over the victualling of the city.

It was he who saw that Sarah's hospital was so well supplied with food—well supplied, that is, in comparison with other hospitals of a similarly independent character. During the siege Sarah saw him frequently, and he went often to the Odéon.

He was greatly enamoured of the young actress, but they were both too busy to give much time to each other, and certainly their humane duties precluded any prolonged love-making. But Berton saw in the Count de Kérartry's frequent visits to Sarah an intrigue that threatened to oust him from his privileged place at her side, and he made many heated remonstrances to that effect.

Paul de Remusat, an author, playwright and educationalist, and withal a most supremely modest and unassuming man, was one of the real forces behind the revolution, but he was not one of the popular figures in it. He seldom spoke in public.

Sarah had been introduced to him, some months prior to the war, by the younger Dumas. She found inordinate pleasure in reading his writings, which were of an inspiring beauty. She would go to his modest apartment in the rue de Seine and sit on the floor at his feet, one arm over his knees, as he read to her his latest works.

It was to Paul de Remusat that Thiers, Favre, Arago,

Crémieux, Gambetta, Jules Simon, Ferry, Picard, Pagès and the rest of the revolutionary committee came in the afternoon with their plan of action (that night the Empire fell).   It was de Remusat who revised this plan, and advised them of the pitfalls that lay ahead.

He could have had anything in the gift of the new Government.   If the times had not decreed that the President must be a military man—the honour eventually went to the Governor of Paris, General Trochu—there it no doubt in my mind that Paul de Remusat would have been offered the highest post possible in the new order of things.   The fact that he had a "de" as prefix to his name was another drawback, for it only needed a "de" to convince some people of one's royalist leanings.

Eventually, it was decided to make him Master of Fine Arts, and a committee was sent to him with this idea in view.   That evening the president of this committee, M. Théophile Besson, sent for Sarah and said to her, despairingly: "It is no use, we cannot move him. You are the only person on earth, mademoiselle, who can make him change his mind!"   Sarah consented to do her best, and saw de Remusat the next day.   He asked to be allowed twenty-four hours to think the matter over, and he then wrote to Sarah to this effect.

"CHERE, CHERE AMI: Allow me to remain, my charming little friend, in the shadow, where I can see so much clearer than I would if smothered in honours!"

In another letter a few days afterwards he said:

"You know well that you have instilled into me an ideal of beauty too partial to be of service to the world, which makes me prefer to avoid worldly strife and ambitions."

Throughout her career Sarah Bernhardt seemed to have possessed this God-given faculty of elevating the ideals and ennobling the ambitions of men. The influence she exerted on her century in matters of art was incalculable. To painters she would say: "If you love me, then paint a masterpiece and dedicate it to me!" To poets she would say: "If it is true that you love me, you will write a poem about me that will live when we both are dead!" And true it is that numbers of famous verses to anonymous beauty had their inception in the ideal which Sarah Bernhardt had succeeded in creating.

Alexandre Dumas *fils* once told me: "She drives me mad when I am with her. She is all temperament and no heart; but when she is gone, how I work! How I *can* work!"

Georges Clairin threw down his tools in his studio one day, interrupting work on a great mural painting he was doing for Sarah Bernhardt's house, and went in search of Sarah. When he had found her, he remained half an hour in silent contemplation of her face. Finally, he jammed his round black velvet artist's cap on his head, turned on his heel without a word and, returning to his

studio, worked savagely on his painting until it was finished.

"Before," he told me, "it used to be absinthe; now it
is Sarah!"

Where other actresses prided themselves on their influence in politics—there was a time when affairs of state
were habitually settled in the salons of the reigning
beauties—Sarah, consciously or unconsciously, exerted her
influence on men of letters and art.

She would not look at a man unless he was doing
something useful with his life. She despised idlers, and
was ever at work herself. Not that she was of severe or
strictly moral character. Far from it. But she used her
beauty and her undisputed hold on men in the finest way
possible: namely by inspiring and creating idealism in
the minds of the clever men who loved her. That may
have been the secret of her hold on men.

It became an axiom in the theatrical world: "If you
want an introduction to So-and-so (naming a prominent
author, playwright, or artist), go and ask Sarah Bernhardt."

Her influence on Pierre Berton was somewhat of a
different sort, but this was his and not her fault. Berton
had an excessively jealous temperament, as I found out
for myself later on.

Victor Hugo had returned in triumph to Paris from
his secret place of exile, and Pierre Berton was asked
to read his poem *"Les Chatiments,"* the daring and
somewhat terrible masterpiece that is credited with hav-

ing been chiefly responsible for the spread of anti-imperialist feeling in France. It was a forbidden work under the Empire and had previously only been read in secret in the clubs.

Berton read the poem in the Théâtre Lyrique, before a great and enthusiastic crowd. Sarah refused to attend. She still felt some bitterness against Victor Hugo, for, though she now called herself a Republican—it was dangerous to term oneself anything else—she had preserved cherished memories of the Emperor, the Empress, and the Court in which her acting had once produced a sensation.

She had never forgotten that simple act of generous courtesy, when the Emperor Napoleon had descended from his throne to kiss her on the cheek, in recognition both of her beauty and her art. He might be a prisoner in Germany and they might call him an imbecile, but she remembered him as a very gentle friend. And the Empress—who had escaped from Paris in the carriage of an American dentist—it was she who had commanded the performance at the Tuileries, and it was she who had personally sent a note of thanks to Sarah at the theatre on the following day.

Sarah's memories of Royalty were inspiring. And she had hardly become accustomed to Republicanism when the existing Government was swept away with the Capitulation of Paris, and the horrors of the Commune introduced.

Sarah saw Paris set on fire by the maniacs who said

they were "saving the nation"; saw many of her friends in political circles shot dead without trial; feared, like many others, that the Terror was come again. And, to add to her trouble, a man whom she had been at some pains to make an enemy was appointed chief of police!

This man was Raoul Rigault, a youngster of thirty. He had been one of that student band who established Sarah's fame, and had presumed on this fact to send her loving verses, and on one occasion a play in bad verse, which she promptly returned through Berton as being "unfit for her to handle, let alone read." Rigault was furious and swore vengeance.

When the Commune came, Rigault was appointed *Préfect* of Police, and he visited Sarah at her flat, situated, after another move on her part, in the Boulevard Malesherbes.

"It depends upon you, mademoiselle," he said, "whether there is war or peace between us."

Sarah, angered beyond measure at this insult, sprang up and struck him on the face with the palm of her hand. Then she ordered him to be shown the door.

When Berton came later in the day, he wanted to seek out Rigault at once and kill him. "The rat!" he kept declaring, "the rat!"

He did, in fact, visit the Préfecture with the idea of meeting Rigault and "calling him out," but could not find him. Before the Communist could wreak his threatened vengeance on Sarah, the Commune was over and he was executed.

Immediately after the signature of peace, Sarah made a long and exceedingly hazardous voyage to Hamburg, *via* Holland, where she met her family and saw her baby boy again. She furiously abused her mother and her aunt for daring to take her son to Germany during that country's war on France, and after their return to Paris she refused for some time to have anything to do with her Aunt Rosine, whom she regarded as responsible for the outrage. She brought her son back with her.

Among her acquaintances before the war had been a man named James O'Connor, a Frenchman of Irish descent. She had had little to do with him at this epoch, and had known him only as a frequenter of several literary salons which she had been in the habit of attending.

Just before the siege of Paris, Captain O'Connor—he had been given a commission in the cavalry—was brought to her hospital at the Odéon, suffering from a bullet wound in the hip Though his recovery was rapid his convalescence was long.

Sarah tended him with her own hands, and their friendship ripened into a warm intimacy. With Berton more and more involved in politics, and passing nearly all his evenings at meetings in the home of Victor Hugo, Sarah saw a lot of the dashing Captain O'Connor, and it was he who, when the Communist rebellion broke out, arranged her escape from Paris with her son, and installed her in a cottage between St. Germain and Versailles.

Almost every day they took long gallops together and once, when riding through the Park of Versailles, they were shot at by a crazy communist who had hidden himself behind a tree. The bullet missed its mark and, turning in his saddle, Captain O'Connor mortally wounded the man. Then he made as if to ride coolly on.

"But you are not going to leave him like that?" asked Sarah, sick at heart, pointing to the man who lay dying on the grass.

"Why not," asked O'Connor, coldly. "He would have worried himself precious little about you and me if he had succeeded in killing us. Every day friends in my regiment are killed in this way by some of these madmen in ambush."

Sarah slipped off her horse and supported the man's head in her arms, where a few seconds later he expired. Then, remounting with a stony face, she gave her hand to O'Connor.

"What's the matter?" he asked in cynical amazement.

"I will not ride any further with an assassin!" she said, and then galloped away.

This unjust accusation deeply mortified O'Connor, especially as Sarah refused to see him the next day when he rode over to offer renewed explanations and to exact an apology.

CHAPTER XIV

THE Paris papers were full of it; the literary and theatrical world talked of nothing else: Victor Hugo was to be played again!

It was *Ruy Blas,* naturally, that had been chosen for the opening of the Hugo season, and it was at the Odéon that the play was to be given. Duquesnel and Chilly, after many long conferences, had come to the conclusion that the decision as to who was to be the chief interpreter of the piece should be left to the illustrious dramatist himself. Sarah Bernhardt saw Chilly.

"I must play *Ruy Blas!*" she said to him.

"But, mademoiselle, there are others whose claim is greater than yours," said the little manager. "Monsieur Hugo cannot and will not be influenced in his choice! I can tell you nothing until I have seen him."

Sarah Bernhardt went to Pierre Berton.

"You are a friend of Victor Hugo's," she said. "Go to him and persuade him that I must play *Ruy Blas!*"

She told me years afterwards: "I felt that it was to be the supreme effort of my life. Something within me told me that, if only I could play this masterpiece, both fame and fortune would come at once. I was so sure of this that I determined nothing should stand in my way—and no other artiste."

Berton returned jubilant from his interview with Victor Hugo.

"The Master says you are *toute indiquée!*" he told the enchanted actress; "he has had you in mind from the beginning."

Rehearsals lasted a month, and Victor Hugo was at each one of them, an indomitable figure of middle height, his grey wiry hair tumbling over his ears and collar. Generally he sat in the front row of the orchestra, but on occasions a chair was placed for him in the wings, and from there he would jump up excitedly whenever he saw something which disagreed with his theories as to how the play should be produced, and would spend valuable minutes trying to demonstrate the right way in which a passage should be rendered.

One evening, after rehearsals were over, he had a new idea concerning the part of Ruy Blas. Without stopping to think, he dispatched this hasty message to Sarah Bernhardt: "Come at once and we will talk it over."

"What! Does he think I am his valet?" angrily exclaimed Sarah, and wrote as much to him. In an hour or so she received the whimsical reply: "No, mademoiselle, it is I who am your valet!—Victor Hugo."

This, of course, appeased Sarah, and when they met the next day they were on cordial terms enough. Two days later Victor Hugo brought Sarah a huge bunch of roses, which he presented to "My Queen of Spain" (Sarah's part in *Ruy Blas* was that of the Queen).

"I know where those roses came from!" declared Sarah, accepting them suspiciously.

"From my garden, mademoiselle!" said Victor Hugo, with a bow.

"No, they came from the garden of Paul Meurice! It is impossible that there should be another rose-bush like that in all France!"

Hugo was extremely disconcerted, the more so as his friend Meurice, who was standing by, burst into a hurricane of laughter.

"I told you she would know them! I told you!" he roared.

Hugo quickly recovered his habitual wit.

"They are, mademoiselle, the finest roses in all Europe!" he assured Sarah solemnly. "I offered to buy them, and Paul would not sell; then I tried to steal them, and he caught me. So I made him give them to me, since with these roses existing it was manifestly impossible for me to give you any others."

Sarah accepted the gift, which was one of a series she received from the great author. Then Hugo said:

"You know, mademoiselle, if we go by the standards of your ancestors, the Dutch, we are not really friends!"

"Why not?" asked Sarah innocently.

"Well, the Dutch have a saying that no friendship is cemented till the two friends in turn break bread together under their own roofs."

"Then come to dinner with me to-night—and you, too, Paul?" she said, turning to Meurice.

"But I cannot do that—I have an important engagement!" said Victor Hugo.

Meurice, his most intimate friend, who knew all his engagements, turned to him in astonishment, and Sarah, seeing his astonishment, naturally thought that Hugo was merely making an excuse so that he would not have to dine with her. She turned haughtily away. But Hugo, running after her, laid his hand on her arm in supplication.

"Do not be angry, *ma petite Reine*," he said, "my engagement is with you!"

"With me!"

"Yes, I have told the cook to prepare a great dinner to-night, and you are my guest!"

Sarah regarded him suspiciously. Stories of his libertinage had been current for years.

"Whom else have you invited?" she demanded.

"Oh," answered Hugo, vaguely waving his hand, "er —lots of people—Duquesnel, Meurice here, and—and others."

Sarah caught the amazed expression on Meurice's face and, excusing herself, sought out Duquesnel.

"Has Victor Hugo invited you to a grand dinner at his house to-night?" she asked.

"No—why?"

Sarah did not answer, but returned to Hugo and held out her hand, smiling.

"Very well, then, it is understood—I shall come at eight o'clock."

Hugo was overjoyed and overwhelmed her with thanks. He was completely taken aback, however, when Sarah Bernhardt arrived at the time mentioned—with four friends!

The table had been laid for two, as Sarah had expected. But Hugo treated the matter as a great joke, entertained them delightfully until midnight with stories of his travels, and went about for days afterwards telling his friends what a "smart woman that Bernhardt was!"

There was never anything but ordinary friendship, and much mutual admiration, between Sarah Bernhardt and Victor Hugo, despite all the rumours that were current then and have been bruited around since. The principal reason for this was, of course, that Sarah was a young woman, while Hugo was nearing the end of his long and active career.

"Victor Hugo?" she answered me once. "A wonderful *vieillard* (old man)."

Ruy Blas was produced at the Odéon on January 26, 1872, before the most brilliant audience the theatre had ever seen. Every seat had been taken days in advance, and hundreds crowded into the space behind the back rows and stood up throughout the entire performance.

Sarah Bernhardt triumphed. She often told me that never again in her long career did she act so well as she did that night. And Paris agreed with her. She was a literal sensation.

When the play was over, she was forced to respond to more than twenty curtain-calls. She tried to make a little speech of thanks, but failed, broke down and ran off the stage sobbing, to the huge delight and thunderous applause of the audience.

Blinded by tears, she was making her way to her dressing-room when she felt two arms placed about her from behind and a gentle voice whisper in her ear:

"What, my queen! Are you going without a word to me?"

The grave reproach made her lift her head and turn. It was Victor Hugo. His eyes, too, were wet.

"Sarah," he said gravely, "I have but one word to say to you, and I say it with all my soul: *merci!*"

Georges Clairin, who was present, sketched the two as they stood there in each other's arms, mingling their tears of happiness.

The sketch was published some days later, under the title of "The Goddess and the Genius." From that day dated the "divinity" of Sarah Bernhardt. Her art had become supreme, a thing to amaze and astound the world.

Sarah Bernhardt's collaboration with Victor Hugo became frequent from that time forward.

In 1877 Hugo saw her in *Hernani* and wrote to her:

"MADAME,

"You have been great and charming; you have touched my heart—mine, the old soldier's—and, at a certain moment, while the enchanted and overwhelmed public applauded you, I wept. This tear, which you caused to fall, is yours, and I throw myself at your feet!

"VICTOR HUGO."

Accompanying the note was the "tear"—a magnificent, pear-shaped diamond, suspended from a gold bracelet.

Years later, when Sarah was visiting Alfred Sassoon in London, she lost the bracelet, and Sassoon, tremendously worried, begged to be permitted to replace it.

Sarah sadly shook her head.

"Nothing," she said, "can ever replace for me the tear of Victor Hugo!"

Every critic in Paris, with the sole exception of Francisque Sarcey the irrepressible, praised with lavish phrases her performance as the Queen in *Ruy Blas*. But Sarcey was brutal.

"She is a scarecrow with a voice," he wrote. "Certainly the public is entitled to be informed of the reasons MM. Duquesnel, Chilly and Hugo had for giving her the rôle in which she appears. She is not yet mature, does not move naturally, and seems to rely exclusively on her talent for recital."

Sarah went into violent hysterics when she read the article. She could not imagine why Sarcey was so venomous. Pierre Berton knew Sarcey intimately, of course, and tried to intercede for her. He met a rebuff.

"Your *protégée* has blinded you with her blue eyes," Sarcey said. "She is not a great success, and she never will be one!"

The critic continued his devastating articles, seeming to find pleasure in tearing down the reputation of the young actress. He had an undisputedly great following, and the management of the Odéon itself commenced to look askance at this unwelcome publicity.

Sarah was particularly concerned over the effect Sarcey's diatribes would have with the management of the Comédie Française, for (secretly) she longed to be taken back into the fold of the theatre which then, as now, was the principal playhouse of France.

Sarcey's articles culminated in a vitriolic attack on Sarah's interpretation of another rôle (I think it was that of Mademoiselle Aïsée). Sarah read the attack during an *entr'acte* on the third night, and became so ill with anger that a doctor had to be sent for. She finished her rôle that night, but her acting was so bad that even critics favourable to her commented upon it.

Girardin, the friend of Victor Hugo and the most famous journalist of his time, came to her on the following day, as she lay in bed exhausted from a sleepless night, and said to her without preamble:

"Of course, you realise why Sarcey is attacking you?"

Sarah looked at him in red-eyed surprise.

"No—why should I know?" she replied. "I have never met him!"

"Think again!" urged Girardin. "He says you and he are old acquaintances!"

Sarah thought, and after a moment she replied: "He is mistaken; I have never met him."

"He tells his friends that he met you once at the home

of Madame de S——," responded Girardin, "and that you were rude to him there——"

Sarah sat up in bed with a bound. "That—that creature—that was Sarcey?" she cried. "Why—he was *ignoble!* He was criticising Camille Blanchet, one of my dearest friends, saying that he was a cow on the stage, and I——"

"What did you say?" prompted Girardin.

"I—I forget; but I think I said that I would rather be a cow on the stage than a pig in a drawing-room! . . . But—I had no idea that he was Sarcey!"

"Well," said Girardin conclusively, "that was he!"

Sarah was pale with dismay. "What shall I do?" she asked.

"There are only two things you can do," answered Girardin. "Either you can ignore him, and let him continue his attacks, in which case you can say good-bye to your chances of re-entering the Comédie—at least for the present; or you can—make friends with the man."

"But how—make friends?"

"I have heard that he is susceptible to a pretty woman!" said Girardin, drily, "and if you meet him, and explain that you did not know that it was he, that day at Madame de S——'s, perhaps——"

Sarah understood.

On the following Sunday Pierre Berton (it was he who told me the story, many years later) saw Sarcey sitting in a stage-box, dressed in a dandified full-dress and wearing all his honours. His expression was so triumphant, as Sarah came on the stage, that Berton "smelt a rat" and decided to watch carefully.

For some months Sarah's attitude to him had been one of increasing coldness—coldness that was the more inexplicable, since he had been her friend and protector from the time she entered the theatre.   He believed now that he held the key to the mystery.

Sure enough, when the curtain fell for the evening, Sarah accosted Pierre in the wings, and said to him:

"Ecoutes!"   I don't feel well to-night; I will go home alone with Blanche."   Blanche was her maid.

His protests only made her refusal to allow him to escort her the more emphatic and irritable.

"I tell you I am ill!   I must go straight home to bed!" she asserted.

Hurrying through his dressing, Pierre ran to the stage entrance, where he hid in the door-keeper's box and watched.   He haid waited some time when word was brought to him that Sarah had left—by the front door. Hurrying round to the front, Pierre was just in time to see her greet Sarcey, who was waiting there, with an affectionate kiss, and then mount into the same fiacre with him.

They drove away together, and from that day on Sarcey's pen ceased to be dipped in vitriol and became impregnated with sugar, in so far as Sarah Bernhardt was concerned.   Things continued thus until the inevitable break came, when Sarcey resumed his rôle of merciless critic.   But by that time Sarah did not care. She was back at the Comédie Française, and not all the

Sarceys in the world could have detracted from her glory nor torn the halo from her brow.

When Sarah quarrelled with Sarcey, she was greater than he.

Afterwards she attempted from time to time to renew her intimacy with Pierre Berton, but Berton, though remaining her friend and admirer, scrupulously kept on that footing and declined to return to his old status of doting lover and slave.

It was his last love affair until, the mother of his five children dying, he met and married me.

CHAPTER XV

SARAH communicated to Francisque Sarcey her desire to return to the Comédie Française. Not that she was unhappy at the Odéon! On the contrary, she had been gloriously happy there and owed everything to the staff of that theatre. It was simply that in those days, unless one had become the great star of the Comédie Française, one was not the great star of France. It was the criterion by which a dramatic career succeeded or failed—a sort of Royal Academy of the stage. And Sarah's engagement at the Comédie as a star would be a double triumph, since it would mean that those who disliked her and were embittered against her by personal quarrels had been forced to engage her because her genius would not let them do otherwise.

It was not an unheard-of thing for an actress to be taken from another theatre to the Comédie and starred; but it was rare. Generally, the stars of the Comédie were *sociétaires*—actresses who had entered the institution as apprentices, and had remained there throughout their careers. It is so even now. For an actress to be invited from another theatre meant a signal honour and a public acknowledgment that she was pre-eminent in her art.

It is likely that Sarcey did not have to use much persuasion with the directors of the Comédie. His influence was unlimited there, and the mere fact that the great Sarcey had changed his opinion of Sarah—even though a majority of Paris suspected the cause—was enough to stamp her with the precious hall-mark of genius.

But Sarah had enemies enough in the House of Molière. Maubant the tragedian, for one, had sworn that she should enter the theatre only over his dead body! Madame Nathalie was still there, together with her group of powerful friends. She had not forgotten the time that Sarah had slapped her face, nor would she ever forget it. The mere rumour that Sarah was to be invited back to the Comédie would send this group into transports of rage.

After *Le Passant,* Sarah's salary at the Odéon had been increased to four hundred francs a month, and following her triumph in *Ruy Blas* she was given a further increase of two hundred francs, making six hundred in all.

This salary, about six pounds a week, was considered excellent in those days—and it was not bad, even considering the somewhat depreciated buying-power of money in Paris due to the war and the Commune.

But it was not nearly sufficient for Sarah, who lived in lavish style in her new apartment in the Boulevard Malesherbes. There she had a suite of nine large rooms, all of them exquisitely furnished, and she maintained a staff of five servants. She had two coaches—one for ordinary driving to and from the theatre, and the other for special occasions, such as Sunday mornings in the

Champs Elysées and the Bois, when all fashionable Paris turned out in their smartest equipages to stare and be stared at.

She was constantly buying things and as constantly signing I.O.U.'s and *traites* (a species of acknowledgment of debt which authorises its collection by a bank). She never knew to a certainty how much money she owed, and was constantly surrounded by a horde of creditors eager to collect.

Among these creditors was a Jew, one François Cohen, a dealer in furniture and one of the most astute business men in Paris. He was not only a good business man; he was an extraordinary judge of dramatic talent, and in fact edited a column of dramatic comment for *Le Monde et La Ville*, a monthly sheet distinguished for its accurate information. He did this, of course, merely as a recreation.

Sarah's attention was first attracted to him by the number of *Le Monde et La Ville* issued after her first performance in François Coppée's *Le Passant*—the charity performance, I mean, before the play became a definite part of the Odéon *répertoire*. In his column Cohen had written:

"It is worth while to report the discovery, on Sunday night, of a new celestial body in the firmament of drama. We have found a poet, you will say; yes, but that is the least of it. Coppée is a master—a master in swaddling clothes—but even he, with his intricate verse, of which

(Photo, Henri Manuel)

Sarah Bernhardt in *Hamlet*.

From the well-known painting by Louis Besnard.

one understands only the beauty without comprehending the sense, would have been lost but for the outstanding magnificence of the most promising young actress on the stage in Paris.   I am speaking of Mlle. Bernhardt.

"Who is she?   I have asked, and nobody seems to know.   There are stories of royal favour, of noble blood, of powerful protection; let us trust that they are untrue, for Mlle. Bernhardt must have the incentive to work which only the necessity to live can give her.   But that she is something new in the heavens is, as I have said, undoubted.

"The question only remains: Will she be a comet, like so many others, flashing for but a brief instant in our bewildered and astonished consciousness, or will she develop into a new astronomical marvel, a brilliant seventh of the Odéon Constellation, destined to shine with increasing brilliance, to dazzle us with her art and to warm us with her voice, until she becomes a fixed sun in the celestial firmament of France?

"No one who saw her performance last night can doubt that the genius is there; it remains but to know whether she also possesses the great gift of ambition and the necessary determination to work which alone can make her success a permanent thing.   It is, perhaps, fortunate that she is not too beautiful. . . ."

It was the most keenly analytical criticism that had appeared—I have quoted only a small part of the article —and, despite Sarah's distaste for the last sentence, she realised that the author of the commentary knew what he was talking about.   This was shown by his skilful delineation of the play.   She carried the paper to Berton and asked:

"Who is 'F. C.' who signs this article?"

"I don't know," said Berton, "and nobody else does either.   It seems to be a sort of secret.   But he is clever."

Sarah sent a note to the paper asking the editor to communicate with "F. C." and ask him if he would call upon Sarah Bernhardt, who wished to thank him.   She named a day and a time.

At the appointed hour a call-boy came to her dressing-room with a card, on which was printed: "François Cohen."

Ah! So this was "F. C."   Sarah's eyes brightened in anticipation.   She knew of a question that she meant to ask him.

The door opened and a little, round-shouldered man, with a hooked nose and beady, sparkling eyes came in. He was dressed in a suit of clothes two sizes too big for him; one of his shoes was unlaced and he kept his hat on.

Without preamble he advanced into the room with a short mincing gait, trotted over to where Sarah sat regarding him with astonishment and suspicion, seized her hand, which he pecked at with his lips, and then thrust a large book on the table in front of her and began to turn over the pages.

"I understand that you are very busy, mademoiselle,"

he said, with a strong accent, "and so I have brought the catalogue that is likely to interest you, and I think we can agree very quickly. The prices are marked, but per-haps——"

Finally Sarah Bernhardt found her voice.

"Who," she demanded, struggling with mingled sur-prise and indignation, "are you?"

The little Jew looked up, astonished.

"Why," he answered, "I am François Cohen! Did not they give you my card? I was told to come up——"

"B—but, I thought that you had come from a paper——"

Cohen's little eyes sparkled. "I am François Cohen, and I sell very fine furniture," he said.

"I do not want to buy furniture!" exclaimed Sarah testily. "I wanted to see a man who signs himself 'F. C.' in *Le Monde et La Ville,* and I thought, when I saw your card——"

"You are sure you do not want to buy any furniture?"

"Of course I am sure!"

"Then, mademoiselle, we may talk of the other matter. I—I am also 'F. C.' "

Sarah regarded him incredulously.

"You are 'F. C.' who writes the theatrical articles in *Le Monde et La Ville?*" she demanded, with frank dis-belief. "I don't believe it! You are trying to lie to me, so that I will buy your furniture."

"I will prove it to you, if you like."

"How?"

"Well, you know what I said in my article—that you would one day be a great star if only you worked hard and had ambition?"

"Yes."

"Have you ambition?" he asked her.

"Yes," returned the actress, wonderingly. "I have—ambition."

"Will you give me your promise to study and work hard?" the extraordinary little man then asked her.

"I mean to do that—yes!" replied Sarah.

"Then I will prove my faith in you by making this agreement: If you will buy from me the furniture that you need in furnishing your new flat" (her old one had been burned out a few nights before), "I will give you credit for six years!"

Sarah could not believe her ears.

"Credit for six years!" she cried. "But that is a long time!"

"Six years!" repeated the Jew impassively.

"But why six? Why not ten—or two?"

"Because I believe that you will be famous within six years and will be well able to pay me," he answered.

The deal was struck. Six years later Sarah Bernhardt's name was the most celebrated in all Paris, and Cohen came to collect his bill—eleven thousand francs, including interest. It took all Sarah's spare cash, and all she could borrow on her salary, but she paid him. It was the only debt I ever knew her to be scrupulous about.

Sarah was in bed one morning when Madame Guérard, who had become a sort of secretary to her, entered the bedroom with a letter in her hand and a mysterious look on her face. Closing the door behind her, she went silently to the bed, and stood looking at Sarah.

Then she handed her the letter. It was in a large, square envelope, and on the back of it was printed "Comédie Française."

Sarah uttered a cry of exultation. It was her summons! She felt morally certain of it before the envelope was opened.

"Open it, Madame Guérard!" she cried, "and tell me what it says!"

The old lady carefully broke the seal, withdrew the letter, adjusted her spectacles and commenced to read:

"Monsieur Perrin, administrator of the Comédie Française, requests from Mlle. Sarah Bernhardt the honour of an appointment as soon as possible."

Sarah jumped out of bed, seized the letter, and did a dance of triumph on the floor. "Tell him," she said breathlessly, "that I will go to see him to-day, at once——"

"It is Monday, and the offices are closed," reminded Madame Guérard.

"That is so. I had forgotten. Well, tell him I will go to see him to-morrow afternoon."

The next day she saw Perrin, who took her hands in his and said to her earnestly: "My child, I know that you are very much attached to the Odéon, but your future belongs to France—and this is the National Theatre of France."

"When Perrin said that," Sarah related to me long afterwards, "I felt that my great moment had come. I was vindicated! My art had triumphed! I had compelled the Comédie Française, my enemies, to admit that I was the greatest artiste in Paris!"

She dictated harsh terms to Perrin, who promised to consider them. In two days came his reply: the administration had met and considered her case, and had instructed him to say that they would pay her an annual *traitement* of 12,000 francs.

With this letter in her hand she sought Duquesnel. That admirable man had long suspected that Sarah was eager to return to the Comédie.

But he only looked at her reproachfully and said: "Our little Sarah wishes to leave us? After all we have done for her? She does not love us any more!"

Sarah burst into a flood of tears, and flung herself into the director's arms.

"It is not true! I do not want to leave you! I love you all! I would like to stay. But you see——"

She could not explain that she felt her glory incomplete as long as she remained only the star of the Odéon.

"Well?" prompted Duquesnel. "Let me say it for you—it is the money!"

Sarah gave a sigh of relief. She had been afraid he would divine her real reason. And, anyway, the money played no small part in her determination to return to the Comédie.

"Yes," she admitted, "of course, it is the money. Perrin offers me twelve thousand francs a year. Give me fifteen thousand and I will remain here."

The largest salary hitherto paid by the Odéon to an artist was the 10,000 francs a year which had been earned by Mounet-Sulley before he, too, was taken by the Comédie Française. Sarah and Duquesnel both knew that it was impossible that she should be given fifteen.

"I will talk to Chilly," said he at last, "but I do not think he will agree."

The next day Chilly sent for her. His manner was abrupt, rude. But Sarah understood the man by this time. She knew that his brusque manner was only his way of concealing emotion.

"So," he said, "you want to leave us—idiot!"

"I do not want to leave," answered Sarah, "but I am offered more money!"

"Your place is here! There is not a theatre in Paris which can offer you more than the Odéon, except the Comédie, and of course you will never——"

Sarah tendered him the envelope she had received from Perrin, and Chilly started as he saw the inscription on the back.

"Ah!" he exclaimed.

Sarah waited.

"What do they offer?"

"Twelve thousand."

"I will give you twelve——"

"No, you must give me fifteen."

Chilly rose from his chair, red with anger. "So, mademoiselle, that is the way you treat your friends! Fifteen thousand francs! It is ridiculous—absurd. . . . Do you then take me for an imbecile?"

His attitude enraged Sarah.

"Yes," she snapped, "I take you for just that—an imbecile!"

And she left the room, banging the door, leaving Chilly wearily staring after her.

Half an hour later she was back in his office. Advancing, she held out her arms to Chilly and embraced him.

"So," he exclaimed joyfully. "You will stay?"

"No," returned Sarah. "I am going! But I want to—to thank you. . . ." And she burst into tears again.

Sarah signed her contract with the Comédie Française the same day. A week later Victor Hugo gave a banquet to celebrate the one hundredth performance of *Ruy Blas*.

It was in many ways a notable dinner. Not only did it commemorate the triumph of his greatest play, but it was Sarah's farewell to the company at the Odéon, her adieu to the stage on which she had achieved renown.

And it was the last supper of Chilly, the director who had helped to mould her fame. He died of heart failure at the table, at the very moment when he was about to reply to the toast of his health.

CHAPTER XVI

THE death of Chilly momentarily saddened Sarah Bernhardt, but did not check her rapid advance to fame. That event indeed once again brought her abruptly face to face with the elemental facts of life; and, like other experiences of the same nature, had a profound effect on her character, while it served as welding material for the art she displayed in her theatrical interpretations.

Her nature was that of the true artist—highly sensitive; once an impression was made on her it remained for ever as a component part of the edifice of her talent. Just as a portrait painter, away from his oils, will observe and remember in its minutest detail some tantalising cast of expression in the face of his model and will later reproduce it on canvas, so Sarah's brain was constantly receiving impressions which she later translated into life, through the medium of the characters she portrayed.

Sarah often told me of the fatal dinner during the course of which the little director Chilly died.

"I shall never forget a detail of that night, as long as I live," she said. "It was so incredibly a masterpiece of the great dramatist, Fate." (She frequently spoke in a figurative sense.) "It all happened as though written, rehearsed and stage-managed for weeks, with every person there an actor word-perfect.

"We were received at the entrance to the restaurant by Victor Hugo himself.   It was summer and extremely hot.   Duquesnel, Chilly, Berton and I arrived all together in my carriage.   Throughout the journey from my flat, Berton and Chilly had been heaping reproaches on me for my decision to leave the Odéon.

"Chilly was hurt and puzzled.   He could not understand why a difference of only three thousand francs a year should make me leave the theatre which had been the birthplace of my celebrity.   Berton was loudly querulous; he insisted on reminding me that it was he who had procured me my first engagement at the Odéon, and once came right out with the statement that it was Sarcey who was at the back of my desire to leave the theatre.

"This latter statement, which was quite untrue and which Berton must have known to have been untrue, angered me to such an extent that I stopped the carriage.

" 'Monsieur,' I said to Berton, 'either you will retract what you have just said, or you will get out of this carriage!'

" 'Well, then, why are you leaving us?' demanded Berton sulkily.   The man was incorrigible.   I laughed at him.

" 'If you insist upon knowing why I am leaving the Odéon, Pierre,' I answered him, 'it is because I can no longer remain at the same theatre with you!'

"Chilly looked at me strangely, but said nothing.   I

know he was aware—the whole theatre was in possession of the main facts by this time—that I had broken with Berton, and I think he may have imagined there was some truth in the explanation I had jestingly given. At any rate, he ceased his complaints and said afterwards not a single word of protest at my leaving.

"I remember that, during the drive to the restaurant, Chilly frequently complained of the heat. He had been working hard all day, and we had, in fact, called at the theatre, and brought him directly from it in his working-clothes. He was the most indefatigable worker I have ever met.

" 'Ah,' said Victor Hugo, on perceiving me, 'here is Her Majesty the Queen!' He seized my hand, kissed it twice and then, drawing me to him, kissed me on both cheeks. It was a characteristic salutation.

" 'I see that she is no longer the Queen, but has become again the artiste of Victor Hugo!' exclaimed Duquesnel.

"Hugo shook his head violently. 'No,' he cried, 'she is more than an artiste, more than a Queen—she is a woman!'

"We dined at a long table—more than sixty persons, including practically the whole *Ruy Blas* company. My chair had been placed at one end, but I had no sooner sat down than Hugo began looking round and running his hand through his hair in the nervous fashion I remember so well. When he saw me, he cried out: 'Ah, no! My dinner will be spoiled!' Then he added, speaking to Essler who was seated immediately opposite him:

'Jane, you are older than Sarah; take the seat of honour at the end, and tell her Majesty to come here!'

"Jane did as he requested, but with excusably bad grace. Before I had come to the Odéon, she had been its bright, particular star.

"The order was given to open all the doors and windows, and everyone was provided with fans, but the heat was stifling. Nobody could eat anything. Duquesnel sat next to me on one side, and Théophile Gautier, the poet, on the other. Immediately opposite to me was Victor Hugo. On his right was Chilly, and on his left Madame Lambquin, who played the part of the Camerera Major, and who was the *doyenne* of the Odéon.

"I remember that I did not touch the first course at all—it was a species of *hors-d'œuvres* made from beet-root, a vegetable which I then detested. Paul de St. Victor, who sat next to Madame Lambquin, apparently adored the vegetable and ate so much that the juice ran down his cheeks. For a poet, he was the fattest and most repulsive being I have ever known. I hated him, and he knew it.

"I managed to eat a little of the fish, which came next, but the horrible manners of St. Victor had completely spoiled my appetite. As I very seldom ate meat—I attribute my long life partly to the fact that I have rarely departed from vegetarianism—I got very little to eat that night.

"When the vegetable course was over, Duquesnel rose to his feet and, in a few words, proposed our host, Victor Hugo's, health. Hugo then replied in a long address, full of sentiment and expression, in which he was good enough to refer to me as the *'animatrice'* of the play.

" 'I,' he declared, 'have only written the piece, but *she* has lived it!' Then, turning to me and bowing, he said: 'Mademoiselle, you have a voice of gold!'

"When I rose to my feet and started to reply, Paul de St. Victor, who had been awaiting an opportunity to vent his spite, brought down his glass so violently that it was broken. I handed him mine.

" 'Use this, monsieur,' I said to him. 'You would not look natural without a glass in your hand.'

"The table laughed, and I was given courage to continue. I was in the middle of a little eulogy of my co-workers in the piece, when my gaze suddenly fell on the face of Chilly, and I stopped short.

"The little director's face was ashen, where a moment before it had been red and perspiring. His eyes were wide open and staring at me, with a glassy look about them that frightened me.

" 'Chilly! *Mon ami!*' I cried.

"His eyes met mine without a shade of expression, though his mouth opened and shut, as if he was trying to speak.

" 'Chilly!' I cried, terror-stricken, and all at the table rose to their feet. I rushed to his side and, kneeling, put my arms about him as he sat in his chair. 'Tell me, what is the matter?' I asked.

" 'Somebody is holding me!' he muttered, in a thick voice. 'I cannot move!'

" 'It is the heat; he has had a little stroke; it is nothing!' said Victor Hugo, with authority.

"Chilly was carried into one of the small dining-rooms, and laid on a couch. Victor Hugo and Duquesnel stood at the door, as guards, to keep the curious away. To everyone they declared that it was nothing and that Chilly would be all right in a few moments.

"I returned to the table and sat down. In my heart I realised that Chilly would not be all right—that it was the end. And I thought of all the times that this little man had befriended me, reviewed in my mind the occasions—yes, even on that very day—when I had been thoughtless and even brutal with him. Ah, I was sorry! If I could but have obtained his forgiveness. . . .

"No sooner had this idea come into my head than I rushed away to put it into execution. I would fall on my knees beside my friend and teacher, and beg his forgiveness. . . .

"At the door I was met by Victor Hugo. One look at his face and I knew that I was too late.

"Raising his voice, Hugo announced to the room: 'Monsieur Chilly has been taken to his home; we hope that he will recover to-morrow.' He could not tell them the truth, as they sat there at his table. Then, to me, in reply to my mute and terrified inquiry, he said, in a low voice: 'He has gone. . . . A beautiful death!'

"Those who did not know the truth remained to finish

dinner. Duquesnel took me home. I cried all night. And the next day a lawyer came to me and told me that almost the last act of Chilly—he had threatened it, but I had never believed that he would keep his word—had been to begin an action against me for breach of con-tract. I lost the case, and was sentenced to pay ten thou-sand francs damages, but this was paid by the Comédie, as provided in my contract."

The death of Chilly was not the strangest event of that fatal dinner. Madame Lambquin became suddenly ill. She told everyone that a fortune-teller, only a few days previously, had prophesied she would die within a week of the death of "a little dark man." Chilly was small and dark, and precisely seven days after his death, Madame Lambquin died.

Victor Hugo, when he heard of this latest tragedy, exclaimed:

"Without a doubt Death himself was at my dinner. I think he aimed at me, but he must be short-sighted, for one of his arrows went to my right, and slew Chilly, and the other swerved to my left, and killed Lambquin!"

A few days later Sarah received a note from Sarcey, asking her to be present at a conference in the directors' office at the Comédie, to decide which was to be her first rôle. Sarah wished to play the part of *Britanicus* as her *début,* and naturally, as Sarcey's note spoke of a "con-ference," she anticipated that her wishes were to be de-ferred to.

On the way to the theatre she confided her desire to

play *Britanicus* to Sarcey, who said nothing. Judge of Sarah's surprise, therefore, when Sarcey opened the "conference" by announcing abruptly: "Mlle. Bernhardt believes that she would prefer to make her *début* in *Mademoiselle de Belle Isle*."

Sarah was so astounded she could scarcely speak, and before she could make an adequate protest she was outside the door of Perrin's office, with the play a *chose jugée*. Then she turned upon Sarcey furiously.

"Why did you do that?" she asked.

"I wish you to play this part! You can have your *Britanicus* afterwards, if you like!"

Sarcey spoke carelessly, and his manner was an indication of the influence he exerted at the Comédie. Sarah was wise enough not to dispute his decision, but she was nevertheless angry with him, and refused to see or write to him for several days.

Her anger was increased when she found that her rôle in *Mademoiselle de Belle Isle* was not in reality the most prominent part in the play. Two other famous actresses, public favourites of the Comédie, were in the cast— Sophie Croizette and Madeleine Brohan. The latter, by her own request, retired from the play during rehearsals. Sophie Croizette was Sarah's great rival for popular favour. She had held the first female rôle at the Française for several years—since before the war, in fact.

Sarah decided that she would play the name part, Mademoiselle de Belle Isle, so extravagantly well that none of the audience would spare a second thought for

Croizette, in her part of the Marquise de Prie, who in
the play is kissed in the dark by the Duc de Richelieu, in
mistake for the lady from Belle Isle. At rehearsals Sarah
was magnificent. Croizette, who was an intimate friend,
despite their rivalry, used to come to her in despair.

"You are splendid—but you give no opportunity to the
rest of us!"

The play was produced on November 6, 1872, and the
first act was a triumph for Sarah. There was indeed
every indication that new glory was about to descend on
the immortal queen of *Ruy Blas* when, at the beginning
of the second act, she caught sight of her mother in a
stage-box.

Julie was leaning back in a chair, her eyes closed, and
beads of perspiration on her forehead. Sarah knew immediately what had happened. Her mother suffered from
a weak heart, and several times before had had a similar
seizure.

The tragic death of Chilly, which she had all but witnessed, was fresh in Sarah's mind, and doctors had told
her years before that she must expect her mother's disease
to end fatally one day. She watched the stage-box in
agonised fashion, while the audience became bewildered
at the extraordinary change which had come over their
star.

Sarah stumbled through the rest of the play, and immediately afterwards, learning that Julie had been carried there from the theatre, hurried to her mother's home.

Meanwhile the danger had passed. When Sarah arrived, she found her mother pale, but otherwise recovered, and taking nourishment.

Returning to her own flat she found a note from Sarcey:

"It was ludicrous. Shall I ever understand you? The first act was wonderful; in the others you spoilt the play!"

Furious that he should not have seen the reason for her agitation, Sarah refused to make any excuse for herself or to give him the slightest explanation. So, when his criticism of the play appeared in *Le Temps,* five days later, he was evidently in two minds as to whether to praise or condemn. His hesitation shows itself in several passages.

At the beginning of his critique he said:

"It must be admitted that, independently of her personal merit, there have formed around the person of Sarah Bernhardt a number of true or false legends, which excite the curiosity of the public. But it was a disappointment when she appeared. Her costume exaggerated her slenderness, and her face had been whitened too much with powder. The impression was not agreeable."

This was because he had urged her to modify her costume and she had not done so. Further on, Sarcey wrote that she "trembled convulsively" during the play, and while admitting that she had "marvellous grace,"

still insisted that she "was lost in the strong passages."
But he added, "were she to possess a vibrant dramatic
quality equal to her enchanting voice, she would be a perfect actress, an actress unequalled at the present day."
This, when his previous articles are remembered, was
quite an admission, and he ended his article with a real
eulogy:

"At the close of the play the artiste apparently found
herself, and for a brief space we could recognise in her
Our Sarah—the Sarah of twenty successes."

By the way, he had not admitted one of those successes himself!

It was only after the publication of his critique—which
in the circumstances Sarah recognised as just—that he
discovered the real reason for her poor performance.
He then had the grace not only to apologise personally,
but to publish an account of what had happened in a
later issue of *Le Temps*.

His apology, however, could not alter the fact that
the public thought her explanation only an artiste's excuse, and the honours of the play went definitely to Sophie
Croizette, who was really one of the most accomplished
artistes who have ever adorned the French stage.

For the next ten years there was a terrific rivalry between these two—not only in Paris, but abroad.

If Sarah created a rôle one week, Sophie created one
the next, and critics were divided in their opinion as to

which was the greater actress. If Sarah went on tour, so did Sophie; and the duel between these two close friends kept Paris perpetually entertained.

It was generally agreed, finally, that Sarah was the greater actress, but that she was also the more eccentric, the more apt to lose her head; nor, it was said, did she have the innate technique that distinguished Croizette's performances.

Croizette had few enemies—and perhaps that is why she has been forgotten, or nearly so, by the public. Sarah, on the contrary, used to say that she counted a day lost wherein she had not made "either a true enemy or a supposedly true friend."

CHAPTER XVII

EPISODE now succeeded episode in the life of the young actress—for she was still not more than twenty-eight years old.

She quarelled with Francisque Sarcey, and fell in love with an old friend of the Odéon—Mounet-Sully, the handsomest actor on the French stage, who, like Sarah, had been taken from the Odéon by the management of the Théâtre Français.

She acquired her famous coffin, which never afterwards left her, and in which her remains now lie at Père Lachaise.

She was sued right and left for debt.

Her sister Régine died.

Her own health became precarious, and a physical examination showed a spot on her right lung.

Most of these events occurred within the first three years of her re-engagement at the Comédie Française. Her eight years at this theatre were among the most eventful of her life.

During them she became the darling of one part of Paris, and the scorn of another part. During them she was credited with having had "affairs" with no less than nine prominent men. During them her fame spread throughout the world.

Her quarrel with Sarcey dated from the moment she felt herself strong enough to stand without his aid. I shall never believe that her liaison with Sarcey was actuated by anything except the motives of professional expediency. In fact, she practically admitted this to me.

"Sarcey," she said, "was one of those highly-gifted but intolerant men whose one aim in life is to mould the opinions of their friends and intimates to suit themselves. He was a brilliant writer, a still more brilliant conversationalist, and there is no doubt that, as a theatrical critic, he was head and shoulders above any other then living in France.

"His judgment was deferred to by most of the theatrical managers, and especially by those at the Comédie, whose political views and connections were the same as those of Sarcey himself. It was said that Sarcey could procure the admission or the resignation of anybody at the Comédie. He was extremely opinionated and very hard to change once he had made up his mind. He hardly ever forgot a slight, and never an insult.

"He was unquestionably an enemy of mine from the beginning, and I made him my friend when it became necessary to do so, but not because I was in any doubt as to his character. I found that, like many geniuses, he was insupportable in private life. He would rave and tear his hair twice or three times a day over matters without the slightest consequence. He usurped the privilege of 'protecting' me, and as a consequence a wrong interpretation was put on our friendship by the theatrical world, to which the word 'protector' meant only one thing—lover.

"People were bound to comment on the fact when a prominent man like Sarcey came night after night to the theatre and insisted on seeing me home. Why, he used to speak of me to his friends as his *protégée*. What actually happened was that my art and my determination to succeed triumphed over his enmity, and, finding that he could not hamper my career, he did his best to make people think he was responsible for it.

"He was subject to fits of extreme jealousy, and would carry on for hours if I so much as accepted another man's invitation to dinner. He acted as though he owned me, and when things got to this pass I decided to demonstrate to him that he did not."

She accomplished this very effectually by yielding to the supplications of Mounet-Sully.

When Sarah re-entered the Comédie Française, Mounet-Sully was the reigning power there. His fame was widespread; he was probably not only the finest but also the handsomest actor on the European stage.

Of Mounet-Sully it was written: "He is as handsome as a god, like a hero of Greek tragedy," and it was of these tragedies that he was incomparably the greatest interpreter of his epoch.

There is reason to believe that Sarah's affair with Sully was secret for many months during which she and Sarcey, who suspected nothing at the time, remained friends.

Later, however, he began to hear gossip linking their names, and once he overheard Sarah address Mounet-Sully by the familiar *"tu."* This may or may not have been significant, for artists of the French stage generally use the second person singular in talking among themselves.

Mounet-Sully also was young, and of a jealous temperament. There came a day when he could no longer bear the covert sneers of the critic. Coming down from his dressing-room after a rehearsal, he found Sarcey striding backwards and forwards on the stage.

"What are you doing here?" he shouted. "Do not deny it—you are waiting for Sarah!"

"What if I am?" demanded Sarcey imperturbably. "Who has a better right?"

"Pig! Son of a pig!" cried the enraged young actor, losing all self-control at the cool cynicism of the critic. "I challenge you to a duel!"

"I do not fight with children!" replied Sarcey, and spat on the floor to signify his contempt.

Sarah had been standing in the wings, and had overheard the dispute. She now came forward.

"Francisque, take me to supper!" she said, darting an angry look at Mounet-Sully. She could never bear these open quarrels between her admirers.

The actor did not speak to her for a month, but they composed their differences later and remained lovers for almost a year, only to separate again as the result of another fit of jealousy on Mounet-Sully's part.

For a short while they were again enemies, and then, once more deciding to make it up, remained friends throughout the remainder of Mounet-Sully's long career. When he married—his grand-daughter recently obtained a *premier prix* at the Paris Conservatoire—Sarah was present at the wedding, and sent the young couple a magnificent gift.

In 1874 Sarah was taken ill, as the result of a cold, which developed into pleurisy. She was in bed for a month, and at the end of this period an examination by three doctors revealed that one of her lungs was slightly affected. She was advised to leave the theatre, and to go to Switzerland for six months.

"How long do you give me to live?" she asked one of the physicians.

"Not longer than five years, if you do not take a complete rest until you are cured," he replied.

"Five years! But that is a lifetime!" she answered. "When I was seventeen the doctors gave me only three years, and I have lived thirteen. I shall continue acting until I die!"

And, despite all remonstrances from her friends, she returned to the theatre as soon as she was able to leave her bed. To the doctors' astonishment also, ten months later the spot on her lung completely disappeared. Perhaps it had never existed!

About this time she was asked by an admirer what he could send her as a souvenir.

"They say I am to die," said Sarah, gaily, "so you may send me a coffin!"

The admirer took her at her word, and a week later she received a letter from a famous firm of coffin makers, stating that an order had been received for a coffin for mademoiselle, which was to be constructed according to her own wishes.

Sarah was most particular in regard to this coffin. She made several designs, only to discard them one after the other. Finally she agreed that it should be constructed of fine-grained rosewood, and that the handles and "hoops" should be of solid silver. She afterwards had these changed to gold, but subsequently, during one of her frequent periods of impecuniosity, she sold the golden hoops and had them replaced with the silver ones that were on the coffin when she was buried.

For the remiander of her life this coffin, *"le cercueil de Sarah Bernhardt,"* never left her, even when she was travelling. It attained an almost legendary fame. She had a mahogany trestle made for the coffin, on which it stood at the end of her great bed, so that she could see it from her pillow, without an effort, on awakening.

"To remind me that my body will soon be dust and that my glory alone will live for ever!" she said.

"How long will it last?" she inquired of the makers when they delivered the coffin.

"For centuries!" replied they.

"It will need to last at least one, for I am determined

to disappoint the doctors and live to be a hundred!" she answered.

She delighted to be photographed lying, dressed in different costumes, in her coffin. More than fifty different photographs and sketches were made of her in this situation. On occasions, when guests came to her house for tea, she would serve it to them on the coffin.

Once she held a mock funeral. The rosewood coffin with its golden ornaments was brought with much pomp and ceremony into the studio-salon at the rear of her apartment, and Sarah, dressed in a long white robe and with a lily in her hand, climbed into it and lay at full-length as though dead.

While I played the "Funeral March" by Chopin on the piano, the poet Robert de Montesquiou ceremoniously placed lighted candles around the coffin; while the other guests, who included Jeanne Bernhardt, Madame Guérard and Madame de Winter, kept up a monotonous chant, reminiscent of the burial service.

She carried the coffin everywhere with her. It was a sight to see it loaded on top of the ancient carriage in which she was wont to make her provincial trips. At hotels in which she stayed, the coffin was invariably taken into her bedroom before she herself would enter it, and placed in the accustomed position at the foot of the bed.

On one occasion when we were touring the South of France, the *personnel* of a hotel at Nîmes struck sooner than permit the coffin to be brought into the hotel. The superstitious proprietor was in tears, and swore that the funereal object meant unhappiness to his family and bad luck to his business.

Nothing daunted, Sarah insisted on the coffin being brought in, and then called together the members of the troupe.

"You and I," she said to me, "will be the cooks. "You," indicating Pierre Berton (then my husband), "will be the waiter."

Other members of the troupe were given their parts as chamber maids, dishwashers, valets and the like, and for a whole day we ran that hotel. The next day the *personnel,* having been given free tickets to the theatre, were so impressed by Sarah's personality that they returned to work in a body, and the manager, declaring that he had never eaten better meals than those prepared by Sarah and myself, refused to accept a franc in payment for our rooms and board.

As soon as it was finished, Sarah had the coffin taken to her flat and placed alongside her Louis XVI bed. Whenever visitors came to call upon her, she would make a point of showing them this strange piece of furniture.

Her sister Régine, who was tubercular, had been sent to Switzerland, but when her disease became complicated with another malady, all hope was given up, and she returned to Paris, to her sister's flat.

Sarah had only just moved into this new home and had only one bedroom, so Régine and she at first shared the same bed. Régine's condition grew so serious, however, that the doctors warned Sarah that she could no longer sleep with her sister without a serious risk of contracting the malady.

Accordingly, Sarah made up a bed in the coffin and slept in that.

When the doctor came he was horrified.

"Take that thing out!" he ordered. "It is not yet time!"

With some difficulty Sarah convinced him that the coffin was not meant for her sister, but was her own bed. A few days later Régine died.

The tragedy had its effect on Sarah's life for a year or more, and she became a devout worker. Her name gradually ceased to be connected by gossipy writers with the scandals of the day. But after a year of mourning she flung off her mask of grief and *"La Grande Sarah,"* as she was known, again became a reigning queen of Paris.

She fitted up one of the rooms of her flat as a studio, and here, when she was not at the theatre or resting, she worked at painting and sculpture.

Sarah Bernhardt, as Charles de Lagrille said, was not simply an incomparable artiste; she was *the* artiste—artiste in the most complete sense of the word. She understood and realised in the most perfect fashion the ideal of Beauty.

Sarah was not only the interpreter of Phèdre,

"La fille de Minos et de Pasiphæ,"

that demi-goddess whom she incarnated so superbly; she was also the wise genius who discovered and launched poets and authors without number—Coppée, Mendès, Richepin, and the two Rostands, father and son. But her love of beauty was not confined to the theatre alone; she was equally at home in all branches of Art; she was novelist, dramatist, painter and sculptor.

Sarah Bernhardt published, in 1878, as we shall see, a book which was greatly appreciated by the literary critics of the time and which was entitled "In the Clouds." Replying to the famous and scurrilous publication "Sarah Barnum," she wrote in retaliation a work called "Marie Pigeonnier." She was also the author of her own "Memoirs," and of two modest works of fiction, one of which was published only a few years before her death, as well as several short stories.

Three successes were recorded by Sarah Bernhardt, the dramatist. They were *L'Aveu,* produced at the Odéon in 1888 by such interpreters as Paul Mounet, Marquet, Raphaele, Sisos and Samary; *Adrienne Lecouvreur,* a piece in five acts, in which she played the title part herself, and in which have since played such distinguished actors as de Max, Gerval, Decœur and Charlotte Barbier; and *Un Cœur d'Homme,* a three-act play, which Henry Roussel and Emmy Lyn produced in 1909.

But the theatre is only one sphere of Art. The great actress was also a great painter. Her pictures, said critics, lacked the masterly technique that only long experience and training could have given her, but they were frank, well-proportioned, and distinguished for their colour values.

Just after she returned to the Comédie Française, she painted my portrait, and this picture, needless to say, is still one of my most prized possessions.

At the Salon of 1878 she showed a remarkable composition entitled "Young Girl and Death." This canvas represented Death clutching at an artiste with a bouquet of flowers in her hand. It was an indication of the morbid strain in her character.

In 1872, after her first triumph at the Comédie, the sculptor Mathieu-Mesnier asked for permission to make her bust. She consented, watched his work, and asked innumerable questions. Thereafter, nothing would do but that she herself must become a sculptress.

Her first attempt in this direction was a medallion bust of her aunt at Neuilly. This was finished in one night and when exhibited astonished the critics by its virility and resemblance to the model. Mathieu-Mesnier continued to instruct her, and she passed most of her nights in modelling.

Her next effort was a bust of her young sister, Régine— made a few days before the latter's death. Others of her best sculptures (many of which were sold at the recent auction in Paris) were "After the Tempest," a group in marble; busts of Victorien Sardou, Blanche Barretta, Busnach (the dramatist who prepared Zola for the theatre), Henry de la Pomoraye, Coquelin, junior; her son, Maurice; Louise Abbema and Edmond Rostand. The last was completed after the poet's death, and was exhibited in the Rostand museum.

CHAPTER XVIII

"LA GRANDE SARAH" had now become an extraordinary figure in the contemporary life of Paris. There were two camps, one composed of her friends, the other of her enemies, and at one time it was difficult to know which group was the more numerous.

The friends of Sarah were called the "Saradoteurs," and cartoons of the great actress surrounded by her court became commonplaces in the metropolitan press. The weeklies were full of real or imagined escapades of the triumphant artiste of the Comédie Française.

It was said that she bathed in milk; that she had made the circuit of the Champs Elysées in the snow, with neither shoes nor stockings on; that she had entered the cage of a lion at the St. Cloud fête, and subsequently purchased the lion; that she had a regular menagerie chained up in her flat and that in consequence the neighbours had complained and that she was to be forced to move; that she had been twice seen on the boulevards with the young Prince Napoleon, who was supposed to be in exile; that she was at heart a Bonapartist, and was secretly working for the restoration of the monarchy; that she had an enormous appetite for strong drink; that she had ordered a coach-and-four in gold and ebony that was to cost two hundred thousand francs; that she had slapped the face of Perrin, the director of the Théâtre Français; that she was not a woman at all, but a boy masquerading in woman's clothes (this was doubtless owing to Sarah's startling success in young male parts); that Gambetta himself had called upon her, and had been received in the actress's *cabinet de toilette,* where she happened to be washing herself; that she had given five hundred francs to a blind beggar, because she thought he resembled a former lover; that she dressed up as a man and frequented public balls in disguise, challenging men friends to duels and then revealing herself to them.

I have no way of verifying any of these tales. From what I myself knew of Sarah and her way of living, I expect that parts of them, at any rate, were true.

It was a saying that there were three celebrated hours in Paris: One o'clock, Gambetta smokes his second cigar; four o'clock, prices fall at the Bourse; five o'clock, Sarah receives for tea.

Every afternoon her flat was filled with a motley assembly of the great and the nearly great. Sarah used to receive them in her sculptor's clothes, a kind of pyjama costume, designed by herself and made of silk. She would stand at the entrance of her workroom, imperious as a queen receiving homage from her people.

The first thing guests perceived on entering was a gigantic dog on a short chain, which growled and sprang at everyone who came in. Many people could not be persuaded to visit Sarah on account of this dog. My aunt was one—I never got her past the door, where she would sit and wait for me patiently, while telling the growling animal, from a safe distance, what she thought of him.

This dog was a great friend of mine, and not the brute which sprang at my throat in the manner related in a preceding chapter. He never growled at me, though I was in and out of Sarah's home at all hours of the day. I used to help her to mix her clay, and several times posed for an effect that she wanted to get perfect.

A flight of five or six stairs led up to the first reception room, where champagne cups usually stood on a small table; and in the hall outside this room a disagreeable surprise awaited the unwary visitor. This was a full-sized monkey, which was fastened by one leg to a chair, but was otherwise free to move about—which he did, with a great chattering and gnashing of teeth.

The little drawing-room had in it two birdcages and a great tank of goldfish, while cats and small dogs roamed about in a most casual way. Philippe, an old waiter whom Sarah had persuaded to leave the Café du Foyer (?) and enter her service, was in perpetual terror of all these animals and eventually left Sarah's service, after he had been bitten in the hand by the monkey.

Sarah usually had something new in the way of statuary to show her guests. I remember well when she did her "Médée," a piece almost as big as she was herself; and once, when I entered unannounced, I found her starting the bust of the famous Adolphe de Rothschild, for which he had promised her ten thousand francs.

Sarah had a lot of trouble with this piece of work. She said it was because the Baron continually changed his expression. At any rate, when the bust was finally achieved, all Rothschild's comment, after looking at it, was to say drily:

"Is that me?"

Then he turned to a writing-table to draw up an order on his bank for the ten thousand francs, only to be arrested by a crash.

Sarah stood in the centre of the floor panting, her eyes flashing and her breast heaving. On the floor lay the bust, smashed to a thousand pieces.

Baron de Rothschild, without a word, turned and left the room. The next day he received his bust—in a thousand pieces—"with Sarah Bernhardt's compliments."

The story became common property and Rothschild never spoke to her again. She remained friends with others of the same family, however, and there came a day when she was grateful for their help.

Sarah fitted up a magnificent studio near the Place de Clichy, in the avenue now chiefly distinguished for the number of night establishments which grace—or disgrace —it. It was a large, bare place, with immense windows, several step-ladders, and a divan covered with skins. For principal adornment it had a single, magnificent, white bear skin, which was the first present Sarah received from Georges Clairin, the painter and mural decorator—of whom more anon. He had been her admirer for years but it was not until 1879 that she yielded to his persistent pleadings and became really intimate with him.

The place was littered with scraps of plaster, old frames, cross-trees, brushes, supports, mallets, chisels and other paraphernalia of the sculptor and painter.

An old man who had once been an actor of repute, but who had been reduced to poverty and disgrace by morphine, was employed as a sort of general factotum. He would be an exemplary servant for a month or so, and then the drug passion would seize him and he would disappear for a week, during which the studio became littered with all kinds of refuse, from broken statues— which had been thrown violently to the floor by Sarah in fits of dissatisfaction, despondency or rage—to empty bottles of champagne and liqueurs, with which she was wont to entertain her guests.

About this time, if my memory serves me right, occurred the famous duel fought by Richard O'Monroy, the writer in *La Vie Parisienne,* and Edouard de Lagrenée, a distinguished young diplomat, whose infatuation for Sarah was like that of so many other men—terrific while it lasted, but of brief duration.

Sarah was in the habit of giving "soirées amusantes" in her atelier on nights when she was not billed to act at the Comédie.

These soirées consisted for the most part of conversation, recitals by poetic friends of the actress, gossip, and sometimes dancing. They were, in the word of Paris, *"très à la mode."*

(Photo, Henri Manuel)

Sarah Bernhardt (aged 30) and her son, Maurice, on the only
occasion when he acted with her.

Sarah's invitations were much sought after, but she never sent a formal one. It was understood that friends of hers were always welcome, and welcome also to bring any friends of their own. Thus Sophie Croizette—who, despite her rivalry with Sarah, had remained a friend outside of theatrical hours—appeared about nine o'clock one night, dragging by the hand a pale, anæmic-looking youngster, who appeared to be extremely bashful and intensely desirious of being elsewhere.

"See what I have caught!" cried Sophie, advancing into the atelier and dragging her young man after her. But the "catch" suddenly twisted his hand from hers and, without a word, turned tail and ran away. They rushed after him, to see his coat tails flying down the street fifty yards away.

"Who," demanded Sarah, when she had finished laughing, "was that extraordinary person?"

"That," answered Sophie Croizette, "was a Consul of France—and he is madly in love with you!"

Sarah looked at her, astonished.

"But," she said, "I have never seen him before!"

"He has seen every performance you have given for nearly six months, since he returned from Rome," explained Sophie.

"But who is he?" demanded Sarah, enormously intrigued, but uncertain whether to be pleased or to be angry.

"He is a young Republican, a *protégé* of MacMahon, and was made a consul. His family is a very distin-

guished one; you will find it in the *Liste des Familles*,"
explained Mlle. Croizette. "He is also a poet, and has
written some fine verses about you, which he has been
afraid to send. He is the most bashful man in all Paris!"

This was enough to excite the interest of Sarah Bernhardt!

A few nights later she perceived the bashful one in
the back seat of a box near the stage. She smiled at him,
but the poor young man was too timid to smile back.
Sarah determined that, by hook or by crook, she would
get to know him. He had, she decided, a face of singular
beauty.

From inquiries she made here and there among her
friends, she found that he had served in the war, and
that he had an enviable record for bravery. It is thus
with many timid, unassuming men.

De Lagrenée was a man of noble artistic temperament,
very much the idealist and the passionate lover—but so
far he had done his passionate loving at a distance.

"Who is the remarkable-looking man with the decora-
tion in that box?" she asked Mounet-Sully, who was
playing with her.

"That is Edouard de Lagrenée," answered Mounet-
Sully. "He is very distinguished in the diplomatic
service."

During the first *entr'acte*, through a hole in the curtain, she pointed out de Lagrenée to a call-boy.

"You see that man?" she said. "Send him to me!"

But her messenger returned without him.

"Monsieur thanks Mlle. Sarah Bernhardt for her courtesy, but begs to state that he is a worshipper on a lower plane, and would not dare to approach the altar of his goddess!" was the quaint reply of the diplomat.

Sarah did not know whether to be offended or pleased. In any case she was immensely interested, and determined at once to bring about an occasion which de Lagrenée would be obliged to meet her.

Accordingly she made inquiries and found that he was in the habit of frequenting the Salon held by Madame Lobligeois in her house in the Avenue des Champs Elysées—a villa set back in what were then woods—which had become a rendezvous of the intellectual set. Through her old friend Duquesnel, still director of the Odéon, she arranged to be invited to one of these exclusive affairs, and that her intention to be present should be kept a secret.

The afternoon came. De Lagrenée, according to his custom, was entertaining the company at the house of Mme. Lobligeois with his views on artistic subjects, when the door opened without warning and Sarah swept in, followed by that cohort of faithful, gay young idolators whom she termed her "performing seals."

As had been arranged beforehand, Duquesnel hastened forward and, on seeing de Lagrenée, cried:

"Ah, my dear fellow, allow me to present you to Her Majesty the Queen of Paris!"

There being no avenue of escape, de Lagrenée, who, although genuinely timid and embarrassed, was none the less a gentleman, found himself pushed forward into the presence of the woman whom he had, for so long and from such a distance, adored.

Sarah at once drew him aside and began an animated, if one-sided, conversation. De Lagrenée was too reticent or too bashful to say much; but under Sarah's friendly smile he gradually gained courage, with the result that when she gave him an invitation to visit her in her dressing-room and afterwards to sup alone with her at her flat, he stammered his acceptance, overwhelmed with a mixture of confusion and joy.

From then on the affair followed the customary course. Sarah made excessive demands on de Lagrenée. She insisted that he should take her everywhere and be seen with her in public restaurants and in society. From a distant worshipper, he became her abject slave. People called him "Sarah's messenger boy," and "Sarah's little dog." Never a day passed without a mass of fresh flowers being sent to her dressing-room by the young diplomat.

At length the scandalous rumour that he was Sarah's latest conquest reached the ears of his aristocratic parents, who belonged to a set which severely disapproved of the stage and everyone connected with it. Aghast, they sent for their son and commanded him to sever his connection with the actress at once.

By nature a dutiful son, he agreed, although not without considerable heart-pangs, as may be imagined. When Sarah heard about his pledge, however, and the arguments that had exacted it, she went to the house of his parents in a fury, insisted on admittance, created a terrible scene, and frightened and astonished them both beyond measure. Finally when de Lagrenée appeared, she overwhelmed his halting objections and carried him off with her in her carriage.

A week later de Lagrenée was directed to join the French consular staff at St. Petersburg, that being the city the farthest away from Sarah that his parents could think of. And the romance was effectually stopped. Before he left for Russia, however, an incident occurred which nearly cost de Lagrenée his life.

Richard O'Monroy, besides writing his weekly chronicles in *La Vie Parisienne*, was one of those society hangers-on who love to boast of their conquests of women. He used to do this, not only in allegedly witty conversation, but, in veiled terms, in the salacious weekly to which he contributed.

He chose this moment to relate—using assumed names, of course, but with descriptions which revealed better than mere names could have done—how, in a quarter of an hour, he had made the conquest of Sarah Bernhardt!

Sarah was terribly offended, not so much at the way the article was written, but at the idea that any man could dare to claim that he had "conquered" her—and in fifteen minutes at that!

Hurrying to de Lagrenée, she laid the article before him. The young consular official was furious, and sent an immediate challenge to O'Monroy, despite the fact that the chronicler was a notoriously expert swordsman, while de Lagrenée was small, physically weak, and no fencer at all.

The duel was arranged according to the code, and was fixed to take place in the Bois de Boulogne one morning at five o'clock. Sarah watched it from the closed windows of her coach. Neither antagonist knew that she was there, the coach being hidden behind some trees in an *allée* usually reserved for riders.

As was to be expected, de Lagrenée was overwhelmed from the outset, and in less than two minutes he was severely wounded in the thigh.

Seeing him lying bleeding on the ground, Sarah would have run to him and covered him with caresses, but she was prevented by her companions.

During his convalescence, she was barred from the sick-room and had to content herself with daily letters and flowers.

As soon as he recovered, he was ordered to his post at St. Petersburg, and the short-lived romance was over.

Sarah never forgot de Lagrenée, and for several years she kept up a correspondence with him. His letters which, according to her custom, she destroyed—were full of tender, poetic messages, pleading love of and faith in her. A man less fitted to be a diplomat probably never existed. Sarah always spoke of him to me in terms of genuine affection.

CHAPTER XIX

NOWADAYS almost anything can be said about a theatrical star and her manager is glad. He knows that the more she is written about, the more she is talked about, the larger will be the receipts of the theatre at which she is playing. Even the ancient and eminently respectable Comédie Française has been obliged to accept this point of view—though not without some pangs, I imagine. Witness the celebrated escapade of Mlle. Cecile Sorel, great and exquisite interpreter of Molière, who two years ago visited a public gallery and smashed an uncomplimentary "portrait" of her by Bib, a young cartoonist. The press of the world was full of the incident, but, so far as is known, the actress was not hauled over the coals by the administration of the Comèdie Française.

But in the seventies and eighties a different view was taken of such matters. An artiste was supposed to be contented with reviews of the plays she appeared in, and the Comédie Française especially deplored any effort on the part of an individual actress to make herself known by any other method than the excellence of her acting.

Thus it may be imagined that Sarah was rapidly making enemies for herself. One could not open a newspaper or a magazine without reading some article devoted to her, without seeing an account of some escapade

of hers. Sarah herself has said in her "Memoirs" that
she regretted this publicity, without being able to sup-
press it, and that she never read the newspapers. Perhaps she may be pardoned this slight lapse of memory.

Many times I have found her in the morning, her bed
covered with marked copies of publications sent her by
friends, and by writers of paragraphs about her. She
gloried in them. She did not care what people said about
her, so long as they said something. She herself, to my
certain knowledge, inspired many of the most far-fetched
stories.

When she found that the cartoonists had seized upon
her slender figure and fuzzy hair as heaven-sent objects
on which to exercise their talents, she wore clothes that
accentuated her slimness, and her hair became more
studiously unruly than ever. When she found that every
foolish thing she did was immediately commented upon
in a score of newspapers, hostile as well as friendly, she
spent hours thinking out new escapades, and made foolishness an art.

She was the first actress who really understood the
value of publicity.

Genius can be as eccentric as it pleases, but eccentricity
without genius becomes a boomerang, to hurl fools into
oblivion.

Had Sarah been a lesser woman all this publicity would
have ruined her, but she really *was* a genius, and not only
possessed a talent for self-advertisement, but had a genuine passion for work. People who had read dozens of

Sarah a constant victim to writ-servers.
Exhibited at the *Exposition des Incohérents*,
1880

Sarah and Sarcey.
By Caran d'Ache. 1880.

The Manifold Vocations of Sarah.
By Moloch, in *La Silhouette*,
1880.

Sarah and Damala in *Les
Mères Ennemies*, by Grimm,
1882.

Sarah Bernhardt in Caricature.

idiotic stories about her would visit the theatre prepared
to scoff—but they remained to applaud her frantically.

She was bigger than all the publicity she obtained.
Her art justified all. But her manager, Perrin, and the
committee of the Comédie could not see things that way.
They were horrified and disgusted at the notoriety that
had descended on the venerable House of Molière, as
the result of the follies of their star.

Perrin used to remonstrate violently with her.

"You are a disgrace to the theatre and to your art!"
he said in my hearing on one occasion. "You will ruin
the Comédie with your insanities!"

"I will resign, then!" said Sarah promptly. And
Perrin immediately became contrite, for Sarah drew more
people to the box-office than any two artists the Comédie
possessed, even including Mounet-Sully and Sophie Croizette.

Louis Giffard was then one of the lions of Paris.
Giffard was a balloonist, and balloon ascensions were the
clou of the 1878 Exhibition. Giffard had long been an
admirer of Sarah's and as he started one of his ascents
he threw a wreath of flowers at her as she stood in a
little group of spectators. For this gentle act of courtesy
she invited him to dine with her.

"*Tiens*, Sarah!" said Clairin, during this festivity,
"there is something you have not done yet—you have not
gone up in a balloon!"

"She has her head always in the clouds!" grumpily put
in Alexandre Dumas, junior, who had had many a lively

passage of arms with his most unruly interpreter.   But Sarah took up the suggestion immediately.

Turning enthusiastically to Giffard, she asked: "It is true?   Can you take me up in your balloon?"

"It would be the crowning point of my career!" responded Giffard gallantly.

"When can we go?" asked Sarah, all excitement.

"To-morrow morning, if you wish!"

Sarah seized Georges Clairin by the arm.   "And you, Georges—will you come into the clouds with me, too?"

"He would be a poor poet who would not follow an angel into her natural element!" answered Clairin, kissing her.

Everyone present was sworn to strict secrecy, and the next morning, at seven o'clock, we trooped out to the space just outside the city gates where Giffard's balloon was in readiness.   He had been there since dawn, making his preparations, and when we arrived everything was ready.

Sarah, as she started to climb into the balloon, turned and saw me crying.

"What is the matter, *ma petite* Thérèse?" she asked, putting her arms around me.   I said that I wanted to go, too.

"There is no room," said Giffard.   "You shall make an ascent with me another time."

"But I want to go with Sarah!" I wailed.

Everyone laughed, and Gustave Doré, the illustrator, caught me up in his arms.   "But, *ma chérie*," he remonstrated, "suppose the balloon falls and you are all killed?"

"I would not care, so long as I was with my Sarah!" I replied stoutly.

There was a roar of laughter, and then Sarah was hoisted into the basket by Clairin and Giffard, both of whom mounted after her. There was a shout of "Cast off," and the next thing I knew the balloon was hundreds of feet above us, the three in the basket shrilling some indistinguishable words of farewell.

Somebody pointed out the balloon to Perrin, who was on his way to his office.

"There goes your *pensionnaire!*" he was told.

Perrin at first did not understand.

"Sarah Bernhardt is in that balloon!"

Perrin angrily rushed to the theatre, called together a special meeting of the committee of administration, announced the news, and said that he had decided to fine Sarah a thousand francs.

"I have had enough of her imbecilities!" he declared.

The balloon did not fly very far and came down seventy miles from Paris; and that evening the three aeronauts were back again, Sarah delighted beyond words with her experience.

In the morning she was informed by Perrin that she was to be fined. Sarah flew into a rage, went home, wrote out her resignation, and sent it to Perrin by a messenger. As usual, the threat prevailed. The fine was withdrawn, and so was Sarah's resignation. But Perrin did not forgive her for a long time.

For a year or more it was open war between Sarah Bernhardt and the directors of the Comédie. Most of the men in the company sided against Sarah. She often complained that her male associates of the stage were far more jealous than the women, and that they would stoop to greater meannesses to revenge themselves. They caused her so many petty annoyances that she finally made up her mind to leave the Comédie.

The idea grew on her. She felt, as she expressed it, a prisoner in a cage of lions. Not only did they want to control her life in the theatre, but her private life was subject to their interference as well.

Time and time again she threatened to resign. Finally, to appease her, they had to promise to make her a "full member" of the company—an honour not usually given till after fifteen or twenty years with the Comédie—and accordingly raise her salary. But still she was discontented. She was making 20,000 francs a year, and spending 50,000.

She decided that space was too restricted in her flat and resolved to build for herself a private house. Private houses in Paris, then as now, were the property only of the wealthy. Over nine hundred out of every thousand people live in flats.

She chose a magnificent plot on the rue Fortuny, in what is now the exclusive residential section of the Plaine Monceau, but which then was practically a desert. Felix Escalier, a famous architect, was called into consultation by the actress, and together they designed a three-story house of noble dimensions and beautiful lines.   Bordering it on two sides was to be a spacious garden.

Sarah could scarcely contain herself when the plans were finally approved and the building begun.   The work seemed to her interminable.   To hasten construction, a call was sent out for more workmen, but none were to be had, so a band of her student friends took off their coats, donned the white aprons of masons, and gave their services free, joyful to be of use.

In a little under a year the house was finished, and Sarah ransacked the shops of Paris for furniture and appointments.

Georges Clairin, madly in love with her, undertook to paint four mural decorations, the largest of which was in the reception hall.   It represented nude figures gambolling on fleecy clouds, and made an enormous sensation.

The sensation came from the fact that the head of the central figure was undoubtedly that of Sarah, and there was considerable discussion as to whether she had posed for the entire body.   Clairin finally settled the argument.

"A professional model posed for the body," he said. "Sarah is much too thin."

The explanation satisfied everybody, for there was no gainsaying the fact that Sarah *was* abnormally thin.

But the gossipy weeklies seized on the affair with avidity, and Sarah's attachment to Georges Clairin soon became public property.   Of course, both were tremendously criticised.   Their denials were not listened to.

Sarah was dumbfounded at the venom of some of the attacks.

"These *canaille!*" she said, contemptuously referring to her critics. "They say that I am selfish—well, what woman is not? They say that I am greedy—but did you ever know me to have a spare franc I could call my own? They say I am cold and haughty, but that is because I will not suffer the presence of fools! They say that I am indiscreet—it is they who are indiscreet! They say that I have never really loved, that I am cruel and ambitious, that I pull men down and climb over their bodies on my ascent to fame—it is not true! I am ambitious; yes, and I am jealous of a success won by hard work; but I am haughty only to those whom I despise, and I am cruel— never! It is they who are cruel to me!"

"They delight in sticking knives into me!" she declared on another occasion.

"I hate them!" she said again, passionately. "I hate them! They tear down gods! All Paris is my enemy and all Paris is at my feet."

On other occasions she was merely scornful.

"Let them talk, these little people!" she would say. "They think they are throwing stones at me, but every stone goes to help in building the structure of my success!"

And it was true. The more people ranted against Sarah, the greater she became. She was by now the greatest feminine personality—I say it in all seriousness —that France had known since Joan of Arc.

Her romance with Georges Clairin was a beautiful thing. She was, I am convinced, genuinely in love with the great painter.

She spent all her afternoons for weeks in Clairin's studio. Sometimes they would work silently for hours, side by side, scarcely exchanging a word. At others they would abandon work and sit and talk to each other, oblivious of their surroundings. Sarah inspired many of Clairin's paintings, and was the model for several.

Once I accompanied her to Clairin's studio. It was a great room, bare of ornament except for easels and pictures that were scattered about. Over a huge sofa hung a white bear skin, similar to the one Clairin had given to Sarah.

Clairin was not there when we arrived, and Sarah astonished me by crossing to the sofa and proceeding to take off her shoes and stockings.

"Whatever are you doing?" I demanded.

"He is going to paint my feet," she answered, and indicated a large unfinished canvas, representing Sarah as a Gypsy boy, in rags, wielding a mouth organ. A tame bear danced to the music, and a greasy Bohemian, presumably the boy's father, turned the handle of a street piano.

Where this canvas went I never knew. It was not exhibited, as far as I am aware. Some said that Sarah destroyed it in a fit of rage, when she quarrelled with Clairin. Her romances invariably had their climax in these terrific disputes.

When the artist entered, clad in a green velvet jacket, Sarah ran to him crying: *"Mon petit Geogotte! Mon petit Geogotte!"*

She fondled him, kissing his face and long hair, scolding him for spots of paint on his black tie, and using little endearing adjectives that were a fresh revelation to me of Sarah, the lover.

Clairin showed her a painting in water-colours which he had done while visiting at Fontainebleau. Taking a crayon, he wrote on the back: "To the Perfect Woman," and handed it to her.

The next day she chose a little statue she had herself modelled, and sent it to him, with the inscription: "To my perfect man, from Sara," spelling her name without the "h," as she sometimes did.

Clairin presented her with fifteen different paintings, all of which she kept until the end of her life. Five were of herself.

These paintings were: "A Portrait of Alexandre Dumas fils," signed by both Clairin and Dumas; "Sarah Bernhardt, Lecturer"—this was done as recently as 1914; "Sarah Bernhardt as Théodora"; "Portrait of Charles Gounod"; "View of Beg-Meil"; "The Toilet of Cupid"; "The Fool and the Skull"; "The Attack on the Fort by the Blues"; "Sarah Bernhardt as Cleopatra"; "Sarah Bernhardt between Comedy and Tragedy"; "Repose on a Rock"; "The Stairway in the Cliff"; "The Virgin of Avila"; "Sarah Bernhardt as Théroigne de

Sarah Bernhardt in *Théodora*.

Méricourt"; "Characters of Comedy."   The last was a
sketch in black-and-white.

These pictures, all of which were signed and dedicated
to Sarah by Clairin, fetched unexpectedly low prices at
the Paris sale of her effects two months after her death.
One was sold for as low as 160 francs—then about two
guineas—while the highest price, fifteen hundred francs,
was paid for the portrait of Sarah as Théodora, which
was conceded to be one of Clairin's greatest achievements.

Their romance lasted for several months.   Then came
the inevitable rupture, the cause of which nobody knew,
and Sarah left for a tour in America, while Clairin went
to a hermit-like seclusion in his home in the *Midi*.

When both returned to Paris they were no longer
lovers, but they remained very good friends, and Clairin,
until he died shortly after the Armistice, was one of the
most devoted of the little court surrounding Sarah.

He was frequently a visitor at her house, and in his
old age spent a few weeks of every year at her property
at Belle Isle, off the coast of Brittany.

Clairin was a year older than Sarah Bernhardt.   He
possessed a nature very similar to hers.

CHAPTER XX

THE publication of Sarah's book "Dans les Nuages," which was at once a defence of her actions, a scornful reply to her critics and a picturesque description of her flight in the balloon, brought down on her head still more criticism, and still further admonishment from M. Perrin, the director of the Comédie Française.

But now she lived a monarch in a little world apart. Her art while on the stage was such that even her sternest opponents were obliged to hold their tongues in reluctant admiration, while she now openly maintained the right to live her private life as she pleased. Every protest from Perrin brought forth the haughty reply that if he was dissatisfied she was perfectly willing to leave the Comédie Française for ever. What made him powerless in any struggle with her was the fact that the Comédie was a government institution, and that Sarah had friends in very high places.

She was a striking figure of a woman, as I remember her at this epoch.

Her extreme slenderness, accentuated by the exaggerated lacing of the clothes she wore, contrived to give her the impression of height; whereas she was in reality no taller than the normal person. Her complexion was naturally pale from her anæmia—a malady which had persisted—but, not content with the effect thus achieved, she must needs paint her face a·chalk white, relieved only by the slender etching of her widely-separated eyebrows, and by a pair of cleverly-reddened lips. Her forehead was high and arched, and her hair was the same riotous and tangled mass of crinkled confusion which had made her remarkable as a child. Her eyes were the singularly lovely blue of the clear sky just after the dawn—light-coloured, but seemingly of illimitable depth.

When she was serious, they would be downcast, shielded by long, curving lashes, mysterious and almost oriental in their pensive languor. When she was interested, they would snap into life with an extraordinary vivacity and play of expression; when she was angry, which was often enough, actual sparks of blue fire seemed to dart from eyes that had miraculously grown into two large, burning pools of wrath. No man I ever saw, except Damala, ever long withstood the challenge of those eyes when Sarah, wistful and imperious, desired to have her way.

After an interview with her and an ineffectual attempt to discipline his wilful star, Perrin invariably ended his lecture by throwing up his hands, uttering a short word of mingled supplication and terror, and escaping into an inner office.

Sarah was a supreme conversationalist. I never knew anyone her match in ordinary talk. She could be eloquent on fifty current topics, and had something original and interesting to say about all of them. The fact that she

could hold such men as Victor Hugo, Alexandre Dumas
fils, Georges Clairin, Gustave Doré, and others like them,
enthralled by the sheer power of her personality as partly
expressed by her skill in conversation, is proof enough
of her many-sided genius.

She was the first great feminine adherent to the capri-
cious cult of *"je m'en fichisme,"* which is best interpreted
as an absolute disregard of convention and an existence
studiously carried along the lines of "the individual before
the crowd."

Sarah was beautiful; she was brilliant.   She was a
genius; she was a hard-worker; she was prodigious in her
handling of men—she seldom had less than a dozen famous ones around her—and her charm, as well as her
antipathetic side, was due to her sublime belief in herself
above everything and everybody.

Perrin, Got and other theatrical celebrities used to beg
and plead with her to dress in quieter and less conspicuous
ways which would be more in conformity with the fashion.

"La mode!" she exclaimed indifferently.   *"Je m'en fiche
de la mode!*   Let fashion follow me!"

And frequently fashion did.   Sarah was thin, narrow-
chested, bony in places and walked with a stride.   The
fashion was for plump women, of rounded and gracious
line.   Sarah remained totally indifferent to the fashion,
and within a few years she found herself a leader of the
mode, with plumpness and *bouffonerie* beating a protest-
ing retreat.

When she was forty, her arms had grown so thin that

they had to be concealed, even with evening dress, so she invented the shoulder-length glove, which immediately jumped into fashion.

She launched several kinds of corsets, one of which still bears her name. Her footwear was seized on and copied extensively. She was the first woman in France to wear high leather buttoned boots with an ordinary street dress.

She was the first woman to bid her dressmaker insert jewels in her slippers. She was the first woman to wear ostrich plumes as an ornament to her evening *coiffure*. She was the first woman audaciously to defy convention, and receive her friends in her painter's garb of silken pyjamas!

She did this, she did that, she did anything she pleased. Whenever anybody started a great outcry against her, others would shrug their shoulders and exclaim, *"Mais, c'est Sarah!"* She was Sarah. That was answer enough. If ever a woman in France has been a law unto herself, it was Sarah at that time—a whole lexicon of law, in fact.

Naturally, she got into numerous scrapes. She was thrice sued for debt, as a result of her lavish expenditure during the building of her house in the rue Fortuny. Whenever she saw anything she liked, she could not rest until she had acquired it. Her salary at the Comédie was only 20,000 francs a year—only £800, even at that time—yet with this, and the small sums left her by her father and by several relatives, she managed to live in a style and with an ostentation surpassed by but few persons of her age.

The furniture in her house had been acquired absolutely regardless of cost, and a lot of it was taken away again when she did not pay for it. Dealers were glad to sell things to her, and to take their money as and when she paid them, for the fact that Sarah Bernhardt had bought an article was certain to start a fad for it.

Her dresses, her hats and her shoes never cost her anything. In later years I even heard it stated that her dressmaker actually paid her to wear his creations! It was a triumph for any dealer to be able to say, "Sarah Bernhardt bought one like that," or, "Sarah Bernhardt was wearing one like that yesterday," or, "Sarah Bernhardt has one in her dining-room."

The mural decorations and the works of art in her house, fortunately, did not cost Sarah anything. They were mostly gifts of such great friends as Georges Clairin, Louise Abbema—of whose paintings, when she died, Sarah possessed more than eighty—Sir Edward Burne-Jones—who had been caught in the siege of Paris, and had then met and fallen captive to Sarah—Ernest Duez, Théodore Fantin-Latour, Maxime Guyon, Hector Giacomelli, Réné Raoul Griffon, Graham Robertson, Luc Olivier Merson, Germain Fabien Brest, John Lewis Brown, Robert Fleury, Vastagh Gezah, Alfred Stevens, and many other great and famous artists of the brush.

Most of the above-mentioned persons frequented her house. I have seen a dozen famous painters and six or

seven great authors all listening to Sarah together—
and finding joy in it.   She ruled her little court with a rod
of iron, but she wrapped the rod in silk.   Victor Hugo,
watching her at work in her studio on one occasion, said:

"Ah! madame, how I wish I could paint!"

"But you can!" replied Sarah.

"No," said Hugo.

"Tu es ridicule!" responded Sarah.   "Anyone who can
write or who can act can paint if he tries!"

Then and there Sarah constituted herself his teacher,
with the result that Hugo became an extremely credit-
able artist, chiefly with pen-and-ink.   His chief delight
was in sketching-tours, which he undertook with Sarah
during her rare holidays—tours in which Clairin and
Doré would generally also take part.   It was a novel and
extraordinary sight to see these three wonderful men and
this single eccentric woman set forth together on foot
from the gates of Paris, huge sketch-books under their
arms.

But things were fast approaching their inevitable climax
at the Comédie Française.

Perrin and his committee had entered into a contract
with Messrs. John Hollingshead and Mayer for a six
weeks' French repertory season at the Gaiety Theatre
in London.   The contract called for the appearance in
the English capital of most of the stars of the Comédie,
including Sarah Bernhardt, Sophie Croizette, Marie
Lloyd, Mounet-Sully, Coquelin and Got.

Sarah was afire with excitement at the idea of playing

before a foreign audience, but a difficulty that seemed insurmountable presented itself.

Sarah was still only a *part sociétaire*. An actress enters the Comédie as a *débutante,* or kind of apprentice. Unless she has extraordinary talent and still more extraordinary luck, she is likely to remain in this decidedly inferior position, both as regards rank and salary, for several years. Then, by decree of the committee, endorsed by the Minister of Fine Arts, she is made a part member, with half or two-thirds of the salary of a full member. Sometimes an actress remained at the Comédie twenty or twenty-five years without being made a full member. Sarah had been there nearly eight years. The salary of a full member was thirty thousand francs a year; Sarah was receiving twenty thousand.

The difficulty arose not so much from the question of salary, however, as from the fact that Sarah Bernhardt would be playing in a foreign capital, and would be in an inferior position as regards the billing and the programmes. The custom of the Comédie was strict in this regard: the name of the oldest *sociétaire* in rank appeared first on the programme, regardless of the rôle she played. This was understood in Paris; it might easily be misunderstood in London.

"If," insisted Sarah, "I go to London, it must be as a full member, with a full member's privileges and emoluments."

There was an immediate rebellion in the committee.

"We have had enough of her caprices!" cried Perrin.

"Let her remain here, if she wants to!   I will not consent to her demands!"

Nothing in Sarah's contract, it appeared, obliged her to travel abroad.   So it was settled that she should not go.

Then Hollingshead and Mayer threw another bomb-shell into the excited and harassed committee of the Comédie Française.   If Sarah Bernhardt was not com-ing, they said, they did not want the troupe at all, and they hereby cancelled the contract!

The end of it was that Sarah obtained her full mem-bership, as did Croizette, and the whole troupe embarked for London.   The first man to greet her as she stepped ashore in England was Oscar Wilde.   He became a great friend of Sarah's some years later—a friendship that only ceased with his downfall.

Sarah's first visit to London was not the triumph which she had anticipated, though she had her share of the laurels.   Her lodgings at 77, Chester Square which were procured for her by William Jarrett, the impresario who later managed her tour of America, were crowded with celebrities, but they came out of curiosity and not to pay homage.

Stories of her eccentricities had long been printed in England.   She was looked upon as a wild woman, and her morals were much discussed and severely commented upon in staid London society.   Everything she did in London during this first visit evoked hostile comment. The papers praised her performances, but criticised her sensational appearances in society, into which she was introduced by Lady Dudley.

Queen Victoria vetoed a suggestion that she should play in a State performance at Court. The Prince and Princess of Wales were not in London on this first occasion, and their tolerant influence did not make itself felt.

Still, there was nothing definite against Sarah, except gossip, and so much was admitted everywhere. All fashionable London fell captive to her art on the stage of the Gaiety. The *Times* acclaimed her as the greatest emotional actress ever seen on an English stage. She made her London *début* in the second act of *Phèdre,* into which she put so much of herself that after the performance she fainted from exhaustion and had to be carried home. "Such a scene of enthusiasm," wrote the *Standard,* "has rarely and perhaps never been witnessed in an English theatre."

Meanwhile, a tremendous campaign was going on against her in the Paris newspapers. They said that by her eccentric actions she had disgraced the Comédie Française abroad, and brought dishonour on her country. It was a despicable campaign, and was founded on practically nothing. But her enemies in Paris were determined to make hay while the cat was away, if I may be pardoned for mixing up two proverbs.

Gladstone, who was much struck by the charming and emotional French actress, introduced her to King Léopold of Belgium, who fell an utter slave to her beauty. She was seen with the Belgian monarch everywhere, and, as Léopold enjoyed probably the worst reputation of any prince in Europe, the fact that he was obviously enamoured of Sarah did not enhance her reputation

This incident, in fact, in Republican France, was only an added cause for dissatisfaction. Léopold was not liked in Paris, and he was barely tolerated in London; yet Sarah seemed to find pleasure in his conversation and amusement in his company. He had, of course, the *entrée* everywhere, and as often as not he appeared with Sarah, generally to the secret dismay of his hostess.

There were houses in London at this period where certain representatives of royalty were looked at askance; and this condition of affairs obtained also in many European capitals. When I was in Moscow I was amazed to find that there were several aristocratic but untitled families who would not have dreamed of receiving a Grand Duke into their homes.

One of the rumours that gained particular credit in London was to the effect that Sarah smoked cigars. She received several boxes from male admirers!

Another story was that she paraded the streets dressed as a man. I doubt both of the stories myself—especially that as to the cigars, for Sarah never smoked at all—but they were widely credited in London, and those of the Paris newspapers that were hostile to the actress naturally seized on them and reprinted them with avidity. Editorials were published severely criticising her conduct, and these finally grew so numerous that Sarah decided to have done with them once and for all.

She accordingly wrote a letter to Albert Wolff, the director of the *Figaro,* announcing that she had decided to resign from the Comédie Française.

Nobody believed she would actually resign—she had threatened it too many times before—but her announcement in the *Figaro* caused huge excitement. The Minister of Fine Arts telegraphed personally to Sarah demanding an explanation. Sarah disdained to reply. The Comédie troupe was recalled from London, and Sarah was warned not to play for a while, as the public, "after the things she had done in London," would be sure to hiss her. She insisted on playing, however, and was given an ovation. It was another triumph for her personality. But she had the critics against her *en masse.*

A few weeks later Perrin refused to postpone the *première* of *L'Aventurière,* in which Sarah was playing Clorinde, despite her statement that she was physically unable to act. The first night was a failure. Sarah was unanimously attacked in the newspapers, and this time, enraged at Perrin, she did resign.

She wrote her resignation, posted it, and then fled from Paris, so that no one could call her back. She was gone five weeks, and nobody knew her address.

When she returned, she found Jarrett waiting for her with a new contract for London, to be followed by one for America. She accepted both, and returned to London with her own company. There the eccentricities of her previous visit were forgiven, and her triumph was complete until she made the serious mistake of taking her son to the home of Lord and Lady R——, where she was invited to play.

Lady R——'s indignation at Sarah's daring action, though Sarah herself probably considered it nothing out of the ordinary, knew no bounds, and she gave secret instructions to her butler. This functionary advanced before Sarah into the huge ball-room, which was crowded with people distinguished in British society, and solemnly announced:

"Mademoiselle Sarah Bernhardt and her son!"

After this she was, of course, unmercifully snubbed, and left in a rage ten minutes later. This was Sarah Bernhardt's last appearance in British society until Queen Victoria, yielding to the entreaties of the Prince of Wales, lifted the ban and commanded her to give a performance of *La Dame aux Camélias* at Windsor Castle.

But this recognition did not come until many long years afterwards.

CHAPTER XXI

"Enough of Sarah Bernhardt! Now that she has finally left the Comédie Française, let us forget her!"

This was the slogan of Sarah's enemies in the year 1880. And many of her friends thought, with a sigh of relief, that they were to be spared for a little while, at any rate, the pain of the extraordinary publicity the actress provoked.

Sarah was now thirty-six years old. Her son, Maurice, had reached his seventeenth year, and was already causing her a good deal of trouble, due to her eccentric way of bringing him up.

She was original in her treatment of his childish faults. When he was six, he persisted in a habit of chewing the tips of his gloves, and no correction, apparently, could cure him of the habit. Exasperated, Sarah one day made him take a pair of gloves to the kitchen, fry them in butter, and eat half of one of them! The cure proved effective.

I do not intend to devote much of this biography to Maurice Bernhardt. He is still alive, and I understand he is writing his own memoirs. It is my opinion, however, that it was not he himself but Sarah's own conception of the boon of motherhood which throughout her life was perhaps its outstanding influence.

Maurice was a wilful, headstrong, nervous child;

strong for his size, and a handful for the various nurses who were engaged to look after him.

Sarah was stern with him at times, indulgent at others; and she educated him to rely upon her, and never once, even in her old age, did she rely upon him.

When he was twelve, Maurice was already quite a "man about town," preferring adult companionship and evincing precocious likes and dislikes. When he was fifteen, Sarah settled a large sum on him and before he was twenty his income from her was 60,000 francs annually. She always told her friends that she did not mind what he did with the money, so long as he dressed himself properly.

Thus, almost from infancy, Maurice was accustomed to an amount of luxury that was far in advance of his mother's real circumstances.

The sole thing on which she insisted was that he should learn the art of fencing, so as to defend his life in case of a duel. This art, when once learned, got the youngster into several scrapes, which cost Sarah a good deal of money.

As a small child Maurice appeared with Sarah on the stage on one or two occasions, but he evinced no great talent for the theatre. He also, when a young man, attempted the art of playwriting, assisted by his mother, but met with no greater success. In later years he tried to persuade his mother to make him general manager of the Sarah Bernhardt Theatre, in her stead. It was the only thing she ever denied him.

Sarah's various studios and flats were always filled with pictures of Maurice at all ages—many of them being sketches or paintings by Sarah herself.

So much for Maurice Bernhardt. He was an affectionate son, and if he has not been exceptionally useful during his long life, it is the fault of his haphazard upbringing. He is now a father, a grandfather, a member of the best Paris clubs, a well-known figure in baccarat rooms and on race-courses, and he still maintains his excellent reputation as a swordsman. Sarah died in his arms.

It was in 1880, before she left for her first American tour—in October of that year—that Sarah Bernhardt first organised a company of her own. This was placed by her under the paternal direction of Félix Duquesnel, Sarah's old friend at the Odéon, and consisted of nine artistes, who had been carefully selected for the purpose of supporting her on tour. They were Madame Kalb, Pierre Berton, Mary Jullien, Jeanne Bernhardt, Madame Devoyod, Jean Dieudonné, L. Talbot, J. Train and myself. I was, of course, the youngster of the troupe.

Our *répertoire* at this time consisted of eight plays: *Hernani, Froufrou, La Dame aux Camélias, Le Sphinx, L'Etrangère, La Princesse George, Adrienne Lecouvreur* and *Phèdre*. Let me now set forth the story of how *La Dame aux Camélias*, one of Sarah's greatest triumphs, proved a failure until she brought her own genius to bear on the play and transformed it into a masterpiece.

La Dame aux Camélias, as a matter of fact, was in its

original form written by Dumas fils after earnest consultation with Sarah. It was never played, however, and lay for some years neglected in a drawer. One day Dumas took it out and read a few pages of the second act to Sarah, for the purpose of eliciting her opinion on the piece.

"Let me take it with me!" she asked, and Dumas gave the manuscript to her.

A few days later she brought it back to him with a third of it crossed out and corrected. New lines had been added to practically all the important passages, and part of the second act had been cut out entirely.

"There!" she told him. "Your play is better like that! If you will revise it as I have marked the manuscript, I will play it and make it a success."

"It is I who am the playwright and not you, mademoiselle!" he said angrily.

Bernhardt turned on her heel.

"Very well!" she flung at him over her shoulder; "a day will come when you will beg me to produce your play!"

Dumas refused to be influenced by such criticism, and eventually the play was produced, in a small way, at the Comédie, and then at another theatre, but had no success at either. Sarah's amendments and suggestions had been ignored.

After Sarah had organised her own company, Pierre Berton one day went to her with the information that Dumas wished to see her.

"What about?" asked Sarah.

"About a play called *La Dame aux Camélias*. We were reading it together last night and I believe it can be played by us with success.   In fact, it is a play absolutely written for you!"

"Did you tell Dumas that?" asked Sarah, grimly.

"Yes."

"What did he say?"

"He said that he agreed with me."

"And that was all?"

"That was all—except that he asked that I should bring the matter to your attention."

Sarah laughed.   "I told Dumas that he would one day beg me to play this thing for him," she said, "and you may tell him that if he wants me to, he must do just that —beg!"

Berton must have taken the message diplomatically to Dumas, for the next day the latter was announced at Sarah's house.

I was not present at the interview, but at the end of it Sarah informed us that *La Dame aux Camélias* was to be included in our *répertoire*.

Knowing Sarah's temperament and her obstinacy, I presume Dumas begged.   At any rate, the book of the play, as it was placed in our hands shortly afterwards, contained all the original corrections which she had made and which Dumas had at first ignored.

We produced *La Dame* (as it was always called) at Brussels, whither we had gone on the earnest representations of King Léopold, who was still greatly enamoured of Sarah.

In Brussels *La Dame* obtained no success whatever. The Belgians much preferred *Adrienne Lecouvreur* and *Froufrou*. It was in the last-named play that Sarah had scored her biggest success in London, on her second visit as an independent artiste. Sarcey, who had written what he called "Sarah's Epitaph" when she left the Comédie, saying that it was "time to send naughty children to bed," was compelled to make a special journey to London in order to write reviews of Sarah's extraordinary productions there.

Instead of her light becoming dimmer, it blazed higher and higher with each month that separated her from her "imprisonment" at the Comédie Française.

Yes . . . imprisonment was what Sarah considered it.

"At last I am free and my own mistress," she said. "Perrin cannot make me work when I don't want to, and all the critics can go to the devil !"

It was predicted that the fine of one hundred thousand francs imposed on Sarah for breaking her contract with the Comédie would be a blow from which she would find it hard to recover.

"We shall hear less of our dear Sarah now! She will go away and leave us in peace !" wrote Paul de St. Victor, her ancient enemy of the *Ruy Blas* banquet.

But instead of sinking under the blow, Sarah only worked the harder. She was absolutely tireless at this period. Her visits to London and to Brussels were organised chiefly to avoid the process-servers, who were hammering at the door of her house in Paris with blue papers ordering her to pay the hundred thousand francs.

Sarah had not then the money to pay her fine, but for one full year her creditors could not legally obtain a judgment against her by default (which would have meant the sacrifice of her house, and of all its treasures). So after they had made the customary three visits to her Paris home, had knocked thrice on the door, and had instituted condemnation proceedings, Sarah returned to Paris and set about organising a whirlwind tour of the provinces, to precede her departure for America.

Sarah met the Prince and Princess of Wales at Brussels, and charmed and was charmed by them. They saw her in *Froufrou* while the guests of the King and Queen of the Belgians. This was the beginning of a long and precious friendship between Sarah and the Princess (afterwards Queen Alexandra) which lasted until Sarah's death.

After Sarah's Brussels visit the Princess—who was by birth Danish, as everybody knows—obtained for us a Royal command to perform before the King and Queen of Denmark at Copenhagen. Five performances only were asked for, and for these Sarah demanded 120,000 francs and our expenses. The sum was immediately agreed to.

Sarah did not like Denmark. She was in a bad humour throughout the visit. We were lent the Royal yacht, on which to make a trip on the fjords. It was a lovely day and I can hear still the beautiful voices of the Upsal Choir, blending so perfectly with the grandeur of the landscape.

Vicomte de Bondy, an attaché then at the French Legation, met us on the trip and begged me to introduce him to Sarah. I agreed, but when we approached her we were dismayed to hear her giving her opinion of the country to a friend, in no uncertain terms.

"Je m'en fiche de leur pays! Ils m'embêtent!" she cried. The nearest translation to this, in English slang, would be: "I'm fed up with their country! They bore me to death!" Only the language was a trifle stronger!

When these phrases reached our ears the Vicomte stopped suddenly. Then he raised his hat, and turned on his heel.

"I do not think I want to meet your Sarah!" he said shortly, and forthwith he disappeared from our party.

I recounted the incident to Sarah the next day, as we sat on deck of a steamer which was carrying us back to France.

"And he was a Frenchman!" she exclaimed. "Why, what you heard me say was nothing! I said a great deal more to the Crown Prince, and he only laughed!"

Sarah's freedom of language was at times embarrassing.

Baron Magnus, the then German Minister in Denmark, was an old inhabitant of Paris, and had known Sarah in the days before the war. But since 1870 Sarah could not bear to look at a German.

When the baron got up at a banquet, therefore, and, raising a glass of champagne, jovially proposed her health, the actress could not restrain her anger. She sprang to her feet and raised her glass high in the air, to the astonishment of the King, tne Queen and various other members of the Royal family who were seated round her—and probably, it must be admitted, to their secret amusement.

"I accept your toast, Monsieur the Minister of Prussia," she cried, "but only on condition that you extend it to include the whole of La Belle France!"

Baron Magnus turned white.   He could think of nothing to say, and he sat down.   The band struck up the "Marseillaise" and then, courteously enough, considering what had passed, he got on his feet again.

Long afterwards, he and Sarah became very good friends.   But he never tired of telling the story of how Sarah had startled a King and Queen and humbled an Imperial Ambassador.

On September 4, 1880, we left Paris on our first tour of the provinces under Duquesnel's managership.   The tour, which lasted twenty-eight days, was a tremendous success, and in October, a few days after our return to Paris, Sarah left for America under Abbey's management.   I did not go with her, my family being unwilling that I should make the journey before having completed my studies.

CHAPTER XXII

As I said at the conclusion of the last chapter, I did not accompany Sarah Bernhardt on her first visit to the United States, and I can therefore give no first-hand impressions of the trip. What is more, she told me so much when she returned, and so mixed were her own impressions, that it is hard for me to say now whether she actually enjoyed her visit to the New World or not

"What a detestable country!" she would say sometimes. "What a marvellous country!" she would exclaim at others. Similar mixed conclusions are often brought back from America by visitors even now.

She adored the scenery, the energy and the extravagance of the Americans, and she thought the American men perfect—all except the reporters. But she hated the American women—and she hated most of them until she died

"Their voices!" she would exclaim, and shudderingly put both hands to her ears. "*Quelle horreur!*"

When she opened in New York, one of her most expensive costumes, she told me, was completely ruined by women visiting her in her dressing-room, who insisted on fondling it and exclaiming over its rich embroidery.

During her visit to London, in the June of the year when she first went to America, she met Henry Irving.

"They tell me, madame, that you are going to the United States?" said Irving.

"Yes," said Sarah. "I must make money, and the Americans seem to have it all!" Even at this period that was the generally accepted idea!

"Madame," said Irving, "what you say saddens me extremely! America is a country of barbarians! They know nothing about the theatre, and yet they presume to dictate to us! If I were you I would not go to America, madame! What you will gain in dollars, you will lose in heart-throbs at their ignorance of your art!"

Irving himself, however, went to America a few years later.

Sarah brought back from the United States six hundred thousand francs, a variety of animals—including a lynx, which bit her chambermaid and had to be killed a week after its arrival in Paris—a profound respect for American enterprise, and the reputation she had long been hoping to make for *La Dame aux Camélias*.

When Alexandre Dumas was told of her intention to play *La Dame* in New York he cried disgustedly: "That's it! Try my play on the barbarians!"

As a matter of fact, Booth's Theatre, where Sarah opened in America, was filled on the first night with almost the entire French colony in New York, which was a considerable one. Practically the only Americans there were the critics, and a few wealthy society people who held regular boxes. The play chosen for the first night was *Adrienne Lecouvreur*.

The next day Abbey, the impresario, rushed into Sarah's bedroom—Sarah usually received her business folk in the morning while still in bed—waving a bundle of papers. His face wore the look of one stricken by some grievous blow.

Stopping short, he gave Sarah a look of indescribable anguish, and then sat abruptly down and mopped his face. He could not speak.

Sarah sat up in bed, fright on her countenance.

"What is it? What is it? The theatre has been burned down, and my costumes are destroyed?"

"No," said Abbey, "but your reputation is!"

The American papers, without exception, said that Sarah Bernhardt was a magnificent actress, but that her *répertoire* was filled with plays which should never be shown on the American stage. "They are doubtless considered all right in immoral Paris," said the *Globe,* "but they will certainly only succeed in disgusting Americans."

And they proceeded to tear poor *Adrienne Lecouvreur* to pieces! A highly improper play, they said, and one which should never be given in the presence of American women. One paper seriously advised the police to descend on the theatre, close the performances, "arrest this woman, and send her back to France."

Sarah was bewildered. She had played *Adrienne* in Paris, in London, in Brussels and in Copenhagen, and everywhere it had been met with tremendous applause. This was her first experience of American methods.

The fact of the matter was that only one of the critics

present at the opening night knew French, and they gathered quite wrong impressions from the few words they
did understand. The play, given at full length in a
word for word English translation, would doubtless have
been insufferably vulgar. In French, it was whimsical,
delightful in its irony, and entirely free from anything
objectionable whatsoever. The American critics, however, could not understand the subtlety of the lines, and
they gathered their opinions solely from the action.

The manager of the theatre followed Abbey into
Sarah's bedroom. He wore a strained, a hunted look.

"You have seen the newspapers?" he asked Abbey.

"Yes!" Consternation was in the eyes of all three.

"What shall we do?" inquired Abbey, at last.

"There is only one thing to do—we must choose another *répertoire!* They will have us arrested soon, if
this keeps up!"

"But that is ridiculous!" angrily said Sarah. "Never
before in my life have I been so insulted! I will either
play *La Dame aux Camélias* to-night, or I will pack up
and return to France by the next boat!"

The two men cried out in protest.

"You can't do that!" said Abbey. "There must be
some way out of the difficulty!"

"I shall play *La Dame aux Camélias* to-night, as arranged!" said Sarah, as if this was the last word on the
subject.

Abbey and the manager of Booth's Theatre took their

departure, after arguing with her for some time, but in vain.

"She will do it!" said Abbey, with conviction. "When Sarah Bernhardt makes up her mind, heaven and earth cannot change it."

"But we *must* do something!" said the manager, in despair.

"I have it!" exclaimed Abbey. "We will play *La Dame,* but we will call it something else. They will never know the difference."

When Sarah Bernhardt arrived at the theatre that night, she was astounded to see huge red placards outside, announcing that she would play *Camille.*

She rushed to Jarrett, the first man she met on the stage.

"What is it, this *Camille?*" she exclaimed furiously. "I know no *Camille!*"

"Oh yes, you do," said Jarrett, smiling urbanely. "*Camille* is—*La Dame!*"

"Oh!" cried Sarah, and burst into uncontrollable laughter.

The theatre was packed to the roof, this time with a most representative crowd of Americans. The publicity of the morning had done its work. Sarah Bernhardt was playing immoral pieces? Well, New York didn't know what to do about it, but New York decided to go and see for itself.

This sort of theatrical psychology is now a well-understood thing. Even in Paris, when a *revue* is not making expenses, they bribe the police to make a complaint about the immorality of one of the scenes—and then its success is assured.   But it was the first time such a thing had been known in America.

New York liked *Camille*—it liked it enormously!

The critics were not fools, though.   Every paper announced the next day that *Camille* was in reality *La Dame aux Camélias,* but with an American name!

They also said that the play had been forbidden in London by Queen Victoria, which was true; and were very severe on the "prudish Queen" for her "narrow-mindedness." Completely forgetting their fulminations of only twenty-four hours before, they said that it was an unthinkable crime that such a beautiful play should ever have been banned anywhere.   It was rather "Frenchy," they admitted, but Sarah's magnificent acting more than made up for that.

Sarah Bernhardt made more than a dozen tours in America, and *Camille* was invariably her greatest success there.   It broke all records for receipts in New York City.

The reputation of the play crossed the Atlantic before Sarah did.   Alexandre Dumas did not know whether to be delighted or dismayed.   The "barbarians" had liked his play!

The success of *La Dame* in America encouraged Sarah to give it a fair trial in France, and elsewhere in Europe. Eventually it became, after *Phèdre* and *Le Passant,* her greatest success.   Even *L'Aiglon*—another play which received its original baptism of success in the United States—could not rival it in popularity.

All of which may go to show that American audiences have a better sense of the dramatic than have audiences in Europe—or it may not!

After witnessing a performance of *Le Sphinx,* which also obtained an enormous success in New York, Commodore Vanderbilt, who was then at thè hey-day of his power in New York, but was not yet accepted in society because of his bluff and hearty—not to say indifferent— manners, was announced to Sarah in her dressing-room. She had heard of this remarkable man, and was anxious to meet him. Her account of the conversation, which took place through an interpreter, was amusing.

"His first words to me" (said Sarah), "were, 'You are a Jewess, aren't you, madame?'

"I was offended at his manner, and replied frigidly, 'No, monsieur, I am a Catholic!'

" 'That's peculiar,' said Vanderbilt, 'I heard you were a Jewess. However, it don't matter. I came to present my respects. You're the only woman who ever made me cry!'

"I laughed—nobody could resist him. 'Yep, by gorry,' went on the multi-millionaire, 'you made me cry! An' I've taken a box for every night you are billed to play!' "

He kept his word. Looking across the footlights, night after night, throughout twenty-three performances, Sarah never failed to see Vanderbilt in his box. Every time he saw her looking at him, he took out a gigantic handkerchief and solemnly wiped his eyes. When she left New York, he was among those who saw her off on the boat.

"Ma'am," he said, "I'd like to give you a present. What would you like the most?"

Some women, hearing such an avowal from a multimillionaire, would have thought of jewels. But Sarah was more original.

"Give me your handkerchief!" she replied promptly.

Vanderbilt was much taken aback, but took out his handkerchief and gave it to her.

Sarah thanked him. "I shall keep this always," she told him, "in memory of the time I made Vanderbilt cry!"

When she got back to Paris, she had it framed and hung on the wall of her boudoir, but on one of the several occasions that her furniture was seized for debt, she lost it, and Vanderbilt had meanwhile died.

Theodore Roosevelt, then a very young man, was another of those who met Sarah Bernhardt during her first visit to New York. He was a firm friend of hers until he died, and invariably visited her when he was on one of his trips abroad.

A letter from Roosevelt, extolling her genius, was one of the few she kept and had framed. It hung until the day of her death in the little ante-chamber outside her bedroom.

In this letter the former President said in one passage: "I have altered my plans so as to arrive in Paris after you return from Spain. I could not come to Paris and miss seeing my oldest and best friend there."

During her tour of America in 1892, Sarah had dinner with Roosevelt, and she loved to recount the experience to her friends on her return to Paris.

"An unforgettable character!" she would say, and then would add: "Ah, but that man and I, we could rule the world!"

They came near to doing it, he on one side as President of the United States, and she, on the other, as the uncrowned Queen of Paris.

Booth, James Hubbard, James Wilcox and James K. Hackett were other Americans whom Sarah counted among her warmest friends. Hackett represented the American stage at her funeral.

It has often been commented upon that Sarah Bernhardt never had an American lover. I heard her speak of this one day with regret.

"I am sure the Americans must be great lovers," she said; "they are so strong, so primitive, and so childish in their ardour. The English are wonderful men to love, because they possess the faculty of bending one to their likes, dislikes and moods without seeming to make it an imposition; but the Americans are greater, for they bend themselves to suit you."

This absence of Americans in Sarah's sentimental life is best explained by the short duration of each of her tours of America and the distances covered during them.

Many towns in America saw Sarah only for twenty-four hours, and the whole period was a ceaseless whirl of arriving, rehearsing, playing and departing. She was a genius at organisation and insisted on attending to the larger details of her tours herself.

After three weeks in America, Sarah learned sufficient English to know the simpler expressions, and before 1895 she spoke it very well. On her tours in America she invariably travelled by special train, the "Sarah Bernhardt Special," but this was not by her own arrangement, and she did not like it.

"They will not put one's special coaches on the fast trains," she explained, "and at night they back one's car into a siding, where one is kept awake by the noise of the goods trains being made up, shunting, arriving and departing."

On her last two visits to America she did not use either a special train or a special car, but travelled in drawing-room sleepers. She said she found it easier and *"beaucoup plus pratique."*

CHAPTER XXIII

SARAH's first tour of the United States and Canada occupied seven months, during which she visited fourteen states and four provinces, played in more than fifty theatres and appeared before the public more than one hundred and fifty times.

When she returned to France, warships fired salutes, the entire city of Havre was beflagged and illuminated, and some of the most distinguished persons in France were on the quay to greet her.

She had departed an *enfant terrible,* to use the *mot* of Sarcey; she returned an idol, feverishly acclaimed. *Enfin,* France was once more to salute its Sarah!

Never before had any woman become such an entirely national character. Others had risen to similar artistic greatness—Rachel was probably as great a *tragédienne* as was Sarah at this epoch, and Sarah always declared that never in her life had she attained the sublime heights of Rachel's art—but none had become at the same time a popular figure amongst the masses, to whom actresses until now had always seemed beings apart.

The theatre has always been a cult in France, much more so than in any other nation, but in the sixties and seventies it was a cult practised only by the few who possessed the requisite education to understand the difficult verse, the delightful satire, the delicate irony of the poets whose work then constituted nine-tenths of the plays performed. Or, on the other hand, there were the so-called popular theatres, but these were vulgar burlesques of what the popular theatre is to-day.

It was Sarah Bernhardt, more than anyone else, who transformed, with her magic touch, the theatre in France from the superior, intellectual toy of the cultured few to the amusement and recreation of the many. This she accomplished not only by her insistence on dramatic values, as much as on literary excellence—on scenic perfection as much as on the handling of phrases—but by her own personal genius in finding the "common touch."

When she returned from the United States, it was to find preparations being made for her to play *Théodora*, the new play by Victorien Sardou, who was just then coming to the fore. But several other matters intervened.

First, she fell in love with Philippe Garnier, an actor of considerable talent; secondly, Garnier persuaded her to make a Grand Tour of Europe; thirdly, she was introduced to Jules Paul Damala, who took her away from Garnier and made her his wife; fourthly, Victorien Sardou, on the advice of Pierre Berton, withdrew his offer asking her to play *Théodora* and suggested that instead she should play *Féodora,* an older play by him and one well-tried by public favour.

These events tumbled one after another into the life of Sarah Bernhardt, and all had their influence on it.

She first became really intimate with Philippe Garnier

at a banquet given to celebrate her return. I remember that Sarah gave a demonstration at this banquet of how the Americans ate with their knives and fingers, and kept us all convulsed by her description of American food.

"*Mon ami,*" she said to the actor Décori, who sat next me, "you would not believe it—the Americans never take more than a quarter of an hour to dine, and they eat in whichever order the cook has prepared the dishes. If the fruit is ready, then they eat that first! Ugh! It was terrible!" She shuddered.

The American *cuisine* was always one of Sarah's pet abominations, and on other visits to the United States she was careful to take her own cook as well as a supply of food, wines and condiments. When Edison invited her in 1890 to one of his country houses, she is said to have arrived there with a cook of her own and an entire kitchen staff!

Though Sarah herself liked to make fun of the Americans, she never allowed anyone else to do so; and when Doré, who had visited America, related a humorous anecdote somewhat too cutting in its sarcasm, Sarah caught him up sharply. Doré replied with equal acerbity, and it was Garnier who distinguished himself by leaping into the breach and smoothing down the ruffled feathers of the two friends.

Sarah noticed him, began an animated conversation with him, and found him *spirituel*—in the French sense of the word—well-informed and charming. She invited him to call and see her.

He called frequently, and a week later was made a star
member of Sarah's company. It was Garnier who insisted that she should exploit the publicity gained from
her American tour by undertaking at once another whirlwind tour of Europe, this time going as far as Russia.

The prospect appealed to Sarah, but she was tired and
not over-anxious to undertake the monumental work of
organising such an expedition. So Garnier did this for
her, and within two months had the itinerary completed.

In the meantime Sarah had made a most tragic acquaintance—that of Damala.

This man was a Greek, of good family, who had originally been destined for diplomacy, and had come to
France to pursue his studies. In Paris he had rapidly
acquired the reputation of being the "handsomest man
in Europe."

He was tall, physically of classic beauty, and with a
passionate, Oriental face, which was dominated by a pair
of warm brown eyes, shielded by lashes of girlish length.
One of his principal attractions to women was his fine,
silky, brown beard, worn in the manner prescribed in
France by fashion of the early eighties.

The "Diplomat Apollo" was the name by which he
was jocularly known among his friends; and jealous hus-
bands and lovers talked of him as the most dangerous
man in Paris.

He had had numerous affairs before he met and fell
in love, after his Oriental fashion, with Sarah Bernhardt.
One was with the wife of Paul Meissonnier, a Parisian

banker, whose reputation he had ruined to the extent of forcing her to leave France.

Another was with the daughter of a Vaucluse magistrate, who left her parents and a comfortable home to follow Damala to Paris, where he deserted her when her baby was born. This girl wrote a book exposing Damala, after he had married Sarah Bernhardt, but the book was suppressed. I never heard what became of her. Perhaps the Seine could tell.

Young, beautiful and a dare-devil, Damala, when he met Bernhardt, was a figure to delight the gods of evil. There was no vice to which he was not addicted, no evil thing which he would not attempt. His Oriental parties, at which those taking part divested themselves of their clothing and plunged naked into baths of champagne, were the talk of Paris.

It was inevitable that Bernhardt, the famous actress, and Damala, the almost equally notorious *bon viveur,* should eventually meet. Each knew the reputation of the other, and their curiosity was only the more whetted thereby.

Each delighted to play with fire, and especially with the dangerously devastating fire which smoulders eternally within the human soul.

Bernhardt prided herself on her ability to conquer men, to reduce them to the level of slaves; Damala vaunted his ability as a hunter and a spoiler of women.

No man, said Bernhardt, could long resist her imperious will; no woman, said Damala, could long remain impervious to his fatal charm—and to prove it he would exhibit with pride the clattering bones in his closet.

Like grains of mercury in a bowl of sand, their two natures were inevitably attracted towards each other. Both were serenely confident of the issue of that coming clash of wills.

Damala boasted to his friends that, as soon as he looked at her, the great Sarah Bernhardt would be counted on his long list of victims; and Bernhardt was no less certain that she had only to command for Damala to succumb.

She was all woman, feline in her charm and attraction for men, but herculean in the labour which was in reality the greater half of her life. Damala was only half a man; he had the exterior, the sexual attraction of one, but he lacked the vital power to live and to endure by the labour of his hands and brain.

He was beautiful and brilliant, but only the shell was left of his manhood, which he had burned out years before his time, for he was younger than Sarah by three years. Sarah, despite all the marvellous things which she had already accomplished, had the best of her span of life before her. Damala was indolent, unambitious except as regards women, hot-headed, quick to take up an insult, and an unscrupulous fiend when his passions were aroused. He had the presence and manners of a gentleman and the mind of a chimpanzee.

Even before he met Sarah, Damala was a victim to the vice of morphine, and in that curious stratum of society which is composed of drug-takers, he met Jeanne Bernhardt, Sarah's sister, who had no right to the name, but who had assumed it at the behest of their mother.

Jeanne had succumbed to morphine before she was twenty-five. She had followed Sarah's footsteps into the theatre, but she had none of the talent of her great half-sister, nor had she the beauty, despite her early promise.

She was a peculiar-looking woman, with dark hair, a thin face, deep green pools for eyes, a weak chin and uncertain mouth. She could fill a small part in a play, with the aid of Sarah's careful coaching, but she could not be depended upon; and at times, under the influence of her special drug, would commit the worst blunders. On more than one occasion she had almost ruined a play.

Poor Jeanne! She had much that was good in her. She loved Sarah with a passion which was extraordinary, to say the least, considering the earlier lack of devotion to one another that characterised the household of Julie Bernard.

That poor lady was now dead, at the age of fifty-one. She had lived long enough, however, to see her unwanted child rise to heights of fame that were almost dizzy, when regarded from her own comparatively small eminence of beauty and coquette.

The baby she had left to the tender mercies of a *concierge's* wife, and all but abandoned; the thin, delicate child who had wanted to be a nun, and whom she had never really understood; that being whom she had created, fruit of perhaps the only genuine passion of her empty life, had become the favourite toast of the world, the darling of two hemispheres, with kings paying homage to her beauty and her art.

It is to be doubted whether Julie ever really understood the miracle that had happened. It is to be doubted also whether she ever credited Sarah with the genuine greatness that was hers. Almost to the day of her death, in fact, she was steadily lamenting her daughter's extravagances and eccentricities—she, of all women, whose foibles had once shocked the gayest city in the world!

It takes a strong will and a cool head to survive the fast life of the theatre, especially when that life is lived as Sarah Bernhardt lived it. Though Sarah might appear strong; though her constitution, which had once been delicate, might now seem to be made of spun steel, in reality she was still delicate—extremely so. It was her will that triumphed, the will to accomplish, to create, to live—the will which is another name for genius.

But little Jeanne, the centre of her mother's fond hopes, had neither strength of body nor power of will. She had not genius, only a facility for mimicry. The life that sustained and exhilarated Sarah, ruined and finally killed her.

Sarah's feeling for Jeanne was the pity which is akin to love, and not the sisterly devotion she might have felt had her earlier history been less unfortunate. She helped the girl all she could, saw that she had work, and that she was able to earn sufficient money. She took her to America, in the hope that travel and the change into a newer, freer atmosphere would work the miracle she so ardently desired.

Sarah's hatred for drugs was one of the abiding passions of her life. She herself had such an unquenchable spirit within her that she could not imagine the plight of those who were compelled to indulge a fanciful morbidity with such artificial stimulants.

Once, shortly after discovering that her half-sister was taking morphine, she thrashed Jeanne with a riding-whip and locked her in her bedroom. There for four days she kept her a prisoner, denying her both food and drug in an unscientific attempt to tame her desires, which, of course, ended in failure. Despite all Sarah's efforts, Jeanne slipped gradually down the hill and into the pit which is the inevitable fate of those who seek the bliss of this artificial paradise.

Morphine had come into general use as a medicine during the war of 1870, and many doctors and soldiers had learned to listen to its dangerous appeal. They taught its use to their women, and the alleged miracles worked by the drug became noised abroad. Its use became almost fashionable!

People who frequented the salons took it shamelessly, just as anyone else would take a glass of champagne. It was said that opium dulled your cares and finally made you forget them, but that morphine kept you conscious of them and actually made you enjoy them!

Jeanne and Damala were members of a group of morphine-takers connected with the stage, who made no secret

of their vice. Damala was a fair amateur actor—it was
in this direction and not diplomacy that his ambitions lay
—and delighted to frequent the *coulisses* (as the French
term the wings), the Green Room, and the other mysterious haunts which lie behind the footlights. Many
were his victories in this half-world of pleasure and of
work.

When Jeanne spoke of Damala to Sarah, the latter
felt herself repelled and yet fascinated. Outwardly she
denounced him, but inwardly she was enormously interested in this notorious man, and longed to meet him.

Unconscious of the insidious spell that was at work,
enchaining their two destinies, Sarah privately determined
to see this arrogant monster, this darling of the drawing-
rooms, this man who was called the handsomest being
since Apollo.

They met finally at the house of a friend who was
curious to see what they would do when brought together.

CHAPTER XXIV

THIS meeting of Sarah Bernhardt, then the greatest feminine personality in Europe, and Damala, who was to be the central figure of the most tragic episode of her life, will remain in my memory for ever.

They were introduced by a mutual friend.

"Damala?" said Sarah, raising her eyebrows, and affecting an ignorance of his name which was in the circumstances really insulting.

"Bernhardt?" replied Damala, in similar accents.

It was flint on stone.

"Sir!" exclaimed the dismayed hostess, "you are addressing the greatest actress in France!"

"And I," said Damala, in a sceptically belittling manner, "am therefore the greatest man in France!"

Bernhardt shrugged her shoulders at this insolence.

"You do not interest me, monsieur!" she said, turning away.

"Wait," said Damala, "you have not heard all. I am also the wickedest man in Paris."

"You sound to me," replied Sarah, "a fool, and the poorest boaster I have ever met!" And she left him.

He laughed, and the laughter reached her. It struck straight at her most vulnerable trait—her vanity.

A man had laughed at Sarah Bernhardt! More, he was laughing still! It was incredible!

Yet it was so, and the memory of that laugh, and of the passage of arms which had preceded it, lingered with her. She was piqued. For the first time in her experience she had met a man who would not humble himself before her.

Sarah was now negotiating for the purchase of the Porte St. Martin theatre, which she proposed to place under the direction of her young son, Maurice Bernhardt. In this capacity, as a possible purchaser, she came face to face with Damala, who had been waiting for her in the theatre.

Sarah would have swept by him, but he stepped in front.

"I have brought you a present!" he said, and held out a bouquet of beautiful lilies-of-the-valley—for it was Springtime, the fête of *muguet*. This flower is supposed in France to be a symbol of good fortune, and many a forlorn lover makes up a quarrel with his sweetheart, on the first of May, by presenting her with a tiny bundle of *muguet*.

Sarah looked at him, astonished. Here was a new Damala!

But the Greek quickly disillusioned her.

"I give it to you," he said, "because you will need it— with me!"

This was even greater insolence than he had shown before. Sarah was angry, mortified—and interested. Within a week she confounded her friends by accepting an invitation to dine with Damala alone.

Although his family in Athens had destined him for the diplomatic service, his own private ambition was to be an actor. As I have said, he was an amateur comedian of no small merit, and when Sarah discovered this she invited him to become a member of her company.

He accepted at once, but his family intervened and— a curious case of history repeating itself—had him sent on a diplomatic mission to Russia, whither young de Lagrenée had gone a few years before.

Sarah was now all ready to depart on her Grand Tour of Europe, during which she was to visit all the principal capitals and was to give performances literally before "all the crowned heads." In fact, many of those crowned heads were destined before long seriously to feel her powers of attraction.

She had already included in her itinerary Spain, Italy, Austria, Holland, Belgium, Denmark, Sweden and Norway. It was an enormous undertaking, having regard to difficulties of transport at that time, when the train services in many countries were the worst imaginable. On this tour, I was again included in her company.

When Damala went to Russia, he begged her to follow, and as her itinerary included Denmark, it was not difficult for her to arrange to go from there to Reval, and thence to St. Petersburg. Russia had always possessed an enormous attraction for her.

Voluminous descriptions of this tour have already been given, and I shall not therefore say much about it, except as regards Sarah personally.

In Lisbon, the actor Décori jumped into the first place in Sarah's affections, and Décori was extremely jealous of another actor named Dumeny, because he had a better part in the piece.

During the rehearsals for *L'Aveu,* however, Décori pretended to be a great friend of Dumeny's, and carried him off every day on fishing trips. As a consequence, Dumeny did not properly learn his part, and his performance on the opening night was farcical.

Sarah called him into her dressing-room for an hour, and gave him one of the most frightful reprimands I have ever heard. It was devastating. When Dumeny came out, he was pale and trembling like a leaf.

That night the company were the guests of the well-known de Rosas at a formal banquet, and one of the hosts proposed a toast to the French artistes.

Sarah sprang to her feet and pointed a shaking finger at her unfortunate subordinate Dumeny, who was sitting quietly at one end of the table with his wife.

"Ah, no!" she cried, "I will not drink your toast if it includes that pig there! When I play with him, I never have any applause!"

There was a dead silence for a few moments, and then Dumeny, very pale and with tears in his eyes, rose and left the room, followed by his wife. We drank the toast.

The next day Sarah bore down on Dumeny in the middle of rehearsals and exclaimed heartily: "Ah, my little cabbage!"—and kissed him on the cheek!

In Madrid I was asked to play the part of Nanine in

La Dame aux Camélias. The Théâtre de l'Opéra at
Madrid is an immense building, and the area at the back
of the stage is a perfect wilderness of gangways, passages, and turnings between the different sets. It was
difficult even for the habitués of the theatre to find their
way about. As for myself, I never did learn the quickest
way from one side of the stage to the other, when a
scene was being played. The distance seemed tremendous, and one was always tripping over something.

I was supposed to make my exit by one door and to
re-appear at another one, where I was to knock and say
a certain line loudly—I have forgotten the exact words.

I made my exit safely enough, but in running round to
the other door I lost my way, missed my cue, and, rendered nervous at the prospect of Sarah's wrath, entered
without saying the line. As I did so, Sarah darted a
furious look at me, and I realised that she had already
explained my absence in such a way that my appearance
created a comic situation. The audience was laughing.

In the last act Sarah "died" and it was my duty to pass
a garment over her. This was the first time I had been
close to her since my *faux pas* of the third act.

Suddenly, as she sank with glazing eyes on her couch,
I was amazed to hear her launch into a perfect stream
of low-toned vituperation, directed at myself.

Her breast heaved, her breath came in short gasps.
Sarah Bernhardt was "dying" in one of the most magnificent scenes she ever played. Her lips moved—and

it is fortunate that the audience could not hear what they said!

They said, in fact: "You ugly cow! You have spoiled everything by your clumsiness! This is not the proper garment!"

And, in truth, I discovered to my horror that it wasn't! I was in such a nervous state that I had chosen the wrong robe. However, I am certain that nobody except Sarah, not even the others in the company, noticed the fact. But, added to my previous grave fault, this error was enough for her.

She kept up her great death scene, taking twice as long as usual, because she kept on thinking of new reproaches to hurl at me. What reproaches they were, too! My ears burned. My cheeks were tingling with indignation.

Finally, when she uttered a really outrageous insult—it was with her supposedly last breath that she said it—I leaned down, and, making the motions of intense and tearful grief, hissed between my sobs:

"You say another word and I'll smack your face here on the stage!"

I meant it, too, and Sarah must have seen that I did, for she "died" properly this time, and never pronounced another word.

And all this while there was the audience out in the mistiness beyond, tense and grief-stricken, held by the marvellous acting of the great *tragédienne* on her stage death-bed!

In Vienna the Archduke Frederick put one of his palaces at Sarah's disposal, and in appreciation of his act of courtesy we gave a special performance for him, to which all the ladies of the Court were invited. The Emperor was away, or ill—I forget which.

The last act in *La Dame aux Camélias,* the very one which I have just been describing, made such an impression on one of these ladies, a beautiful Hungarian, that she fainted dead away and had to be carried out of the theatre.

"Had I been a woman I would have fainted too!" said the Archduke, when Sarah expressed her regret at the occurrence.

He gave her an emerald pendant, set in natural gold which had been obtained from a mine on his estate near Bugany in Hungary. For a long time Sarah wore this emerald more prominently than any other jewel. Finally it went the way of most of her precious possessions. Sarah gave out that it had been "lost." Perhaps it had been, but I think I know the man who found it—and who paid Sarah handsomely for the privilege!

We were asked to play in Prague, but Sarah had refused to go there, as she had refused to go to Berlin. A few years later, in fact, she declined an offer of one million marks to play in Berlin. "Never among those swine!" she would say.

Eventually, however—some sixteen years later I believe—Sarah appeared in Berlin and secured triumph. Germany, as I have stated in an earlier chapter, acclaimed her as one of the Fatherland's own children.

Finally, after returning to France through Switzerland, we went to Holland, and from there to the Baltic states. We played in Stockholm, Christiania and Copenhagen. Our greatest reception was in Stockholm, where Sarah became an idol of the people. I have always thought that the Swedes understand dramatic art better than any other nation except the French.

We passed through Finland, but did not play there. Sarah was anxious to get to St. Petersburg, where a grandiose demonstration and welcome, not to mention Damala, awaited her.

Word came that the Tsar was to command a performance in the Winter Garden, and the whole company was tremendously excited. None of us had ever seen the Tsar. But so many stories had reached us about him that, in our imaginations, he had become a sort of god. Tales of the munificence of his entertainments, the sumptuousness of his Court, the power that he wielded, had combined to weave about his person a truly romantic glamour. And we were to play before this mighty personage!

But Sarah was not thrilled—at least, not in anticipation of playing before the Tsar. She might have been, and probably was, thrilled at the prospect of again meeting Damala, the one man who had met and vanquished her with her own weapons.

And, when we actually saw the Great White Tsar, we felt the edge taken off our thrill, too. He was the most insignificant looking monarch in all Europe!

CHAPTER XXV

We made our entry into St. Petersburg under the most propitious conditions. The sun was smiling, and the effect on the towers, domes and spires of Russia's wonderful city was indescribably lovely. The Nevski Prospekt was a never-to-be-forgotten sight, with its splendid shops, its magnificent palaces, and its succession of fashionable people in their smart turnouts.

Rooms had been reserved for us at the Hotel du Nord, but on arriving there we found that it had not sufficient accommodation for all of us, so a part of the company, amongst them myself, went on to the European.

Being extremely tired after the long journey, I went straight to my room to get some sleep, though it was only four o'clock in the afternoon. I was awakened by a knock on the door. I lit the gas, and found that the clock said midnight. Who could be knocking on the door at that unearthly hour?

It was a maid, with a message from Hugette Duflos, one of the women members of the company, who had remained at the Hotel du Nord.

"Sarah is ill and wants you," the message said.

I dressed at once, and asked the maid whether a conveyance could be found to take a very young girl in safety through the streets at night. The maid laughed.

"Oh, yes!" she answered. "Evidently madame is not acquainted with our customs! This is tea-time!"

"Tea-time!" At midnight! I must have looked incredulous, for the maid went on to explain:

"Fashionable people do not rise until twelve o'clock in St. Petersburg, and the shops and restaurants therefore keep open very late. When you are having your supper in Paris, we in Russia are taking our tea!"

Going out into the brilliantly-lighted streets I saw that she was right. They were alive with people, and most, if not all, the shops and of course the restaurants were open. It was a novel scene that amused and enchanted me.

We arrived in a few minutes at the Hotel du Nord, and there another surprise awaited me. Sarah Bernhardt herself, accompanied by none other than Jacques Damala, advanced to meet me. Right and left were other members of the company, arriving in a similar state of bewilderment.

"We are going to have a real Russian party!" announced Sarah.

"But—I thought you were ill?" I said.

"Just an excuse—to get you out of bed, *ma petite!*" she said, to my astonishment. "I knew all of you were so tired that you would never get up for a mere invitation to a party, so I invented the excuse that I was ill!"

Some of the party, especially the men, were very angry and returned to their beds, after telling Sarah what they thought of her. Sarah only laughed. I myself felt nervous and annoyed, and Sarah must have seen this, for she passed her arm round me and led me to a buffet, where she gave me a little hot tea with cognac and lemon in it. This warmed and strengthened me, and I decided to stay.

The party kept on till four o'clock, with Sarah and Damala behaving like two children in their teens. There was a fearfully fascinating Prince there—Dimitri something, his name was—and he devoted himself to me, as the youngest and therefore the most innocent of the party. I was sixteen or seventeen—I forget which. At any rate, it was all perfectly wonderful to me.

People kept arriving and departing as casually as they had come. All St. Petersburg seemed determined to make the acquaintance of Sarah Bernhardt, and the throng round her was tremendous, with the result that many who wanted to talk to her had to content themselves with the other members of the company.

My Prince was courtesy itself. He was quite young, and very distinguished-looking; and I heard it stated that he was related to the Royal family. But I never found out the exact relationship . . . in fact, Russia was such a whirl for me that I carried away very few facts and decidedly mixed impressions. Everyone was charming.

We were fêted night after night in the most gorgeous way. The Grand Duke Michael—I think it was he— opened up his palace, which looked like a fortress, to us one night and we gave a brief performance there. After that we danced. Several of the Grand Dukes were there, and so was my Prince, who presented me to his wife, a gracious lady with that air of innate breeding which only the Russians, the English and the Danes seem to possess. The fact that Prince Dimitri had his wife there did not prevent his paying attention to me, and I had a wonderful time. I could have stayed in Russia for ever.

We did not play in the Winter Palace, but gave a gala performance for their Imperial Majesties at the National Theatre. It was private, in that no seats were sold and could be obtained only through invitations sent out by the Court Chamberlain; but when we saw the vast throng crowding the theatre it looked as if all Russia was there. And all wealthy and titled Russia probably was, for we heard that special trains had been made up to bring "Sarah Bernhardt sightseers" from Moscow and other famous cities. We were not to visit Moscow on this trip.

I have heard many people say that anyone who has visited Russia can talk of nothing else and always longs to return there. I can testify that this is true in my case; and I know also that it was true in the case of Sarah Bernhardt who returned to Russia three times and always spoke of the land of the Tsars with the warmest affection and feeling.

I remember a gracious remark made by the Empress, a woman of no great stature and with evident marks of trouble on her sweet and modest face. When Sarah was presented and dropped her curtsey before her, she said:

"I think, my dear, that I should be the one to bow!"

I thought it one of the most exquisite tributes I had ever heard.

Sarah Bernhardt in *Adrienne Lecouvreur*.

We played François Coppée's *Le Passant, La Dame aux Camélias, Hernani,* and *L'Aventurière.* The Emperor chose *Le Passant* for the Command Performance, and Sarah greatly appreciated his choice.

"He must be a poet himself! He looks like one!" she said.

This observation came to the Emperor's ears, and after the Command Performance was over he came down from his box on to the stage and shook hands with Sarah warmly.

"You are the most wonderful actress we have ever seen in Russia, mademoiselle!" he said, "and one does not need to be a poet to appreciate you!"

Alexander II presented her with a magnificent brooch, set with diamonds and emeralds, as a remembrance of the occasion. She "lost" it on one of her trips to South America.

What jewels that woman lost or sold! The total would have staggered belief, had it ever become known. I suppose no actress ever possessed, at varying times, such wonderful jewels as did Sarah Bernhardt. Yet when her collection of gems was sold by auction in Paris after her death, most of the articles were found to be paste, and the whole collection fetched only a few thousand francs, and that chiefly for sentimental reasons.

Damala and Sarah were seen together everywhere. He took her about, introduced her into that class of society to which he belonged by virtue of his official position, and seemed wildly infatuated with her. Whether it was really infatuation, or simply the desire to capture the love and be seen in the company of the most famous woman of her epoch, I shall leave to my readers to judge.

To me Damala was the most cold-blooded, cynical and worthless individual whom I had ever met. I could not bear the sight of him. His very touch revolted me. And my feelings were shared by most of the company, so that when Sarah casually announced one day that Damala had resigned his official position in order to join her company, we were all more indignant than astonished. It had been evident from the first that he meant leaving St. Petersburg when she did.

What Sarah saw in him I am at a loss to imagine. He was still extremely handsome—"beautiful" would be a better description. He affected extreme dandyism in dress, and was eccentric in many of his habits.

He was still coolly nonchalant in his dealings with Sarah and in this he was wise, for it was this cynical attitude of his, this disdain of her greatness and success, which had first attracted her to him and which continued to hold her interest and pique her curiosity.

Once get a woman curious about a man, to the extent of wishing to seek his company, and the rest follows as night the day. . . .

To other people, Damala would praise Sarah wildly.

"She is the sun, the moon and the stars!" he would exclaim. "She is Queen of the World! She is divine!"

Sometimes these verbal extravagances reached Sarah's ears, but she never believed he had uttered them! This was comprehensible enough, for when he was with her his attitude was as different as possible.

On some occasions he actually treated her as an inferior! He would criticise her dress, her manner of doing her hair, her acting, her views on any subject, her deportment, her speech. He was always finding fault with her, and Sarah would fly into the most frightful rages when he carried his sarcasms too far.

A hundred times she would cast him from her, with stormy admonitions never to come near her again, a hundred times she declared violently that she could not bear the sight of him, despised him, and refused to take such treatment from anybody, let alone a "Greek Gypsy." This was her pet piece of invective, for, as she was aware, it had the merit of piercing Damala's thick hide. As a matter of fact, Damala was every inch an aristocrat, even though he was a particularly degenerate one.

In reply to these wild outbreaks on Sarah's part, Damala would adopt a peculiarly irritating attitude. He would take her at her word, leave her, and then send a note to the effect that he was glad to have rid himself at last of such an incubus!

Then he would stay away from her until she came to him and begged to be forgiven. That was what he wished and liked; that was the pleasure his liaison with Sarah Bernhardt gave him—the idea of a proud and beautiful creature, idolised by two continents, crawling to him, Damala, on her knees, for forgiveness!

He would let people know about it, too.

"I had my proud Sarah on her knees last night," he would say, "but I refused to forgive her; she has not yet been punished enough!"

What a brute the man was—but how well he knew women!

The worse he treated her, the more she became his slave. The more sarcastic he became, the humbler was she. It had from the first been a struggle between two arrogant natures, and Damala had won—for the time being. There came a day, however, when his victory seemed empty enough.

St. Petersburg talked much of Sarah's affair with Damala, as may be supposed. The two were so open about it. The Court, and the gentle little Empress, were shocked. There were no more command performances. Russian high society was beginning to look askance at this beautiful genius, who was so scornful of convention.

The code in Russia was that a man could do what he liked. If his rank was high enough, he could commit murder without losing caste. But a woman had to walk within a strictly defined circle, which was drawn by the Empress herself. Once she stepped beyond that circle she could never get a footing inside it again. Sarah had stepped outside, and she did not care.

Soon after this we left St. Petersburg, but not before an incident occurred which will bear relating, even though Sarah was not directly concerned in it.

We were playing one night when, during the third

entr'acte, I received a message from a call-boy who looked very awed and yet very important.

"The Grand Duke V—— desires that you will go to his box," was the message.

Grand Dukes counted for little in my life and I, a Republican to the backbone, was vexed at the peremptory fashion in which the request was framed.

"Tell His Imperial Highness that I am not in the habit of going to private boxes during a performance!" I said.

The boy looked a little startled, but took my reply. In a few minutes he was back.

This time there was no mistaking the character of the message.

"His Imperial Highness presents his compliments to Mademoiselle Thérèse, and wishes to inform her that he will await her for supper, after the performance."

In consternation I went to see Sarah.

"What shall I do?" I asked. "I can't go to supper with the man!"

"Tell him to go away, then!" suggested Sarah, who had not taken much interest in my story. But another member of the company, who knew Russia well, held up his hands in horror.

"You can't do that—it would be disobeying a Royal command!" he exclaimed. "When a Grand Duke puts a message in that form, it admits of but one reply. You will have to go to supper with him!"

"I won't!" I replied, obstinately decided.

"Then you will be thrown into prison!"

"What! Thrown into prison because I refuse to sup with a Grand Duke? What a ridiculous idea!"

"It's true, none the less. These men wield an enormous power. A mere word from them, and you would disappear and never be heard of again, and Grand Duke V—— is the worst of the lot. You must remember that this is Russia!"

I was now terribly frightened. I looked for Sarah again, but she had disappeared.

"What shall I do?" I inquired of Pierre Berton, who had always been most kind to me.

"I will go to His Highness and tell him you are ill," he suggested. But I would not hear of Pierre getting himself into trouble over me.

So, after the performance, I waited in fear and trembling in my dressing-room. Several other members of the company were there also, curious and disturbed as to the outcome, while Pierre Berton had a positively ferocious expression on his face. He looked as though he would like to eat all the Grand Dukes in Russia.

This was the first intimation I had had regarding the true state of Berton's feelings towards me. His declaration of love and our marriage did not come until years later.

Finally the Grand Duke came in. He was in full evening dress, and when seen near at hand appeared a most amiable gentleman.

He bowed to the company, and when one of the ladies dropped a curtsey, his eyes twinkled. I was thoroughly frightened, but when he held out his arm to me, I stepped forward in spite of myself. He was so thoroughly courteous! Berton blurted out something indistinguishable, but fortunately did not interfere. I went out with my Grand Duke.

Well, the story has not the ending the reader may have been led to expect. The supper was a gay one, but all the men present behaved themselves quite properly and the Grand Duke was more like a father to me than a lover. Afterwards, he took me for a ride in his open barouche, and then accompanied me home.

At the hotel, when they saw who had brought me back, they received me with open mouths. It was the Hotel Demouth, a little place but very smart, opposite the statue of Catherine the Great. I had moved there because the European was too noisy.

The manager himself escorted me upstairs to my room and bowed me in. I had become a personage!

I told Sarah about it the next day, and she complimented me.

"However," she said, "nothing would have happened to you if you had not gone! That same Grand Duke wanted me to dine with him the other night, and I said I would if I could bring Damala, and that finished it!"

CHAPTER XXVI

OF all the tragic episodes that abounded in the life of Sarah Bernhardt, her marriage was probably the most tragic.

The one man whom she adored sufficiently to marry betrayed her love, made her a ridiculous spectacle in the eyes of her theatrical comrades, ill-treated her to the extent of actual cruelty, and, after spoiling her life for seven years, died a victim of morphine.

Nobody knows what caused their decision to marry. I know only one thing, namely, that not a member of the company was aware of their intention until a few hours before the actual ceremony; and then only Pierre Berton, Jeanne Bernhardt, Mary Jullien, and Madame Devoyod were let into the secret.

I was taken ill on the voyage home from Russia and Sarah thought it best for me to return to France. Thus I did not go on to London with the company, and joined it only when it returned through Paris, on its way to Italy.

What I know of Sarah Bernhardt's marriage is therefore hearsay—only what Pierre Berton told me. The event must have made him miserable, poor man! I am sure he adored Sarah still, although weary of her caprices.

Berton was a very conscientious and honourable man;

and his was the restraining influence in the Bernhardt company, whereby many pitfalls were avoided owing to his sage counsel. Sarah Bernhardt's once tender feeling for him had changed into one of extreme respect. She recognised the power of his intellect and admired his wisdom, and never forsook him, both because he was a marvellous actor of great drawing power and because he was a counter-balance in the scales to outweigh her ruinous escapades.

A great many of the company, having very good reason to hate Damala, desired to leave at once, when Sarah married him; and it was Pierre Berton who persuaded them to stay on in order to support Sarah in the trials which he knew she would shortly have to endure.

Sarah and Damala may have decided to marry during the voyage from Russia; but knowing them both as I did, I am inclined to believe the thing was arranged on the spur of the moment.

One could and can do such things in London. They are impossible in Paris, where the consent of parents is obligatory, even in the case of those who are no longer minors, and where at least a month is always consumed in absurd preliminaries and red tape.

I firmly believe that, had it been necessary for Sarah to get married in France, she would never have done it! Such a decision, in her case, required to be made and carried out practically on the spot, while she was under the influence of one of her fantastic moods. Marriage to her, I am sure, was not the solemn, semi-religious event that it is in the lives of most women. For her it was merely another escapade—the crowning one, if you like.

Almost everything else on the list of follies she had committed. Why not marriage?

That, at any rate, is the opinion I have always held. But Berton had a graver conception of the matter.

In his view Sarah was so tremendously infatuated by Damala that she married him to make him wholly hers. He used to say:

"She lived in constant terror that Damala's fancy would change, that some other woman would cross his path, and that he would leave her.

"She was completely under the fellow's domination. If any good man, of high and noble principles, had offered Sarah his name, she would have refused him scornfully; she would have answered that she would tie her life to no man's.

"But with Damala it was another matter. It was she who desired passionately to hold him—not the reverse. At least, such is my belief. Sarah, too, when she remembered how easily she had fallen a victim to it herself, was often much perturbed at seeing how quickly women were captured by Damala's fatal charm.

"She could think of no way to bind him to her except by marriage. So, despite her distaste for the orthodox union, she determined on the ceremony.

"She waited until we got to London, where such things can be done over-night, and then took advantage of one of Damala's affectionate spells to persuade him to marry her. He agreed; a priest was sent for, and they were married—all in the space of a few hours."

Damala always declared this version to be true—that it was Sarah who proposed to him and not he to her. Moreover, in fits of temper, he would tell her so before the whole company.

"If I had not been crazy I would not have been caught so easily!" he would cry, beating the air with his arms.

By marrying Damala, Sarah thought to bind him to her. It was the supreme mistake of her life. Instead of keeping him, she lost him.

She simply exchanged a lover for a husband, and many women have found to their cost what that means. Sarah's disillusionment came only three weeks later.

Until the marriage, Damala had been more or less faithful to Sarah—as faithful as a nature like his allowed. But he had scarcely stepped down from the altar with his bride, than he began betraying her right and left.

He demanded that she should change her stage name to "Sarah Damala" in his honour, and when she refused he walked out of the house and disappeared.

Performances had to be abandoned during the three days he was away. Sarah was absolutely frantic. She was ready to believe anything—that he had deserted her for good, that he had fallen into the Thames, that he had run away to France, that he had committed suicide, that he had gone away with another woman.

This last theory—and Sarah would rather have lost an arm than that it should have been found true—was the correct one. Damala, previous to his marriage and unknown to Sarah, had struck up a friendship with a Norwegian girl whom he had met on board ship. It was with her that he spent those three days, scarcely a week after his marriage to Sarah.

Paris, which had gasped at the news of the wedding, was in spasms of mirth at this new unhappiness which had overtaken Sarah. It so perfectly agreed with what everyone had predicted.

"She is mad!" said Auguste Dane, the writer, when he heard of the marriage through a letter that Berton wrote to me. "He will leave her within a week!"

I remember the words so well, because they so nearly came true.

In a few days Damala returned, to find Sarah ill from anxiety and bruised pride. God knows what his excuses were, what methods he took to win his pardon! A woman in love is ever ready to believe, and Sarah was no exception.

The next day they were together again as usual.

The company went to Ostend, where it played five nights. On the last night Damala disappeared again, and was heard from two days later in Brussels, whither he had gone with a pretty Belgian acquaintance.

He rejoined Sarah in Paris, and Sarah forgave him again. He would pretend to be ill and win her pity; and once pity takes the place of resentment in a woman's heart it is not difficult for a clever man to obtain everything he wishes.

With every month of their married life, Damala's behaviour deteriorated. It began to be said of him that he was the most unfaithful husband in all France, which was saying a good deal.

"I saw Damala at the theatre last night," somebody would say.

"With Sarah?"

"Sarah? No, of course not, imbecile! Sarah is now his wife!"

And so it went on.

Accustomed to facile successes with women, Damala carried his infidelities to extremes. In almost every town they visited there was a new betrayal to register; and Damala now scarcely took the trouble to conceal his double life from Sarah.

One can imagine the mortification all this caused to such a proud nature as hers.

From being the idol of two hemispheres she was fast becoming (as she knew well) the laughing-stock of France; and the sole reason for her misfortunes was her insane action in marrying a man who did not understand even the first principles of honour. In place of a ring he had given her a cross to bear; and the cross was the condescending amusement of the multitudes who, a few months previously, had been ready to fall down and worship her as a demi-goddess.

"She cannot be much, after all," said the man in the street. "See, her husband betrays her right before her eyes!"

"All those stories about her must have been true!" thought the staid and virtuous members of society. "Even her husband cannot live with her for more than a month!"

The cruellest fact about mob-psychology is that a mob is invariably ready to believe the worst. The Parisians now discovered with intense satisfaction that their idol's feet were made of clay.

"C'est le ridicule qui tue," declared a great French essayist. Ridicule was killing Sarah.

Never before had I seen Sarah Bernhardt suffer so fearfully from the ravages of jealousy, nor did she ever suffer so again.

Her face, within a few short months, lost that girlish look which had been its greatest charm. Lines came to features that had previously been clear of them. She became dispirited; could not be consoled; would sit for hours by herself; seemed to take little interest in what was going on about her.

Then Damala would return, like a truant schoolboy; and, after the usual scene of anger, all would be well—until the next time.

"Tu es folle—il faut prendre ton parti!" ("You are foolish—you should make up your mind to make the best of it!") I told her repeatedly.

One day at Genoa, Damala and an actress, whom Sarah had dismissed on suspicion of a liaison with her husband, left the company and went to Monte Carlo.

Sarah was seized with a frantic fit of jealousy, stopped

(Photo, Henri Manuel)

Sarah Bernhardt in *Les Bouffons,* 1906.

all performances (in spite of the tremendous loss this occasioned her); and wrote letters every hour pleading with Damala to return.

The only reply he made to these overtures was a curt note in which he informed her that he had lost 80,000 francs gambling at baccarat, and that if she would send him this money he would come back at once.

Sarah sent the enormous sum and Damala kept his word. He returned—but still with the actress!

There was a tremendous scene in the lobby of the Genoese hotel where we were staying. Sarah's rage was directed against the woman. She ranted against her, threatened her with everything from physical violence to criminal proceedings, and ended by ordering her out of the hotel.

"She has come back for the money you owe her!" said Damala.

C'était le comble! Sarah went straight into hysterics. But when she recovered the woman was still there, and, moreover, had a legal claim on her for her wages, so that Sarah was forced to pay.

After this incident she had a respite from matrimonial storms for several weeks. Her world revolved in and about Damala, whom (at his own request) she created managing-director of the company, with his name, as such, billed in large type everywhere.

This request of Damala's was his undoing. It opened Sarah's eyes as nothing else could have done to the real worthlessness of the man she had made her husband.

Damala she knew to be congenitally unfaithful, but her pride could not endure the further discovery that she had married an incompetent.

As manager of a theatrical company on tour he was a miserable failure. He wasted thousands of francs, became tangled in his accounts, could not handle other people, had no genius whatever for organisation. Had it not been for their affection for Sarah, the members of the company would have voted that it should be disbanded.

Foolish contracts were made with theatres in strange towns, hotel arrangements omitted, trains missed, properties lost—all those incidents occurred which indicate bad management and which demoralise a company.

To avoid a crash, Sarah allowed her business sense to dominate her other feelings, and there was a welcome return of her old authoritative character. We greeted with enthusiasm her domineering ways in place of Damala's blundering and bullying incompetency.

From Head of the Company, Damala became a mere Prince Consort.

There was a disgraceful scene when she made her decision known to him. He called her horrible names—"long-nosed Jewess" was one of the milder ones.

Then, characteristically, he had his revenge by making open love to one of Sarah's lesser rivals.

"If a man quit me for a Queen," said Lady Dudley, in the days of Elizabeth, "then I will be proud, for it will have taken the Queen to tear him from me; but if a man quit me for a Duchess, then am I like to die of shame."

Damala had quit his Queen for a Duchess, and Sarah was "like to die of shame"; but she cured herself by writing Damala a letter, telling him never to return.

Damala did return the next day, however, and in Sarah's absence carried off several articles of considerable value belonging to her. This happened in Paris after he had played with her in a piece at the Porte St. Martin theatre, which she had just purchased.

Damala then returned to his abandoned diplomatic career, but his habits soon forced him to give up active work.

Despite the fact that she had been born a Jewess and was only baptised into the Catholic faith, Sarah had strict ideas of a sort about religion. She refused to divorce Damala, contenting herself with a semi-legal separation whereby, in return for certain sums she sent to him monthly, he agreed never to re-enter her life.

Five years later, however, Damala sent a message to Sarah saying that he was dying in Marseilles and imploring her to forgive him and take him back.

The strength of the love which she must once have borne him is shown by the fact that, immediately she received this message, she abandoned her performances in Paris, rushed to the bedside of her husband—whom she found wasted from disease and drugs—and nursed him back again into some semblance of health.

Damala promised to leave morphine alone and they went on tour together; but the drug, to which Jeanne

Bernhardt had already succumbed, proved too strong for him.

Once, at Milan, he was nearly arrested for exhibiting himself naked at the Hotel de Ville (which is an hotel and not a town hall). His body was a mass of sores occasioned by the drug.

I was a member of the company on the famous tour Sarah made with Damala in Turkey. We played in Constantinople and Smyrna, and on taking the boat for Cairo we ran into a terrible storm.

Three times we tried to get into the Bay of Alexandria, and each time failed. Finally the ship was anchored until calmer weather came. Sarah was violently sick, and, on recovering, asked the steward to bring her the delicacies she had had brought on board for her own special use at table.

These delicacies included several cases of champagne and others of fruit and *pâté de foie gras,* of which Sarah was particularly fond.

Imagine her fury when the steward returned with the information that Damala had eaten all the fruit and had consumed all the champagne, and that nothing was left for Sarah except the regular rough fare of the steamer.

Shortly before his death, Damala was given a part by Sarah in the play *Lena,* at the Théâtre des Variétés. During the second performance he was so drunk that he could not say a word.

A few weeks later he died. Sarah was with him until the last. This was in 1889.

CHAPTER XXVII

EXCEPT that those seven fearful years left their inevitable traces upon her appearance and mind, Sarah's imprudent marriage had wonderfully little effect upon her after life.

Moreover, she never renounced the name of Damala, which remained her legal name until she died, though few people knew it.

During the war the fact that she was legally a Greek caused her much annoyance, and once when there was a danger that King Constantine might throw his country into the war on the side of the Germans, she saw herself actually refused a visa to her passport by an officious nobody in a consular office at Bordeaux.

"But I am Sarah Bernhardt, sir!" she exclaimed.

"My orders are not to grant visas to Greeks," said the official stolidly. "This passport is a Greek one and I will not endorse it."

It required a special telegram from the Minister of the Interior himself before the obstinate clerk could be persuaded to change his mind.

Sarah wore mourning for Damala for a year, but his death did not put a stop to her theatrical activities. If anything, she cast herself into her work with more eagerness than ever.

The seven years of her marriage with Damala had been

317

distinguished by Sarah's first essay in theatrical management. Towards the end of 1882 she acquired the lessee-ship of the Ambigu Theatre—the play-house where, fifteen years earlier, she had been refused a part by Chilly. It was announced that her son, Maurice Bernhardt, was to be manager.

It is doubtful whether Maurice ever did any active management. He had little aptitude for such work, and Sarah was the supervising genius both at the Ambigu and the other theatres which she subsequently acquired.

It was at the Ambigu that Sarah launched Jean Richepin. She mounted his play *La Glu*, which obtained an enormous success. She also played *Les Mères Enne-mies,* by Catulle Mendès.

Exactly on what occasion Sarah Bernhardt and Jean Richepin were brought together I cannot say. I think they had known each other for a considerable period before their real association began. Sarah was much attracted to Richepin, who had a temperament very similar to hers by all accounts.

Richepin's life had been almost as fantastically varied and adventurous as Sarah's own. He had been born of rich and influential parents, and educated at the Paris Normal School, an institution of considerable importance.

He gave many evidences of precocity during his schooldays, and, after graduating, scandalised his former teachers and schoolmates by impertinently opening up a fried-potato stand just outside the school gates. It was a way of expressing his individuality and his scorn of pedantries.

After that he became a vagabond, journeying through the provinces of France on foot, sometimes begging his bread and sometimes working at odd trades for it.

Of an extreme suppleness of body and delighting in acrobatics, he finally obtained a job in a travelling circus, where he was destined to meet the woman whom he afterwards made his first wife.

From then on he became an actor, unattached to any particular theatre at first, but gradually taking parts of increasing importance until he wrote *Nana Sahib,* in which he played with Sarah Bernhardt. This play laid the real foundations of a fortune and celebrity which to-day are both considerable.

While they were playing together in *Nana Sahib,* Sarah's great rival on the stage was Marie Colombier, the friend of the author Bonnetain.

The whole city was divided into two camps, the Bernhardt camp and the Colombier camp, and there was tremendous venom displayed on both sides.

Performances at the theatre in which Marie Colombier was playing would be enlivened by bands of "Saradoteurs," who, taking possession of the galleries, would hoot and hiss and whistle until the curtain was rung down.

The next night there would be, as like as not, a similar scene in Sarah's theatre, and often the police would be obliged to interfere to prevent a battle royal between the opposing factions.

Two-thirds of the contents of Sarah's letter-bag consisted of flowers and presents; the other third of insulting anonymous letters.

A score of times Richepin offered to challenge Bonnetain to a duel on Sarah's behalf, but was dissuaded from doing so.

Finally Bonnetain wrote a book about Sarah, which was signed by Marie Colombier and entitled "Sarah Barnum." Barnum and Bailey's Circus was then the greatest attraction of Europe.

None of the names in the book were real, of course, but they were so cleverly disguised that everyone in Paris knew for whom they were intended, though any proof might be impossible.

Sarah had no remedy in the courts, so she took her revenge in another way. She and Jean Richepin—at least, the way in which the book was written certainly greatly resembled Richepin's well-known style—wrote and published a volume in reply which was entitled "Marie Pigeonnier," and in which exactly the same tactics were followed.

The two books convulsed Paris and the several editions were quickly exhausted. Sarah's friends bought up "Sarah Barnum," and Marie Colombier's friends purchased all they could find of "Marie Pigeonnier." Sarah herself spent 10,000 francs in buying up every copy of the "Sarah Barnum" book she could lay hands on.

A few copies escaped, however, and these can be found in certain Paris libraries to-day.

They were really very clever books, beautifully written and full of very effective satire.

Marie Colombier, in "Sarah Barnum," accused Sarah of drinking too much whisky, and Sarah Bernhardt retorted by asserting that Marie Pigeonnier delighted in absinthe. It was an amusing although scarcely polite controversy!

Jean Richepin is now one of the great and respected men of France. His romantic youth is almost forgotten in the eminent respectability of his age. He is probably France's most prolific classic author, and though he quarrelled bitterly with Sarah Bernhardt, his warm regard for her persisted until her death.

Richepin is one of the most distinguished living members of the *Academie Française* and of the *Institut de France*. He is credited with having obtained for Sarah Bernhardt the Legion of Honour, after a long discussion as to whether an actress could be awarded a distinction which had hitherto been reserved for men.

Sarah soon abandoned the Ambigu to play at the Vaudeville in *Féodora,* a play by Victorien Sardou. This had been arranged before Sarah left for America. Raymond Deslandes, director of the Vaudeville, paid her 1,500 francs—sixty pounds—per performance.

Later on, when Sarah took over the management of the Porte St. Martin, she made Duquesnel director, and Sardou and Duquesnel wished her to launch *Théodora,* another play by Sardou. Pierre Berton was against the innovation, and urged that *Féodora* should again be played. Sarah and Berton were now at daggers drawn.

"My compliments" (wrote Sardou to my husband at this time). "You are right about *Féodora*—that is better than a new piece, which I know will be a failure.

"But why do you wish Sarah to play *Féodora* where Garnier has no part? It is Sarah, which is to say Garnier, who leads everything to-day in this lunatic asylum of which Duquesnel thinks he is the director but of which he is only a *pensionnaire*."

This is an interesting revelation of Sarah's renewed friendship for Garnier, whose place Damala had usurped a few years previously.

Sardou's letters to my husband, never before published, throw a light on the dealings of the great actress with her dramatists.

Here is one showing Sarah's distaste for Berton's persistent advice:

"Mon cher ami,

"Je reçois une lettre de Sarah, *fulminante contre vous,* et qui n'a aucune raison d'être. Je ne sais pas ce qu'elle s'est figuré et j'insiste sur le mot.—Car je me suis borné à dire à Grau que je vous avais vu, et que vous m'aviez dit qu'elle allait jouer *La Dame* (*La Dame aux*

Camélias) décidément, et que vous jouiez Gaston—rien de plus! C'est ce que j'écris à Sarah, en lui déclarant que sa colère est insensée en ce qui vous concerne.

"En même temps je lui dis ce que je pense de la Dame dans ces conditions, et de Duquesnel, qui la *force* à la jouer et qui ne voit pas qu'en cela il nuit à tout le monde, à Sarah, à moi, à *Dumas,!!* et à lui-même."

After this Sardou had a long and stormy interview with Sarah, urging her to play *Théodora* instead of *La Dame aux Camélias,* on which she and Duquesnel had decided. It ended in the great dramatist's defeat, and while his anger was still hot he sat down and wrote to Berton:

"Mon cher ami,

"Il n'y a rien à faire avec cette folle qui tue la poule aux œufs d'or. Je connais ses projects—une Maria Padilla de Mailhac!!! Maria Padilla!! Et de Meilhac! Et une pièce de Dumas! Elle n'aura ni l'une ni l'autre, et compte alors se rattraper sur *Froufrou.* Elle va jouer *Froufrou* alors de septembre en mars!

"Elle est folle, et plus on veut la tirer de l'affaire plus elle s'enfonce. Quant à moi j'en suis saoul et ne veux plus entendre parler d'elle. Si vous avez quelque chose d'utile à me dire, venez me voir dimanche vers quatre heures, car je suis pris tous les autres jours. Demain je vous aurais bien indiqué une heure à Paris, mais je n'aurai pas un moment à moi, et samedi j'ai conseil municipal.

"Poignée de main,

"V. Sardou."

I give these letters in the original French, partly because they would lose greatly in translation, and partly because they have never before been seen in print, and are therefore an interesting contribution to the intimate story of Sarah Bernhardt's life.

Some phrases in the above are worth noting: "Nothing to be done with this idiot who is killing the goose that lays the golden eggs"; "She is crazy, and the more one tries to save her the deeper in she sinks"; "As to me, I am drunk of the whole affair and don't wish to hear her name again!"

Previous to the production of *Théodora* Sardou wrote to Berton:

"Mon cher ami,

"Il faudrait plusieurs pages comme celle-ci pour vous mettre au courant des négotiations relatives à Théodora et au mouvement tournant opéré par Sarah. Là encore une fois Duquesnel à recueilli le fruit de son irrésolution. Il fallait signer avec Grau le lendemain du jour où il m'avait dit que c'était chose faite. Mais vous connaissez l'homme. Pour ce que vous concerne ça a été plus simple. Sarah m'a déclaré qui si vous deviez jouer Andréas, elle ne jouerait pas Théodora en tournée, et comme il avait

Letter of Congratulation from Victorien Sardou.

déjà fortement question d'y renoncer, vu la certitude de
ne pas la jouer en Belgique et en Russie, la dépense du
matériel à transporter etc., etc., la menace ne laissait pas
d'avoir un côté sérieux. Cela pouvait se traduire pour
moi par une perte d'une vingtaine de mille francs; j'ai du
capituler, en exigeant toutefois que si vous jouez Justinien,
le tableau du iv acte, qui est à lui, fût maintenu, *condition
formelle*.

"Il est bien entendu avec Bertrand qu'il vous engage
pour l'Eden, et nous avons, *in petto,* prévu le cas Andréas.
Faites-vous payer. C'est bien le moins qu'on vous
dédommage des sottes humiliations que vous infligent les
caprices de cœur de la grande artiste. J'espère que le
vent tournera, dans le cours de ces neuf mois, et que nous
verrons une fois encore Damala renvoyé à l'office. De
toute façon, ne vous brouillez ni avec elle, ni avec Bertrand, en vue l'avenir. Mille bonnes amitiés.

"V. Sardou."

The interesting thing about the above letter is, of
course, the proof that Sarah, during her disagreements
with Damala, went back to Berton, with whom she subsequently quarrelled after her reconciliation with Damala.
The phrases which stand out are: "Sarah declares
that if you play Andréas she will refuse to play Théodora
on tour . . . which will mean a loss to me of 20,000
francs . . . I was thus obliged to consent"; "Make her
pay you. It is the least return they can make for the low
humiliations which the caprices of heart of the great

artiste inflict on you." "By all means, do not break with Sarah or with Bertrand, because of the future."

There came a day, however, after he had married me, when Pierre Berton could no longer stand these humiliations heaped on him by Sarah. He retired definitely from the stage to devote himself to dramatisation, his most successful play being *Zaza,* which was an enormous success both in England and America.

CHAPTER XXVIII

DURING the rehearsals of *Théodora* at the Porte St. Martin, Richepin invariably accompanied Sarah Bernhardt to the theatre. This enraged Victorien Sardou, for it was then and has since remained a matter of unwritten theatrical law that one dramatic author should not visit the rehearsals of another's play.

Eventually Sardou made a scene one afternoon in the office of Duquesnel, the manager. I happened to be present, having had a previous appointment with Duquesnel.

Beside himself with anger at the slights she was constantly heaping upon him, Sardou abused Sarah and Richepin, coupling their names in language of considerable vigour.

Sarah, as it happened, was in an office next to that of Duquesnel, and heard every word. Bounding forth, she rushed into Duquesnel's office and cried:

"I have heard all! You are animals and pigs! Richepin is an *être délicieux!* I will not remain in your odious theatre another instant! I refuse to play this pig's piece!"—indicating Sardou, who was too much astounded to say a word.

With that she flounced out of the theatre, leaving us in doubt as to whether the play could continue.

On returning to her house, however, she was met by her maid, who said to her:

"Monsieur Richepin has just been here and has taken away his things. He has left madame a note."

Sarah tore open the note feverishly. A cry of mingled rage and despair escaped her. It was a note of adieu!

Immediately Sarah sat down at her writing-table and wrote to Sardou and to Duquesnel:

"MY DEAR FRIENDS,

"I have reflected, you are quite right; Richepin after all is only the latest of these *voyous* whom I have put out of my door. All shall be as you wish.

"SARAH."

It was only later that we learned from Richepin the true story.

The one and only pantomime that Sarah Bernhardt ever played in was *Pierrot, Assassin,* by Richepin.

This was a complete failure and only brought hisses and cat-calls wherever it was produced, but Sarah insisted on retaining it on her *répertoire* so that Richepin could have the author's royalties. These were considerable, for Sarah cannily would only produce the pantomime once in each city, and her name alone was sufficient to fill the theatre.

She took the thing all over Europe. When we were in Scandinavia she would tell us that the play was not a success because: "These Northerners do not understand the art of pantomime; it is an art of the South; you will see how they will applaud us in the south of France!"

But when we played in Montpellier, the students were so indignant that they demolished the interior of the theatre, and we had to steal out of the city in closed cabs during the night in order to escape their wrath!

Since that day *Pierrot, Assassin* has not been played.

All this time she had kept up her friendship with most of the people who had surrounded her during her years at the Comédie Française in the seventies, and among these was Gustave Doré, the immortal illustrator of the Bible and of Dante's "Inferno."

Her romance with Gustave Doré was one of the really illuminating episodes of her life.

One night she was playing Clorinde, in *L'Aventurière*. Doré, who was in the audience, was so charmed that he sent her the next day the original sketches he had made for the Gospel of St. John, considered among his finest work. In reply, she wrote to him and asked him to come to her dressing-room after the performance.

When Doré came, he had scarcely opened the door before she characteristically threw herself into his arms and kissed him on both cheeks. Doré was so astounded that, for a moment, he could not speak. This was the first occasion on which he had seen Bernhardt at close quarters, and in fact it was the first time he had ever been behind the scenes of a theatre.

When Doré did not move nor speak, so great was his astonishment, Sarah flew into a temper.

"Ah, you regret, you are sorry you sent me your pictures!" she stormed.   "You despise me."

Doré threw himself at her feet, and kissed her satin slippers.

"Madame," he said simply, "I do not permit myself to love a being so far above me; *I adore!*"

This was not the beginning of their romance, however, for Sarah was then held in ties of intimacy with Georges Clairin, Doré's friend.

But Doré joined Sarah's little intimate circle, and after the death of Damala he ventured to reproach her for abandoning her painting and sculpture.

"It is because I have no teacher," she said sadly.   She had quarrelled with Clairin, who had gone to live in the Midi.

"Let me accompany you!" suggested Doré.   "I cannot teach you, but we will teach each other."

Less than a week later it was common gossip in Paris that Gustave Doré and Sarah Bernhardt experienced a tender passion for each other.   It is questionable, however, whether this was not a passing passion with Sarah —although a very genuine one all the same.

Doré was a handsome man of singularly fine physique. He was quiet, studious, and in his own field as famous as Sarah in hers.

He used to work on exquisite miniatures of Sarah, several of which are now to be found in private collections.

Sarah and he spent one August sketching together in Brittany. They both wore corduroy trousers and carried easels, and people who did not know them took them for an old painter and his apprentice, never dreaming that the "apprentice" was the most famous actress in France.

Sarah told me of an amusing incident that occurred during this painting odyssey. They had been walking all day, and dusk found them near a farmhouse. Entering, they asked for shelter for the night.

After dinner Doré was shown to a bedroom, and the painter supposed that Sarah had been given another. But the next morning, on looking out of the window, he was amazed to see her washing herself at the yard pump, her clothes full of straw and filth. She was in a merry mood.

"They took me for your boy pupil, and gave me a bed with the cow in the barn!" she told him.

During the first twenty-five years of her career, Sarah Bernhardt earned considerably more than £200,000. Most of this was made after she left the Comédie Française to become her own manager. At the Porte St. Martin, when she leased it, her profits were 400,000 francs annually.

But she made her largest sums on tour. Altogether she brought back from the United States alone considerably more than six million dollars.

But she was one of the most extravagant women who ever lived. She nearly always spent more than her in-

come, and, when she was in debt and besieged by creditors (as often happened) she would organise another
Grand Tour of America, or Australia, or Brazil, or Europe—anywhere that promised her sufficient money.

This was the real reason for her repeated tours, which
made her internationally famous.

She was still, despite the fact that she was advancing
towards middle age, wonderfully beautiful and full of
high spirits.

In fact, these high spirits sometimes translated themselves into practical jokes, the point of which we might
be pardoned sometimes for not seeing.

When I was a young girl, and none too rich, she saw
me with my shoes sodden from walking in the rain

"Let me put them to dry," she exclaimed, removing
them gently.   Then, in a burst of her peculiar humour,
she threw them in the fire!   And I had to walk home in
my stockinged feet.   She promised to buy me another
pair of shoes, but I am bound to say that she never did.

When Catulle Mendès gave Sarah the principal part
in *Les Mères Ennemies,* he was the friend of Augusta
Holmes, the celebrated composer.   They were both poor,
and with his first profits from the piece Mendès bought
his friend a green cloth gown, with long sleeves and a
high collar.

When Sarah saw the gown she cried: "What! A fine
woman like you, to hide your arms and shoulders! How
ridiculous!"

And, seizing a pair of scissors, she cut off both sleeves

and sliced off the collar, while poor Augusta stood by, terrified to death. The gown now had a square *decollété*, it was true, but it was completely ruined.

When a male friend came to see her, wearing a tall hat, it was a delight to Sarah to throw it on the ground and playfully dance upon it!

She was a trial to all who loved her, and she had tremendous difficulty in keeping domestics. Despite this, she finally established a household which remained with her for most of her later years.

Her secretary was Piron, formerly of the Opéra Comique, who could play on almost any instrument. Her personal maid was Dominga, a Buenos Ayres dressmaker, who threw up her business to follow Sarah. Her valet was Antonio, a Tunisian Jew who spoke five languages and who was discovered by Sarah in far-away Chili. Her butler was Claude, and her dresser was Félicie.

It was during a performance of Jeanne d'Arc at the Porte St. Martin, in 1890, a year after Damala's death, that the accident, which eventually cost her her right leg, happened to Sarah.

She injured the right knee in falling while on the stage, and during the resultant illness, which was complicated by phlebitis, there was much talk of amputation. (This did not come until 1915, however, and for the time being Sarah's limb was saved, thanks to the genius of the famous Doctor Lucas-Championnière.)

An American impresario then in Paris (I think it was

P. T. Barnum) went to Sarah and said that he had heard her leg was to be cut off.

"I offer you 10,000 dollars for your limb for exhibition purposes," was his astounding proposition.

Sarah's reply was to raise her skirts and to display wistfully the member, which had shrunk a good deal owing to the injury.

"I am afraid that you would lose on your bargain," she said. "Nobody would believe that that was the leg of Sarah Bernhardt!"

In 1887 she made another Grand Tour of Europe, and in the following year left for a tour of the United States and Canada, which she repeated in 1889.

At the conclusion of this latter tour she took over the Porte St. Martin, where she distinguished herself chiefly in the rôles of Jeanne d'Arc and Cléopatra.

In 1893 she acquired the management of the Renaissance Theatre, and in 1894 launched there another great dramatist—Jules Lemaître, whose play, *Les Rois,* she starred in herself, and in which she obtained a great triumph.

Her friendship with Jules Lemaître was one of the most abiding and beautiful things in her life. It lasted from those successful days at the Renaissance right up to his death, which occurred only a few years before her own.

She helped and encouraged him in his dramatic work, appeared herself in several of his plays, and, in his declining years, invited him for long months to Belle Isle, her home on the shores of Brittany.

Jules Lemaître was the one man with whom she never quarrelled. His was such a perfect character, so sweet a spirit, that a dispute with him would have been impossible.

And now Sarah was growing old herself, even though her spirit was still young. When she produced *Les Rois* she was just fifty years old.

It was perhaps because her friendship with Jules Lemaître was a spiritual association, rather than a love affair, that it lasted so long. They adored each other, but their mutual interest lay in their work together.

Never a play of Lemaître's was produced or a criticism of his published which Sarah did not see first; and never a literary effort of Sarah's saw print without first having been subjected to the kindly criticism of Jules Lemaître.

It was a beautiful chapter in both their lives, and the last sentimental episode for each. For, after she became fifty years old, Sarah Bernhardt became more and more a worker, an apostle of energy, and less and less the ardent lover.

Her affair with Edmond Rostand was the last great affair of passion in the life of Sarah Bernhardt.

It merits a chapter to itself.

CHAPTER XXIX

THE first time Sarah Bernhardt's name was publicly linked with that of Edmond Rostand was prior to the production of *L'Aiglon*.

Sarah still pursued her studies as a sculptress, though not so assiduously as before. Sometimes a whole year would go by without her putting chisel to stone, and then she would have a burst of trenchant energy and work furiously on a bust for days and nights together.

She was possessed of great determination, a trait which is generally allied to obstinacy, and she was remarkable among her friends for always finishing anything she started. She might, in the fits of temper which now were becoming rarer, break her sculptures or rip up her paintings after she had finished them, but she invariably completed them first.

She liked to have famous men to pose for her. She seized on Victorien Sardou, a man of great irritability— as demonstrated by his letters reproduced in a previous chapter—and compelled the great dramatist to sit for her twenty-one times, during which she completed her famous bust of him in black marble. This is considered by many to have been her finest work.

Occasionally, when people refused to sit for her or pleaded various excuses, she would trick them into submission. This was the way she managed to get Edmond Rostand and Maurice Maeterlinck to pose together.

Rostand and Maeterlinck were friends, and one night they accepted an invitation to dine at the home of the Countess de B——, the occasion being in honour of the President of the Republic.

Having some time to spare beforehand, the two men, who were then not nearly so celebrated as Edmond Rostand was when he died, or as Maeterlinck is now, called upon Sarah Bernhardt. It was three o'clock in the afternoon, and the Countess's dinner was fixed for nine o'clock at night.

Nine o'clock came and passed, and then nine-thirty, and finally 10 p.m. The Countess gave orders for the dinner to be served, at the same time sending messengers to the homes of the absentees, to inquire if there had been any accident.

To her astonishment the messengers came back with the news that nothing had been seen or heard of the two poets since they had departed, shortly after lunch, to take tea with Madame Sarah Bernhardt.

Containing her anger, the Countess returned to her guests and explained that Rostand and Maeterlinck had been unavoidably detained. Then she privately sent two young guests to Sarah's house, with strict instructions not to return without finding out whether the distinguished and errant couple were still there.

They had no sooner reached the portals of Sarah's

home than the *grille* opened and out came Rostand and Maeterlinck, in a great hurry.

"The Countess and the President of the Republic have been waiting for you for three hours!" cried one of the messengers.

It came out that, during their visit, Sarah had been seized with one of her modelling fits and had persuaded them to sit to her. When it was time for them to go, she had enticed them into a room she called her studio, which had glass doors, and turned the key on them there.

When they turned round they perceived Sarah sitting on the other side of the transparent doors, calmly continuing her modelling.

They rapped on the door, made faces at her, shouted, all to no purpose. Sarah went on working with her clay, rounding the figures into shape.

"But the President is waiting for us!" cried Rostand finally through the key-hole.

Sarah's "voice of gold" came sonorously through the door:

"It is a far greater honour, messieurs, to be a prisoner in Sarah Bernhardt's hands, than to be a performing lion for the President of France!"

Rostand's courtship of Sarah Bernhardt remained one of the great episodes of his career. Though Sarah refused him repeatedly, and he afterwards married the famous Rosamonde, his friendship with the actress continued, and she was at once his inspiration and his mentor, as well as the co-author of his fame.

Sarah was the first woman invited to see little Maurice Rostand on the day that he was born.

And when Sarah herself lay dying, Rosamonde and this same boy Maurice were among the last to be admitted to her bed-chamber.

Rostand used to write Sarah frantic letters, pleading his love for her. He sang her praises everywhere he went, even in the cafés on the boulevards where he and his fellow litterateurs were wont to gather.

"She is the Queen of Attitude, the Princess of Gesture, the Lady of Energy," he exclaimed once, in a poem dedicated to Sarah.

In 1896, after *L'Aiglon* was produced, he wrote:

"The existence of Sarah Bernhardt remains the supreme marvel of the nineteenth century."

As was the case in all her love affairs, except that with Jules Lemaître, her high-strung temperament clashed frequently with that of Rostand, who was a wild and erratic youth.

He was in the habit of meeting Sarah and supping with her after the theatre. Sometimes they would go for long drives together, Sarah sitting and listening attentively, while Edmond declaimed his latest poems.

It was thus she heard for the first time the verse of *L'Aiglon,* which he and she created. She would criticise the dramatic construction of a play, and was no mean authority on verse. Rostand admitted afterwards that he owed everything to her shrewd coaching during those midnight drives through the Champs Elysées and the Bois de Boulogne.

Once he arrived at the stage door of the new Sarah Bernhardt Theatre—the old Opéra Comique, which Sarah had leased from the City of Paris—five minutes late. They had had something particularly important to talk over in regard to a forthcoming production, and Sarah could not brook delay.

She left him a short, imperious note stating that she would not produce his play, since he took so little interest in it, and, moreover, she did not wish to see him again!

The next morning, when Sarah left her house to take her accustomed ride in the Bois, she discovered a haggard figure sitting on the doorstep.

It was Rostand. He had stayed on the doorstep all night, hoping by thus humbling himself to be forgiven.

Sarah was struck by his devotion, but more by the fact that he was shivering with fever. She took him into the house, and had him put to bed in her private apartment, and for three days she ministered to him while he recovered from a severe cold.

She would not allow a domestic to approach the bedroom, even carrying Rostand his food and hot-water bottles with her own hands. During these three days she did not go near the theatre—and nobody in Paris knew where Rostand was!

It was during this sickness in Sarah's house that Rostand conceived (as he admitted afterwards) the first idea for *L'Aiglon,* which he composed for and dedicated to Sarah. *L'Aiglon,* as everyone knows, is the story of the King of Rome, Napoleon's son, who dies in exile.

It had a moderate success when Sarah first produced it in her own theatre at Paris, but was an absolute triumph in London and New York. In the play Sarah takes the part of the young King of Rome.

To me she once said: "L'Aiglon is my favourite part. I think I like it better than Tosca. At any rate, a poet wrote it with me in mind."

"So did François Coppée write *Le Passant,* with you in mind!" I reminded her.

Sarah was wistful. "Yes, that is true," she answered. "Poor François. He is a genius . . . but—he is not Edmond Rostand!"

L'Aiglon was not the first play of Rostand's that Sarah produced.

In 1896 the door-keeper of the Renaissance came to her with a worried look.

"There is a wild man outside who wants to see you, madame," he said.

"Who is he?" asked Sarah.

"He said Jean Richepin had sent him—but I doubt it myself; he looks like a savage."

"Send your wild man to me," commanded Sarah, laughingly, and turning to me explained: "It is this boy Rostand, whom Jean spoke of. It appears that he is a poet, and quite a good one."

I made as if to go, but Sarah stayed me. "Wait, we will see what he looks like!" she said.

It was thus that I was present at the first meeting between Sarah Bernhardt and Edmond Rostand.

Sarah had her own fashion of greeting visitors. Her leg pained her if she used it too much—the phlebitis persisted—so she would remain seated. When anyone was announced—especially a stranger—she would hold out her hand with a word of greeting, bid him sit down, and then cup her chin on her hands and look at him steadily, without a trace of expression.

Few men there were—or women either, for that matter—who could withstand the hypnotic appeal of those glorious blue eyes, which at fifty retained all the sparkle and fire of youth, together with the mysterious inscrutability of approaching age!

Sarah received Edmond in her customary manner, with myself an interested and, secretly, much amused spectator.

Rostand sat down, placed his hat and gloves on the floor beside him, and then turned to await Sarah's instructions to proceed.

I saw then why the door-keeper had called him a "wild man." His hair was at least five inches long and was in the most indescribable tangle, as though it had not been brushed for months. It was matted over his forehead, on which beads of perspiration were standing.

Rostand turned and looked at Sarah. Sarah, chin on

(Photo, Henri Manuel)

Mme. Bernhardt's Sitting-room at her Last Home,
56, Boulevard Pereire, Paris.

hands, was steadily staring at him. It was an awkward moment for a young, aspiring poet!

Tremendously nervous, Rostand moistened his lips and twice tried to speak.

"I——"

Sarah stared as before.

"I——"

Sarah's expression did not change.

Finally Rostand could stand it no longer. Seizing his hat and gloves he rose precipitately and dashed from the room without having spoken a word regarding his mission.

Sarah screamed with laughter.

"Eh bien!" she exclaimed. "So much for our young poet!"

But when she went out of the theatre she was met by her coachman, who was in great agitation.

"If it please, madame," he said, "there is a man sitting in your carriage, and he won't get out!"

A man sitting in her carriage! It was like a pagan mounting the steps of an altar!

Sarah hastened outside. Sure enough, there was her carriage, and there was a man in it. One look at his mass of hair and Sarah realised who he was.

It was Rostand!

"Throw him out!" commanded Sarah, while we stood by aghast at this sacrilege committed by an unknown poet.

Then Rostand to my amazement found his voice. He stood up in the carriage and bowed to Sarah.

"I don't wish to have to knock your coachman down a second time," he said, "so, madame, it will save time if I explain that I am going to ride home with you!"

"*You* are going to ride home with *me!*" said Sarah. For once even her ready wit had forsaken her.

"I came here to read you a poem, and I am going to read it!" continued Rostand firmly.

Sarah burst out laughing.

"So be it!" she cried cheerfully. "Jean told me that I should hear your poem, and if you cannot read it to me anywhere except in my carriage, why, you may do it there!"

And she got into the carriage with him, and it drove off—much to our amusement, of course.

But we were not astonished. Nothing that Sarah Bernhardt did had the power to astonish us any more.

The poem which Rostand read to Sarah as they drove about in her carriage—it was the first of a score of similar rides, for which it established the precedent—was part of his play, *La Princesse Lointaine,* one of the sweetest poetical dramas ever penned.

Sarah produced it six months later and it was a great success. In fact, it made Rostand as a playwright, and paved the way for his triumph in *L'Aiglon.*

He was enormously grateful to Sarah and his gratitude was the foundation of his love for her.

Sarah's association with the Rostands did not cease

with the death of the great Edmond.   When he died he directed that if ever his famous property, Arnaga, near Biarritz, was sold, Sarah Bernhardt should be given the first opportunity to acquire it.   But when it finally went under the hammer it was bought by a South American, and this happened a few weeks after Sarah died.

When it was first put up for auction there were no bidders, since the reserve price had been set at two million francs.

"I am too poor even to purchase a lot in a cemetery," Sarah said at the time, and, in fact, she was at that moment having difficulties over payments for work on the tomb built for herself at Belle Isle—a tomb in which she will perhaps never lie because, five days before her death, the property was sold.   There is talk now that the purchasers, who are transforming the property into a Bernhardt Museum, will petition that her body may be brought to its ordained resting-place.

Sarah early recognised the budding genius in the boy Maurice Rostand, son of Edmond.   She encouraged him in every way, and she returned to the stage after the Great War in order personally to appear in his *La Gloire,* which is conceded by critics to be a masterpiece.

Maurice Rostand is a peculiar individual to look at, and there are many stories about him; but there is no doubt about it—he is Edmond Rostand's son and a worthy successor of his great father.   Maurice Rostand is a genius.   And Sarah Bernhardt was the first to recog-

nise genius in him, as she had been the first to recognise
it in his father.

Let me read to you what Maurice Rostand wrote the
day that Sarah Bernhardt died:

"Since yesterday, Poesy and her Poets are in mourning.   The muse of Shakespeare and of Musset carries
crêpe upon his shoulder of gold!   Phèdre has died a second time!   And a poet feels in the shadows about him
a thousand wounded heroines who cry; and their immortal verses, like useless bees, search in vain for lips
whereon to rest!

"Permit me, however, to render homage to Her who
has taken with her to a radiant tomb all the lyricism of
an epoch!   Permit me to render homage to the living
poesy of Sarah Bernhardt!

"Yes, she herself was the *théâtre poétique!* The heroes
of poets, on the dangerous road of the centuries are in
danger of succumbing, and more than one disincarnated
heroine would not reach the far country without the
helping hand of genius such as Hers.

"To affirm their existence, it is necessary from time to
time that a heart of fire and passion cause their passions
and their pains to live again.   Lorenzaccio, the young
débauché, for having one night taken this voice of crystal,
is launched to more than eternity!   The sister of Ariane
and her great sob of *bête divine* fills the world more profoundly.

"The Poets are not so niggardly that they do not recognise to what horizons a voice like that can hurl their songs.   You knew it, Musset?   You knew it, my father! . . . Thou knowest it, my heart.

"I write on the first midnight of her death, her first glacial night, when shaken by Her I have contracted from her passage an insulation which is the proof itself of her astra.   This insulation the whole of an epoch has received, and the trace of her passage has glorified the poets, even when she was not saying their verse.   The beauty and the genius of Sarah Bernhardt made the shadow of Herself penetrate into all the arts she epitomised.   Who knows in what measure the genius of Gabriele d'Annunzio has not warmed itself at that Great Flame?   I have recognised in more than one of these sisters of voluptuousness and of fever She who was Divinity in *La Ville Morte!*   One finds her everywhere. Here in a poem by Swinburne; there in prose by Wilde, in an arabesque by Beardsley, in a motif by Claude Debussy, in a song of Maeterlinck. . . .

"Burn, immortal tapers, before her great Memory!"

Who shall say that this was not the voice of Edmond Rostand, living again through the charmèd pen of his son?

CHAPTER XXX

SARAH signed the lease with the civic authorities of Paris to run the Théâtre de l'Opéra Comique, on the Place du Châtelet, in November, 1898. She immediately changed the name to Théâtre Sarah Bernhardt, and on January 18, 1899, she opened it with *Adrienne Lecouvreur*.

This was a curtain-raiser, so to speak, and it soon gave place to *L'Aiglon,* which has been consistently included in that theatre's *répertoire* ever since.

By a singular irony of coincidence *L'Aiglon* was being played at the Théâtre Sarah Bernhardt on that sad night, the twenty-sixth of March, 1923, when the world of art and drama was thrown into mourning by her death.

It was at the Théâtre de l'Opéra Comique, it will be remembered, where Sarah saw her first play as a little girl. And it was there that she played her last.

Although it was to be nearly a quarter of a century before the final curtain fell, Sarah found her energy, though not her fortitude, diminishing. Further and further her sentimental life was being pushed into the background, as the cares of business and of management weighed on her.

She moved to a little red-brown house on the Boulevard Pereire, and there at last, after all her wanderings amongst the different quarters of Paris, she found a permanent home. Into it she brought the accumulated treasures of a lifetime spent in travel, including gifts that had come to her from every corner of the globe.

She installed herself in this house alone with a secretary, for her son was married now and living in a street near-by, in a home of his own.

Here also she brought the waiter Claude, who loved to call himself *"l'écuyer de Sarah Bernhardt,"* or "Sarah Bernhardt's butler," and Félicie, her maid.

Sarah was very particular over her table. She insisted on the best. Although she herself ate frugally, her guests were always given the choicest that could be procured.

Sarah was a vegetarian—she remained so, in fact, all her life although on one or two occasions perhaps she may have pecked at a bird, a slice of venison, or a similar dainty.

In the morning, at eight o'clock, she would partake of an orange, a light roll, and drink a cup of weak tea. The orange-for-breakfast habit she acquired in America, where fruit customarily precedes the first meal of the day.

Then she would work until noon, when she would be served with her only real meal—an omelette, perhaps, and a piece of fish, and more fruit. Until she was thirty-four she never tasted cheese—it offended, she said, her æsthetic sense!—but when she grew old, a light gruyère or a Pont-l'Evêque was a favourite dish of hers.

At five in the afternoon she had an invariable glass

of champagne, and at seven an *œuf soufflé* or something similarly light. For years her diet was prescribed by doctors, and never a week went by after 1890 that Sarah Bernhardt was not examined by a physician.

Despite the accident to her leg and the subsequent phlebitis, which grew more serious with every recurrent attack, Sarah continued to act in the plays she produced at the Théâtre Sarah Bernhardt. One after another she produced *L'Aiglon, Hamlet, La Sorcière, Le Procès de Jeanne d'Arc, La Belle au Bois Dormant, La Beffa, La Courtisane de Corinthe, Lucrèce Borgia, Les Bouffons*, and *Jeanne Dorée*.

Thrice, after she opened her theatre, she undertook long, fatiguing tours of America and Europe, and once she went to Australia, South Africa and New Zealand. "Bernhardt's Circus" was what her travelling company was facetiously nicknamed by the Paris press—the fun and criticism of which, however, had grown considerate and kindly.

"Sarah Bernhardt is a national institution; to criticise her is like criticising the Tomb of Napoleon," said *Le Journal des Débats* one evening.

The Prince of Wales, who was shortly to become King Edward VII was a warm friend of Sarah Bernhardt, and on one well-remembered occasion paid an informal visit, together with the Princess of Wales, to her home in Paris.

"What did you talk about?" I asked, the next day.

"Dogs and dresses," said Sarah promptly.

"The Prince," she continued, "is tremendously interested in dogs, and there we have a common ground."

Once the Prince called on Sarah in her dressing-room —this was when she was at the Renaissance.

Word was sent in advance, of course, that he was coming—and she was requested to be ready to receive him at ten o'clock. At that hour she was customarily on the stage, and her entourage was excited at the possibility of her not being there to receive the Royal visitor.

The stage-manager suggested advancing the time of the whole piece, so that the third act would be finished by ten, but this did not suit Sarah, who knew that such an arrangement would make many people who had purchased seats miss a part of the first act.

She settled it in her own characteristic fashion.

"Let him wait," she said. "After all, he isn't King yet!"

At ten o'clock—punctuality is the politeness of kings —the Prince arrived. When Sarah returned, she found him in the wings, watching the life behind the scenes with intense interest. It being draughty there, he had not removed his hat.

He advanced his hand, but Sarah kept hers at her side. She was in one of her haughty moods that evening.

"A King may wear his crown, but a Prince must remove his hat in the presence of a lady," she said loftily.

The Prince snatched his silk hat from his head, blushed deeply, and murmured a confused apology. It was probably the one occasion in his life when a woman treated him with such scant consideration for his Royal dignity!

After the famous dinner *"en famille"* given to the Prince and Princess of Wales by Sarah—it was supposed to be strictly secret, but Sarah saw that it leaked into the papers!—she received a note from one of the ladies-in-waiting to the Princess, who, with her Royal husband, was living at the Hotel Bristol in the Place Vendôme.

"Her Royal Highness was much interested in the gown which Madame Bernhardt was describing to her last night, and wonders whether Madame Bernhardt could spare her a few minutes this morning to consult with her regarding it."

Truly a strange message to be sent by a Princess to an actress!

Sarah visited the hotel and had another long chat with the Princess, whose beauty and grace were the talk of Paris. They talked of a good deal besides dresses. The Princess loved to speak of her beloved Denmark, which Sarah knew well, and they recalled the first occasion on which Sarah went there, just after she left the Comédie Française, when the Princess was also visiting her native country.

Sarah gave the Prince a Swiss shepherd-dog, and he, after becoming King Edward VII, sent her an Airedale puppy. This puppy came to an unfortunate end shortly afterwards. It died in agony as the result of being bitten by Sarah's pet panther.

After he came to the throne, King Edward VII and Queen Alexandra invariably "commanded" a perform-

ance whenever Sarah was in London.   It might be at
Windsor, or at Sandringham, or in London, but afterwards the kindly King and the lovely Queen of England
would carry Sarah off for a confidential chat in the home-
like atmosphere of their private apartments.

Sarah had hundreds of reminiscences to relate regarding her two Royal friends.   How she loved Queen Alexandra!

In 1904 Sarah had another and severe attack of
phlebitis while on tour in America, and lay ill for a long
time in San Francisco.   It was thought then that she
would eventually lose her limb.   The poison was gradually creeping upwards, and she could not put her foot to
the ground without intense pain.   She remained a fortnight in bed, with her leg held up by a pulley.

Sarah's fortitude throughout her long trial was amazing.   As soon as her foot became sufficiently well to
stand upon, she insisted on returning to the theatre.

Finally, when she was playing in Bordeaux in the early
spring of 1915 she had another and more critical attack,
and was taken to Dr. Moure's private clinic.

Dr. Pozzi, the famous surgeon, was sent for from
Paris, but after examination he shook his head.

"Amputation cannot save her," he said, and he refused
to undertake the operation.

Another doctor was sent for, Dr. Denucce, also a great
surgeon.   Dr. Denucce put the situation squarely before
the actress.

"There is one hope for you—amputation—but it is a

chance in a thousand, for the infection has reached the spine," he told her.

Sarah heard her sentence calmly.

"Cut it off!" she said.

When they laid her on the operating table, they tried to cheer her with words of encouragement, but Sarah's brave smile shone wanly.

"I have already faced death seven times," she said. "If this is when my light is to go out, I shall not be afraid!"

She was in a terrible condition, not only physically but financially. The operation was a success, but she had not a cent with which to pay the clinic or the doctors. The Rothschilds and their friends finally came to the rescue.

"All my life, it seems, I have been making money for others to spend!" she said, but with no complaint in her voice.

She faced her future then, penniless after the millions she had earned, and with one leg, as courageously as she had returned to face a jeering Paris after her first visit to London.

By the irony of fate her sick-room at Bordeaux was filled with flowers worth literally thousands of pounds, that had been sent from all quarters of France by her worshippers.

"If I only had the money these flowers cost!" she remarked resignedly.

The war was on, and the ambulance in which she was being taken to the station on her way back to Paris overtook regiment after regiment of soldiers on their way to the Front.

"La glorieuse blessée," the papers called her, and the soldiers thronged about the ambulance and her car on the train, taking the flowers that decorated their bayonets and throwing them at the indomitable genius who sat inside it with tears in her eyes.

Within six months Sarah herself was at the Front, playing from an armchair for the *poilus* who were battling to check the invader.

She was then seventy-one years old.

CHAPTER XXXI

WHEN she was asked by a journalist in 1898 to describe her "ideal," Sarah Bernhardt replied:

"My ideal? But I am still pursuing it! I shall pursue it until my last hour, and I feel that in the supreme moment I shall know the certainty of attaining it beyond the tomb."

In these few words lie the expression of Sarah Bernhardt's whole life.

Indefinable as perhaps her ideal was, it was the star that guided her throughout her long career. It was that grasping after the unattainable, that desire to take the one more step ahead, that *culte du parfait,* as Rostand expressed it, that inspired her battles and illuminated her art.

Shortly after she moved to the Boulevard Pereire, she purchased the Fort des Poulains, on Belle Isle-sur-Mer, on the coast of Brittany, and here she spent the summers of her convalescence, surrounded by faithful friends and members of her family.

She built a magnificent house at Belle Isle, and another building on the farm adjoining it. This she called "Sarah's Fort," and it was consecrated to the great tragedienne. Here she would spend hours in the company of her son, or with Jules Lemaître, or some other trusted friend, and here she was safe from the cares and worries of her business in Paris—for she still retained the active management of the Théâtre Sarah Bernhardt.

"It is," said the *Illustration* recently, "with a real sentiment of satisfaction that we learn that the Fort des Poulains, the property of Madame Sarah Bernhardt at Belle Isle, is to become a museum consecrated to the great tragedienne and is not to become a tourist hotel and dancing-place, as had been reported. By a sentiment of respect and piety, the group which has purchased the property has so decided. They will try to bring to the property a collection of souvenirs of the great artiste, and tourists will thus be able to visit the surroundings which were so dear to Sarah Bernhardt's heart. . . . What souvenirs are attached to Belle Isle, where *La Princesse Lointaine* will sleep one day perhaps her last repose!"

Once when in Florida, Sarah expressed the desire to hunt an alligator. There was no alligator in that region, and the local admirers of the artiste were in despair until it was remembered that the druggist of the town possessed a baby alligator, which at the moment (it being winter) was tranquilly asleep.

He consented to give the creature for the purposes of the hunt, and it was placed secretly in a marsh near-by. The next day Sarah was told that the hunt had been organised. She was delighted beyond measure and gaily walked the five miles to the spot, where the sleeping alligator was captured without any difficulty.

Maurice Bernhardt was at Belle Isle at the time and Sarah sent him the alligator, together with a letter telling her son that he did not need to be afraid of it, for it was a "quiet little thing" and had not even made a move since it had been caught.

But, unfortunately, when the alligator arrived at Belle Isle, it was its time to wake up, and it became a formidable customer—so dangerous, in fact, that before Sarah could arrive to view her capture in its new home it had to be killed.

Sarah had a regular colony of dogs, horses and birds on the farm.

After the war she announced her intention of returning to the stage, one-legged though she was. There was a chorus of protest, which, however, had no effect upon her.

Money had to be earned, and it seemed as though she was the only member of the family who could earn it! So she returned to the stage, in *Athalie,* and was given on the opening night what was possibly the greatest ovation of her career.

Then Louis Verneuil, a talented young poet who had married her beautiful grand-daughter Lysiane, wrote a play specially for her—*Daniel.* It was the story of a young author, victim of opium. In it Sarah had no need to move, but spoke her lines sitting in an armchair and lying on a couch.   Even thus, her tremendous personality and her magnificent voice dominated the house.

Sarah next played in a one-act play, *Le Vitrail,* by Réné Fauchois, at the Alhambra.   Then she produced *Régine Armand,* and, finally, created *La Gloire,* by Maurice Rostand.

Not content with this almost superhuman labour, she was arranging to play with the Guitrys' at the Théâtre Edouard VII when, just before Christmas, 1922, she was seized with an attack of her old enemy, uremia.

I was among those who called at the little house in the Boulevard Pereire on the night of December 31, when it was thought that she must die.   But she rallied, and though all her friends and her family and she herself knew that it was but a temporary reprieve, she insisted on going back to work.   Not this time, on the stage, but in her own house before the motion-picture camera.

A syndicate organised by a young American in Paris and directed by another American, Leon Abrams, made her an offer of, I think it was, 5,000 francs per day. She was, as usual, penniless, and the offer was a godsend.

She posed for the film, with her chimpanzee, in the studio at the rear of her house.

So needy was she that, just before lapsing into unconsciousness for the last time, she demanded that the moving-picture men should be admitted to the bedchamber.

"They can film me in bed," she said, her voice scarcely audible, so weak was she. "Now, don't object," as Professor Vidal remonstrated, "they pay me 5,000 francs each time I pose!"

Her insistence on fufilling her contract to play in this cinema play was, according to the doctors, the cause of her last collapse. It was more than her strength could stand. She was really dying when she faced the camera on the last two occasions. But her indomitable will triumphed over her body almost to the last, and, until the dreadful malady paralysed her, she continued acting.

My tears are falling as I write these last lines. They are difficult sentences to fashion. I am no poet, and words could not add to the drama of that night when the divine Call-boy came for Sarah Bernhardt.

She died at five minutes past eight o'clock, her snow-white head pillowed in the arms of her son, Maurice.

"Be a good boy . . . Maurice." These were her last words. . . . The curtain descended. . . .

That day, Monday, the twenty-sixth of March, Victor Hugo died for a second time.

Even before she died, Sarah Bernhardt had outstripped Glory and had become Legend.

Nothing of hers had faltered: not her intelligence, not her heart, not her talent, not her genius. She was complete.

She was the glory and the light of the French theatre. The light that is extinguished will not flame again. How dark it seems!

Dead, she is greater than in life. Who of us would not accept her luminous night?

Her epitaph, by Jacques Richepin:

✝

CI-GIT SARAH

QUI SURVIVRA

THE END

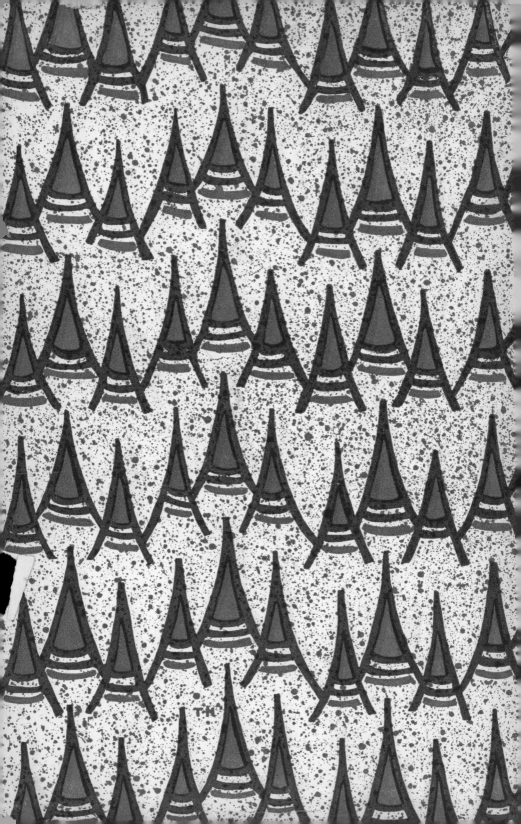